Using

The Internet
Second Editon

Using

The Internet
Second Editon

Jerry Honeycutt

Using the Internet, Second Edition

Library of Congress Catalog No.: 96-70786

ISBN: 0-7897-0963-5

98 97 96   6 5 4 3 2 1

Interpretation of the printing code: the rightmost double-digit number is the year of the book's printing; the rightmost single-digit number, the number of the book's printing. For example, a printing code of 96-1 shows that the first printing of the book occurred in 1996.

All items mentioned in this book that are known to be trademarks or service marks have been appropriately capitalized. Que cannot attest to the accuracy of this information. Use of a term in this book should not be regarded as affecting the validity of any trademark or service mark.

Screen reproductions in this book were created using Collage Complete from Inner Media, Inc., Hollis, NH.

Composed in *ITC Century*, *ITC Highlander*, and *MCPdigital* by Que Corporation.

Credits

President
Roland Elgey

Publisher
Joseph B. Wikert

Publishing Manager
Jim Minatel

Editorial Services Director
Elizabeth Keaffaber

Managing Editor
Sandy Doell

Director of Marketing
Lynn E. Zingraf

Acquisitions Manager
Cheryl D. Willoughby

Product Director
Steven M. Schafer

Production Editor
Bill McManus

Editors
Patrick Kanouse
Patricia Kinyon
Julie MacLean
Jade Williams
Aaron Gordon

Assistant Product Marketing Manager
Christy M. Miller

Strategic Marketing Manager
Barry Pruett

Technical Editor
Bill Bruns

Technical Support Specialist
Nadeem Muhammed

Acquisitions Coordinator
Jane K. Brownlow

Software Relations Coordinator
Patty Brooks

Editorial Assistant
Jennifer Condon
Andrea Duvall

Book Designer
Ruth Harvey

Cover Designers
Dan Armstrong
Jay Corpus

Production Team
Michael Beaty
Marcia Brizendine
Erin M. Danielson
Heather Howell
Daryl Kessler
Paul Wilson

Indexers
Robert Long
Greg Pearson

Cheryl, thanks for your support and encouragement.

About the Author

Jerry Honeycutt provides business-oriented technical leadership to the Internet community and software development industry. He has served companies such as The Travelers, IBM, Nielsen North America, IRM, Howard Systems International, and NCR. Jerry has participated in the industry since before the days of Microsoft Windows 1.0, and is completely hooked on Windows 95 and the Internet.

Jerry is the author of many Que books, including:

Using Microsoft Plus!

Using the Internet with Windows 95

Windows 95 Registry & Customization Handbook

Special Edition Using the Windows 95 Registry

VBScript by Example

Special Edition Using the Internet, Third Edition

He is also a contributing author on *Special Edition Using Windows 95*, *Special Edition Using Netscape*, *Platinum Edition Using Windows 95*, and *Visual Basic for Applications Database Solutions*, all published by Que. He has been published in *Computer Language* magazine and is a regular speaker at the Windows World and Comdex trade shows on topics related to software development, Windows 95, and the Internet.

Jerry graduated from the University of Texas at Dallas in 1992 with a B.S. degree in computer science. He currently lives in the Dallas suburb of Frisco, Texas, with Becky, two Westies, Corky and Turbo, and a cat called Scratches. Please feel free to contact Jerry on the Internet at **jerry@honeycutt.com**.

Acknowledgments

The Internet community moves at a faster pace than the rest of the world. I've heard it called Internet-years, much like dog-years—each four Internet-years being about one human-year.

Internet-related books, such as *Using the Internet, Second Edition*, have to keep just as frenetic a pace as the Internet itself. And that's not easy to do. Writing an Internet-related book is the easy part. What you often miss is the incredible amount of detail-oriented work that goes on behind the scenes. I can't acknowledge every person involved, but you should know about a few individuals:

- Cheryl Willoughby, to whom this book is dedicated, keeps cracking her whip in order to get things done.

- Steve Schafer's wisdom and good humor guided this book into what you hold in your hands. Thanks.

- Bill McManus had the unenviable task of coordinating all the chapters and figures. Though his schedule usually suffers at the hands of technical editors and errant authors, he remains steady.

- The copy editors, Patrick Kanouse, Julie MacLean, Jade Williams, Aaron Gordon, and Pat Kinyon, made sure that the gibberish I banged out on the keyboard was readable and conformed to some sense of English structure.

We'd Like to Hear from You!

As part of our continuing effort to produce books of the highest possible quality, Que would like to hear your comments. To stay competitive, we *really* want you, as a computer book reader and user, to let us know what you like or dislike most about this book or other Que products.

You can mail comments, ideas, or suggestions for improving future editions to the address below, or send us a fax at (317) 581-4663. For the online inclined, Macmillan Computer Publishing has a forum on CompuServe (type **GO QUEBOOKS** at any prompt) through which our staff and authors are available for questions and comments. The address of our Internet site is **http://www.mcp.com** (World Wide Web).

In addition to exploring our forum, please feel free to contact me personally to discuss your opinions of this book: I'm **sschafer@que.mcp.com** on the Internet, and I'm ID**71034,3406** on CompuServe.

Thanks in advance—your comments will help us to continue publishing the best books available on computer topics in today's market.

Steven Schafer
Product Director
Que Corporation
201 W. 103rd Street
Indianapolis, Indiana 46290
USA

Contents at a Glance

Table of Contents

Part II: Getting to Know Your Tools

Part III: Using the Internet for Business and Pleasure

12 Get Your Software Fix Online

Introduction

My, how things change. The previous editions of this book explained that the Internet is actually a huge network of networks. You were informed that you can use a variety of services on these networks with different tools such as a Web browser, a newsreader, and a mail client. The previous editions also helped you pick the best tools available and showed you how to use those tools.

The only problem is that simply helping you pick and use the best Internet tools is like writing a book about rock-and-roll that only discusses CD players, amplifiers, and speakers. It does a great job covering the tools you can use to listen to the music, but it never shows you how to appreciate the music and find artists that suit your own tastes. I won't have any of that here, not in the second edition of *Using the Internet*. This book isn't going to bore you with my favorite rock-and-roll artists, but it is going to focus more on "using" the Internet, rather than using the Internet tools.

The first editions of *Using the Internet* and *Using the Internet with Windows 95* have helped thousands of folks, such as yourself, get onto the Internet and use its resources. This book is different than its predecessors, however, because it doesn't focus on a particular platform or, for that matter, on particular Internet tools. Instead, this edition shows you how to accomplish things on the Internet. Real things. How to plan business and personal trips, for example. How to shop. How to educate your children. How to get answers to virtually any questions you have. It's all here.

You and this book

I wrote *Using the Internet, Second Edition* with the beginner in mind. You don't have to know anything about the Internet. TCP/IP? Domain names? Phooey. You don't need to know any of it before using this book. I promise not to swamp you with more details than you need. You don't give a hoot about how the Internet works or how it has evolved. You just want to use the Internet, right? So, this book leaves out a lot of the Internet jargon that you don't need to know right away.

I didn't leave out all the experienced users, though. If you're an experienced user, you will get a lot out of this book, too. You'll appreciate this practical guide to getting things done on the Internet. I've dedicated the bulk of this book to showing you how to use basic Internet tools to accomplish everyday tasks. However, you will learn how to do them *better* on the Internet. In addition to the hints I just dropped, you will learn how to use the Internet as a research tool, how to find the best free programs on the Internet, and much more.

Why should I learn about the Internet?

Tough question. Everyone's situation is a bit different. For now, the most important reason you should learn about the Internet is that it's great fun.

Beyond getting your jollies on the Internet, I believe that, in the very near future, the Internet will have important social and economic impact—impact that effects you directly. It will change how you work, play, and relate to other people. The change is already starting, too, as you see in the following examples:

- A major grocery chain in the Dallas area will soon accept your shopping list via the Internet. They'll bag your groceries and deliver them right to your doorstep. All for a fee, of course, but it's worth it if you spend less time at the grocery store and less money on gas. Oh, yea, no checkout lines—yippee!

- Students in my local school system get extra credit on their homework if they can show that they researched it on the Internet. Students who have Internet connections at home fare much better than those who have to wait in line to use the computer lab.

- For professionals in a national company for whom I consult, Internet mail is replacing the telephone as the communication tool of choice. It's quicker to use and it makes tracking people down easier. You're much more likely to get a reply to your queries if you fire off an Internet mail message than if you leave other types of messages. Internet mail also gives you better organization and a better paper trail because it records the date and time of each message.

- Many companies in the Dallas area have found that they don't have enough cubicles in which to stuff their employees. Thus, they're gradually allowing employees to work at home, using the Internet to connect to the office (Dilbert would be proud). The result is lower costs and, I hope, more productive employees.

- A number of technology companies in the Dallas area give preference to candidates who have experience using the Internet. Why? A huge number of online resources are now available only on the Internet. Besides, learning the Internet also makes you look more technically hip and up-to-date. You can increase your odds of landing a great job by learning how to use the Internet.

Sold. What do I need before using this book?

You need two things to use this book: a basic computer system and a little bit of knowledge. First, the computer system. This book is for Windows users. Windows 3.1. Windows 95. Windows NT. It doesn't matter which flavor you prefer, but you must have a computer running one of the Windows platforms to follow the examples in this book.

You don't need an Internet connection to use this book. In fact, you might want to put off signing up with a service provider until you read the first few chapters. These chapters first show you how to find the best service provider in your area. Then, they show you how to easily connect your computer to the service provider.

And the knowledge? This book requires that you understand a handful of really basic topics. You should understand how to use the different parts of Windows. In Windows 3.1, for example, you should understand how to use the Program Manager. Likewise, in Windows 95, you should understand the task bar, Start menu, and Desktop. You also should understand how to use windows, menus, and dialog boxes. If you're not familiar with Windows or your computer, take a look at some of these QUE resources to help you get going:

- *Using Windows*
- *Using Windows 95*
- *Using Your PC*

Got any suggestions for using this book?

Once you're connected to the Internet, you don't have to read this book front to back. You can jump around all you like. The Table of Contents is a great place to look for an area to dive in. Also, look at the Action index in the back of the book if you have a particular question or problem. Here are some additional tips for using this book:

- If you're brand new to the Internet and don't yet have an Internet service, I suggest that you read the first two parts of this book in sequence. You'll learn the basics before moving on to the more complicated material.

- If you're brand new to the Internet, but are already connected to the Internet, you can start with Part II, "Getting to Know Your Tools." You'll learn how to access and use the basic Internet tools.

- If you have an Internet connection and you're comfortable with the basic tools, flip around this book all you like. I *would* take a close look at Part III, "Using the Internet for Business and Pleasure." This part shows you how to really get things done on the Internet.

How this book is put together

Using the Internet, Second Edition has 4 major parts, which include 21 chapters, 3 appendixes, and two indexes. Part I introduces you to some basic concepts and shows you how to get on the Internet. Part II shows you how to access and use the basic Internet tools. Part III shows you how to do specific tasks on the Internet. Here's what you'll find in each of these parts:

- Part I, "Getting Started," contains the first four chapters of this book. These chapters introduce you to the Internet. Chapters 1 and 2 describe the Internet and give you just enough technical background to understand the rest of the book. Chapters 3 and 4 help you get connected to the Internet.

- Part II, "Getting to Know Your Tools," contains seven chapters that show you how to access and use the basic Internet tools. Chapter 5 shows you how to download the tools. Chapters 6 through 10 show you how to use them. Chapter 11 shows you how to use the Internet search tools.

- Part III, "Using the Internet for Business and Pleasure," is the heart and soul of this book. Chapters 12 through 21 show you how to accomplish a variety of tasks on the Internet such as doing research, planning a vacation, and shopping.

- Part IV contains the appendixes and indexes. Appendix A contains additional resources you can use to learn more about the Internet. Appendix B contains information about using my Web site in conjunction with this book. Appendix C provides a comprehensive list of Internet Service Providers and information on how to contact each of them. Finally, the indexes include a standard index for the entire book, as well as an action index, which will help you quickly find where you want to go.

Information that's easy to understand

This book contains a variety of special features to help you find the information you need. For example, it uses formatting conventions to make important keywords or special text obvious, and it uses specific language to make keyboard and mouse actions clear.

Tips, Notes, Cautions...

You'll find a number of special elements and conventions in this book that will jump right off of the page. These elements will provide just-in-time information.

 TIP Tips point out things that you can do to get the most out of the Internet. Often, these tips are not found in books or online help, but come from personal experience instead.

 NOTE Notes are chunks of information that don't necessarily fit in the surrounding text but could be valuable nonetheless.

 CAUTION Cautions warn you of possible trouble. They warn you about things that you should avoid or things that you need to do to protect yourself or your computer.

What are Q&A notes?

These elements anticipate your questions and provide advice about how to solve problems or to avoid bad situations.

  Plain English, please!

These notes explain technical terms in a manner that you can understand. **99**

Keyboard conventions

In addition to the special features that help you find what you need, this book uses some special conventions that make it easier to understand:

Element	Convention
Hot keys	Hot keys are underlined in this book, just as they appear in Windows 95 menus. To use a hot key, press Alt and the underlined letter. The <u>F</u> in <u>F</u>ile is a hot key that represents the <u>F</u>ile menu, for example.
Key combinations	Key combinations that you must press together are separated by plus signs. For example, "Press Ctrl+Alt+D" means that you press and hold down the Ctrl key, then press and hold down the Alt key, and then press and release the D key. Always press and release, rather than hold, the last key in a key combination.
Menu commands	A comma is used to separate the parts of a pull-down menu command. For example, "Choose <u>F</u>ile, <u>N</u>ew" means to open the <u>F</u>ile menu and select the <u>N</u>ew option.

Sidebars are oh-by-the-ways

Sidebars provide useful and interesting information that doesn't really fit in the text. You'll also find more technical information.

In most cases, special-purpose keys are referred to by the text that actually appears on them on a standard 101-key keyboard. For example, press "Esc" or press "F1" or press "Enter." Some of the keys on your keyboard don't actually have words on them. So, here are the conventions used in this book for those keys:

- The Backspace key, which is labeled with a left arrow, usually is located directly above the Enter key. The Tab key usually is labeled with two arrows pointing to lines, with one arrow pointing right and the other arrow pointing left.

- The cursor keys, labeled on most keyboards with arrows pointing up, down, right, and left, are called the up-arrow key, down-arrow key, right-arrow key, and left-arrow key.

- Case is not important unless explicitly stated. So "Press A" and "Press a" mean the same thing. This book always uses the uppercase version, though.

Mouse Conventions

In this book, the following phrases tell you how to operate your mouse within Windows 95 or Internet Explorer 3.0:

- **Click**   Move the mouse pointer so that it is in the area of the screen specified and press the left mouse button. (If you've reversed these buttons—as many left-handed people like to do—whenever the instructions say to press the left button, press the right button instead.) Sometimes the buttons are referred to as the primary and secondary mouse buttons, which would be the left and right buttons, respectively, unless you have reversed them.

- **Double-Click**   Press the left mouse button twice rapidly without moving the mouse between clicks.

- **Drag**   Press and hold down the left mouse button while you're moving the mouse pointer. You'll see an outline of the object as you drag the mouse pointer.

- **Drop**   Release the mouse button after a drag operation.

Typeface Conventions

This book also uses some special typeface conventions that make it easier to read:

Element	Convention
Bold	Bold indicates Internet addresses, new terminology, and text that *you* type.
Italic	Italic indicates placeholders, which you substitute with appropriate text.
Monospace	Monospace indicates file names and text you see on-screen.

Part I: Getting Started

1

What Is the Internet?
Is It for Me?

● **In this chapter:**

- **Here's a brief Internet history lesson**

- **Just about anyone can, and must, use the Internet**

- **How do I know that the Internet is right for me?**

- **Is the Internet safe for my kids?**

- **What's causing all this hype about the Internet?**

- **How can I tell one dialog box from another?**

The Internet is quickly becoming a fact of life, and there's no better time than now to get with the program . . . . ▶

Technology that actually changes how we live doesn't come around all that often. Thinking back, I can point to the telephone as a major change to our lifestyle. I can also point to the television (good or bad), the automobile, and the computer—among a handful of other innovations.

The Internet falls into the same ranks. It promises to change how we interact with the rest of the world—for both the good and the bad. How we buy things. How we communicate with other people. Where we go for our entertainment. Where we work. All of these things are, or soon will be, affected by the Internet.

Don't panic if you're not on the Internet yet. You shouldn't feel as though you've been left behind, however, because the train has just left the station— you can still catch up. You've picked a great time to pick up this book and get yourself online.

Poof! And there was the Internet

So, just what is the Internet? The Internet is a gigantic network of computers (it's actually a network of networked computers, but I won't fuss with the details right now). Some of the computers on the Internet provide a variety of services, which folks like you and me use through our computers. These computers publish documents, for example, or provide forums for communicating with other people. Thus, my definition of the Internet actually has two parts—computers and people:

- The Internet is a vast network of computers to which anyone can connect their computer.

- The Internet is also the vast community of people that connect to the network.

The Internet, as we know it today, is still very new. It started out as a way to help researchers and educational types collaborate and do more things, faster. However, it has recently evolved into much more. All those people and businesses on the Internet have generated a lot of fuss. And the more fuss it generates, the more people and businesses are drawn to it.

It's sometimes hard to remember that the Internet has been around for quite a while. It's worthwhile looking at a bit of Internet history before you go forward to the "how to" stuff. I'll keep it brief, though.

In the beginning...

In 1969, the Advanced Research Projects Agency (ARPA) was created by the Defense Department. The Defense Department, in its infinite wisdom, decided that it needed a communications network that could survive a war. The goal was to design a network that, if part of it got nuked, could still send a message that would find its way to its destination. The successful result was ARPAnet.

Q&A *Sounds cool. Does it work?*

Yep. In the Gulf War with Iraq, the United States had trouble knocking out Iraq's communications network because Iraq was using the same commercially available technology found in the Internet.

The eighties witnessed the evolution of the Internet as we know it today. ARPAnet was neat, but it wasn't the Internet. In 1983, mostly for pragmatic reasons, ARPAnet split into two different systems called ARPAnet and MILNET. ARPAnet was reserved for civilian use, such as research, and MILNET was reserved for military use. Both networks were connected, so users could exchange information; this became known as the Internet. While all this Defense Department wrangling was going on, other networks, such as BITNET (Because It's Time) and CSNET (Computer Science Network), started springing up. They were initially totally separate networks, used for educational and research purposes, but over time, they connected to the Internet to facilitate sharing information across organizations.

One of the most important advances for the Internet came in 1986, when folks over at the National Science Foundation decided that the existing network wasn't good enough anymore. As a result, they created NSFNET to connect several high-speed supercomputers across the country—mostly for research purposes. ARPAnet was dismantled, and NSFNET became the main pipeline (**backbone** for those in the know) of the Internet.

You are here ...

The growth of the Internet has been explosive. In 1985, there were about 2,000 host computers on the Internet. Now there are well over 9 million host computers, which support many millions of users. All of these users aren't necessarily connected directly to the Internet. However, they can still exchange e-mail with other Internet users.

NSF is in the process of farming out parts of the Internet to private industry. They can't afford to continue funding it due to both economic and political reasons. Economically, it has become too expensive for NSF to maintain. The Internet has grown far beyond what NSF originally anticipated (although they're quite happy with the results). Politically, when NSF was funding the Internet, it was used primarily for educational and research purposes. Now that the Internet is growing more commercial every day, some folks are a bit resentful of a government agency funding a commercial enterprise.

 Q&A **If NSF was funding the Internet, does that mean they owned it?**

Nope. The Internet is owned by no one. It's not possible to claim ownership over all the private networks that are connected to the Internet. There are a handful of regulatory and advisory groups that oversee the Internet, but there remains no central authority or ownership. The lack of ownership and the variety of participants are two of the primary reasons that the Internet is as open and diverse as it is.

The future looks bright

The amazing growth of the Internet is going to continue. Each month, the Internet welcomes millions of new users. Many people try the Internet and decide that it's not for them. But most hang around. This includes folks who are connected directly to the Internet, and folks who are connected to the Internet through online services, employers, and schools.

All this growth and attention have not escaped the notice of the venture capitalists (vulture capitalists) and big corporations. A vast percentage of the venture capital spent these days is spent on the Internet. Companies such as Microsoft and AT&T are jumping into the fray, too. To truly understand what the future holds for the Internet, you need to understand where all this loot is going and what type of technology is springing up from the nerd-herds at the companies that are driving the Internet. Then you can envision the types of things you'll be able to do on the Internet in the very near future.

- **HTML**   You'll soon see much more dynamic content on the Internet. Why? Because HTML (the language Web developers use to create Web pages) is all grown up now, with features such as style sheets.

- **Objects (Java, too)**   Web developers are no longer limited to text and graphics on the Web page, so you can rest assured that you're going to see a lot of really cool content on the Web. A number of recent advances make it possible to distribute objects, including controls or complete programs, via the Web. You'll read a lot more about two types of objects in this book: ActiveX and Java.

- **Scripting**   Scripting lets Web page developers liven up their Web pages by scripting what happens as you interact with the Web page. They can validate a form when you click a button, for example, or provide help to you if you seem to be stuck.

- **Multimedia**   Multimedia on the Internet keeps getting more and more exciting. Countless vendors have sprung into action with programs that let you experience a variety of multimedia within a Web page. RealAudio, Macromedia ShockWave, Microsoft ActiveMovie, and VRML (Virtual Reality Modeling Language), are just a few examples. Simply breathtaking.

- **Security**   Security issues are finally getting their due. The powers behind the Internet are making it safer to buy things on the Internet by providing transaction security. They're making it safe for your children to play on the Web by providing ratings. And, they're making it safer to run distributed applications by providing code authentication.

- **Conferencing**   A lot of advances have been made in video conferencing and other types of conferencing. For example, technology is available that enables you to collaborate on documents across the Internet. Likewise, you can have audio conferences and even share a whiteboard where conference participants sketch out ideas for all to see.

One of the most important, but often overlooked, advances is **bandwidth**. In particular, I'm talking about personal bandwidth. I remember when 1200 baud modems were thought of as blazingly fast. Then came the 2400, 9600, 14.4K, and 28.8K modems. Now, I have ISDN, which is like a 128K modem. Personal bandwidth is rapidly approaching the point at which video conferencing, video on demand, amazing multimedia, and distributed applications are becoming quite practical.

> **6 6** *Plain English, please!*
>
> **Bandwidth** is another way of saying "how big is your pipe." That is, bandwidth refers to the amount of data that you can send and receive through your Internet connection. **9 9**

Who can access the Internet?

Anybody can access the Internet. Schools provide access, as do some churches and employers. You'll even find public access to the Internet in libraries and coffee shops. If you have a computer and a modem, you can find an independent service provider or commercial online service to use, too.

The Internet isn't just a U.S. thing, either. People all over the world have access to the Internet. I've communicated with folks in Russia, Australia, United Kingdom, Germany, China, and Japan. Sure, most of the people who connect to the Internet are in the U.S., but it's still available all over the world.

How do other folks use the Internet?

Julia Richardson, a Conference Administrator at Softbank COMDEX, is one of the hardest working folks I know. She helps pull off trade shows such as Windows World and COMDEX. I recently exchanged messages with Julia about how she uses the Internet, and here is what she had to say:

"The Internet is a great entertainment guide, and I use it at least once a week. You can access local magazines and newspapers to see what will be going on in the upcoming days, and if you want more information, you can also access theaters, clubs, galleries, and restaurants. You can get a full picture of what is happening in your city in a half

hour or less, without the hassle of calling all over the place.

"I also find it a source of entertainment in and of itself. Whatever your interests, you can bet there is someone who shares them and has been nice enough to present information on it in a neat, concise package. And no matter how much I surf around, it is always a pleasant surprise to see listings for other pages of interest. You can't, for example, go into an antique store and expect the clerk to say, 'Sure, we've got that, but Joe's Antiques down the street has a better one.' I find the Internet a welcome change from our ordinary competitive world."

Take the leap—the Internet is right for you

Having been on the Internet for a while, I'm pretty much convinced that the Internet is right for you—and everyone else out there. I know, however, that you may need a bit of convincing before you make that leap into cyberspace. Let's take a look at the types of things that you already do during a normal day, and see how they relate to what you can do on the Internet. The items in Table 1.1 are not made up. They are all possible on the Internet, and you'll learn about them in this book.

Table 1.1 Do it on the Internet instead

Do you do this?	Do it this way on the Internet
Use couriers	Send files to the office with e-mail, if they're on the Internet
Send letters/postcards	Save postage—send e-mail instead
Call long distance	Use Internet Phone or NetMeeting and call for free, as long as the person you're calling is online
Read the newspaper	Use Internet news services
Play the stock market	Get stock quotes and trade online
Read trade rags	Stay current with newsgroups or a variety of industry newsletters
Read magazines	Read their online editions
Socialize/chit-chat	Socialize in Internet chat rooms
Shop at the mall	Shop using online catalogs
Call product support	Get product support through the Web
Go to the movies	Preview movies before paying
Watch news for weather	Get current weather reports online
Use a dictionary	Use an online dictionary
Subscribe to *TV Guide*	Get an online version sent to you

Table 1.1 touches only the tip of the proverbial iceberg. There is so much more to the Internet. It's very hard to summarize in a table the benefits that

you get from being able to connect with people who have similar interests or problems. If you're having teenager problems, you'll find advice and consolation on the Internet. If you want more information about your favorite self-help author, look on the Internet. Want to learn how to brew your own beer? Look on the Internet. And on, and on, and on.

Q&A *The Internet may be right for me, but is it right for my kids?*

The Internet has received a bad rap recently for its seamier side. Still, Internet access will be a necessity for your child to be competitive in our fast-paced world. If you're feeling uncomfortable, consider a product such as Surf Watch, which blocks access to the more indecent bits of the Internet. It is very important, as well, to understand what your child is doing while online. Chapter 16, "How Do I Protect Myself and My Computer?," contains more information about making your children safe on the Internet.

What's causing all the hubbub about the Internet?

Few folks will argue with me if I say that the most-used resource on the Internet is e-mail. It's a workhorse. Many people have access to Internet e-mail, but not the rest of the Internet. As with any workhorse, however, it's there when you need it, but kind of dull.

The next most popular resource on the Internet is the World Wide Web. Nothing dull about that at all. It has multimedia, shopping, useful information, and more. In fact, many people confuse the Internet with the World Wide Web. If you were to ask ten people at random to define the Internet, they would probably describe the World Wide Web. When a company decides that it's going to "have a presence" on the Internet, it doesn't decide to start a gopher server, a mailing list, or a chat server. It goes straight for the throat—the World Wide Web.

What's causing all this hubbub about the Internet? In short, the World Wide Web.

Publishing

Many of the nation's top publications are making their presence felt on the World Wide Web. *Time Magazine. PC Week. Sports Illustrated. The Wall Street Journal.* They're all there. Figure 1.1 shows the *USA TODAY* Web page, featuring the complete daily edition of one of the most popular national newspapers. *USA TODAY* exemplifies one of the biggest advantages of publishing on the Web: It's updated as events occur throughout the day to reflect the latest news, weather, and financial news.

Fig. 1.1
The *USA TODAY* Web site contains the news that you need, updated throughout the day.

Advertising

The Internet old-timers really scorn advertising on the Internet. It violates their concept of "acceptable use." Phooey. As the Internet grows and more commercial services are provided, advertising becomes an unavoidable fact of life. Figure 1.2 shows an example of advertising on the Web.

Fig. 1.2

Microsoft is one of the many sponsors that keep Yahoo! a free Internet service.

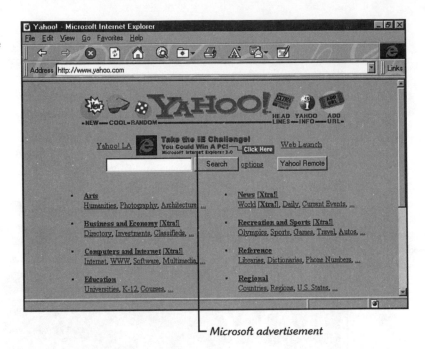

— *Microsoft advertisement*

66 *Plain English, please!*

Yahoo! is an Internet search tool that you can use to find things on the World Wide Web. If you just can't resist, and you want to learn more, see Chapter 11, "Find Things on the Internet." 99

It works just like television. You don't have to pay for the big three networks: NBC, CBS, and ABC. They are free. So, how do these companies make money? They sell advertising. Someone's going to have to pay for all those cool things on the Web, and nobody's willing to pay subscriptions (especially not me). What's an Internet developer to do? Give away his or her services to the public and sell advertising space to sponsors. Everybody's happy. You get great content, the content provider makes a bit of money, and the sponsor gets to target its advertisements to a specific group of people. You do have to spend money to connect to the Internet, however, just like you have to spend money to purchase a TV or receive cable. You learn about the costs associated with an Internet connection in the next chapter.

Services

The press has really dinged the Web a few times because it lacked real services such as bill payments and so on. I'm sure these were fine journalists, but they obviously didn't do much research. The Web is full of very useful services. One of my favorites is AT&T's 800 directory, shown in Figure 1.3. Just as its name implies, you provide the company name and it provides the 800 phone number.

Fig. 1.3
You can also browse the 800 directory rather than search for a specific company.

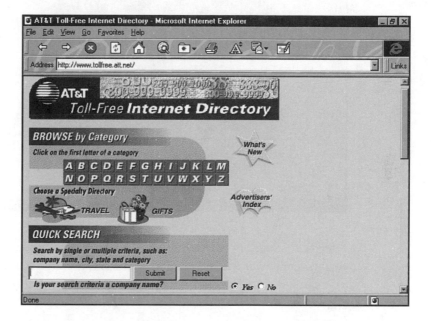

There are many other services available on the Internet. Aside from shopping, which you'll find in the next section, there are weather, business information, employment, and dictionary services available on the Web, too.

Shopping

Online shopping is one of the great potentials of the Internet and the Web. Many companies already offer catalogs, such as 1-800-Flowers, shown in Figure 1.4. You'll also find many catalogs popping up on the Web. You browse the catalog, place your order, and you receive your goods via the mail.

Fig. 1.4
Don't forget Mother's Day. Pick just the right bouquet, pay for it online, and 1–800–Flowers will send it to Mom.

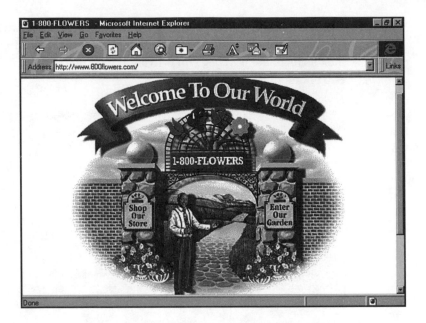

Microsoft, Netscape, and other companies are busily setting standards for how transactions will be handled on the Internet. It's to the point now that you can use a credit card on the Web without worrying about someone ripping it off.

Research

The original intent of the Internet was research, right? Maybe for students and scientists, but real research that regular folks could use is a relatively new thing. The Web has recently seen the addition of the *Encyclopedia Britannica* (see Figure 1.5), several good online dictionaries, travel information, and more. There are also some very powerful search tools that'll help you find even the remotest facts hidden on the Web.

Fig. 1.5
Britannica is now available to the entire public for a subscription fee.

What Do I Need to Know About the Internet?

● **In this chapter:**

● **The Internet doesn't have to be intimidating**

● **You don't have to learn a single buzzword**

● **Here's what you should know before getting started**

● **No special gizmos are required to use the Internet**

● **Choose the service that's best for you**

Sorting out everything you've heard about the Internet can be tough if you don't have a friend, like me, to help you. . . . .

For a lot of people, including myself, getting on the Internet can be intimidating. A lot of things are probably running through your mind, such as:

- Where in the world am I going to get service?

- If I ever do get on, how am I going to find my way around?

- I'm sure it's only for nerds because no one else could understand all that jargon

- I bet I have to spend tons of money buying all sorts of fancy equipment

- How am I going to install all that complicated Internet software?

Don't sweat it. It'll all work out. No one ever intended for the Internet to appear so complicated; it just happened that way because there's so much going on behind the scenes. But this chapter will help you cut through all the nonsense and get online straight away. Then you can safely ignore a lot of the techno-babble (your first technical term) and focus on the important stuff, such as having fun on the Internet.

You don't need to know a bunch of buzzwords, but...

Nerd types deserve blue ribbons for inventing and using buzzwords. Worse, they use all those acronyms that mean even less to you, such as TCP/IP, PPP, URL, and HTTP. To get on the Internet for the first time, you don't need to know a single one of these acronyms. You probably don't care how Windows 95 works, for example; you just want to get the job done. Likewise, you don't need to know a bunch of buzzwords to have fun on the Internet.

Don't get me wrong, it wouldn't hurt you one bit to learn a few concepts and technical terms. And, in this section, I'll gently introduce you to some. But you don't need to feel as if you have to memorize every bit of it before you can get online. Feel free to skip the rest of this section and come back to it when it'll make more sense to you.

The Internet isn't just a big network of networks

You'll frequently hear the Internet referred to as a network of networks, and it's true. There are many types of networks joined together to form the Internet: small businesses, large corporations, the government, universities. They connect in many different ways, too. Some connect through the phone lines, whereas many more organizations connect with permanent lease lines (expensive, permanent connections), satellites, or microwaves. Whatever ways exist to connect two networks, they've been used on the Internet.

 Plain English, please!

> A **network** is a bunch of computers that are connected to share resources and move information between computers.
>
> A **LAN** (Local Area Network) is a network in one geographical location.
>
> A **WAN** (Wide Area Network) is a network that spans many geographical locations. The Internet is a WAN network.

The physical characteristics of the Internet are only part of the story, though. It wouldn't be very helpful to connect to a bunch of networks if you couldn't do anything useful, or if you couldn't interact with other people. Therefore, I'll add my own two cents to the definition of the Internet:

- The Internet is a huge collection of **services** that people can use, such as e-mail, UseNet, the World Wide Web, and IRC Chat. Don't worry yet about what these services do; you'll learn about them later.

- The Internet is also the millions of **people** all over the world who have come together to share ideas, opinions, and resources. Their contributions have built the Internet.

 Q&A *Who governs or controls the Internet?*

No one, really—it governs itself. The Internet is like a country without a government. The participants govern themselves by the sometimes vague agreements that they make for how networks will behave on the Internet. However, there are groups, such as the InterNIC, that facilitate the day-to-day management of the Internet.

How does all this information get around?

To use all those services and hobnob with all those people, you must have a way to move information around the Internet. The problem is complicated by the fact that every computer on the Internet isn't a PC clone running Windows 95. Although I hate to admit it, there are also UNIX, Macintosh, Amiga, and huge IBM mainframes on the Internet. And they all have to talk the same language if they're going to get along with each other.

That's where **TCP/IP** enters into the action. If I speak English and you speak Spanish, but we both know some Greek, we can communicate. TCP/IP serves as a bridge in the same way. It stands for Transmission Control Protocol/Internet Protocol. This is the protocol that all the computers and networks on the Internet understand, regardless of what language they use internally.

 **Plain English, please!**

A **protocol** defines the rules for how two programs or computers will interact—just like a protocol that defines how two diplomats interact.

TCP/IP, however, is really two different protocols:

- **IP** Special computers, called **routers**, use the Internet Protocol to move bits of information around the Internet. Every **packet** of information has the IP address of the computer that sent it and the computer to which it's going. An **IP address** is the unique name of the computer as it's known by the other computers on the Internet. IP addresses are four numbers, separated by dots, that look similar to 198.175.1.12. Que's computer, for example, has the IP address 206.246.150.10.

- **TCP** The Transmission Control Protocol defines how the actual information will be broken up into packets and sent across the Internet. Imagine ripping the first three pages out of this book and sending them to a friend. You put the first page on a bus, mailed the second at the Post Office, and sent the last via Federal Express. They'd all get to your friend at different times and in the wrong order. So, how would your friend put them back together again? The page numbers. TCP handles packets of information the same way.

The Internet has friendly addresses, too

As you just learned, every single computer on the Internet has an IP address. But I'd hate to try and remember the IP address of every computer to which I wanted to connect. Thankfully, there's a human-friendly way to address a computer, called a **domain name**. Microsoft's domain name, for example, is **microsoft.com**. Likewise, it's a lot easier to remember **whitehouse.gov** than it is to remember the IP address 198.137.241.30. Remember Que's IP address (206.246.150.10)? The domain name for that address is **www.mcp.com**—a lot easier, huh? If you're eager to learn more about Internet addresses, see Chapter 6, "The World Wide Web," and Chapter 7, "E-mail and Mailing Lists."

Computers on the Internet, however, still use the IP address to send stuff. So, how does a domain name that you type turn into an IP address? **Domain name servers**, that's how. They translate a domain name into an IP address. It all happens behind the scenes, though.

TIP **How do you pronounce a domain name, such as honeycutt.com,** so as not to sound foolish? Like this: "honeycutt dot com."

Bits and pieces of a domain name

A domain has several words stuck together by periods. The right-most word is the **top-level** domain and usually defines the type of institution or country it's in. In the U.S., there are six top-level domains defined:

Top-level domain	Type of institution
.com	Commercial company
.edu	Educational institution
.gov	Government agency
.mil	Military
.net	Internet service provider
.org	Anything that doesn't fit

A domain name can be more than just two words separated by dots. As you move to the left of the name, it gets more specific. The domain name **onramp.net**, for example, is the name of my Internet service provider. The domain name **www.onramp.net**, however, is the name of a specific computer on my service provider's network.

Tying it all together

You're going to learn about a lot of cool things you can do on the Internet. The World Wide Web, e-mail, and UseNet newsgroups are examples of Internet **resources** available for you to use. All of these resources require two things to work: a client program and a server.

- A **client program** is a program that you run on your computer to access a resource on the Internet. It hides the nasty details behind an easy-to-use interface.

- The client program sends a request to an Internet **server**, asking it to do something or send information back. The server accepts the request and sends a suitable reply back to the client program.

You can't just mix and match clients and servers, though. Each particular type of server requires a client program that talks the same language. You need an FTP client program to talk with an FTP server, for example. Likewise, you need an e-mail client program to talk to an e-mail server.

Every resource on the Internet has a protocol that the client program and the server use to communicate. FTP client programs and servers talk by using the **File Transfer Protocol**. E-mail client programs and servers talk by using the **Simple Mail Transfer Protocol**. And, Web client programs and Web servers talk by using the **Hypertext Transfer Protocol**.

Which Windows do you do?

If you use Windows 3.1, you can access the Internet just fine. Windows 3.1 users have been logging on to the Internet quite happily for years. If you're in a position where you can choose between Windows 3.1 and Windows 95, though, I strongly recommend that you upgrade to Windows 95. Here's why:

- Windows 95 has support for the Internet built right in, whereas Windows 3.1 requires that you go outside the operating system to get onto the Internet.

- If you use Windows 3.1, you won't be able to use all the resources available to Windows 95 and Windows NT users because some programs and features are only available on those platforms.

While Windows 3.1 users have to look outside of Windows for all their Internet needs, Windows 95 users don't. Windows 95 has support for the Internet built right in. Here are some of the ways Windows 95 supports the Internet:

- Windows 95 is a networking operating system, which includes support for a variety of network adapters and protocols, such as TCP/IP.

- Windows 95 includes Dial-Up Networking, which allows you to connect to a network, such as the Internet, via the phone lines.

- Windows 95 includes Microsoft Exchange. When combined with the Internet Mail Service, Exchange becomes a powerful Internet e-mail program.

- Windows 95 includes a handful of other Internet utilities, such as a Web browser, FTP, and Telnet, to get you started.

 Q&A *Can I use Windows 3.1 Internet programs in Windows 95?*

Yep. You'll have very few problems using tools designed for Windows 3.1 in Windows 95. In fact, many Internet tools don't have Windows 95 versions available yet.

You'll need Internet service to get online

For many people, the scariest part of getting onto the Internet is figuring out how to get Internet service. A few years back, it was pretty difficult because there wasn't much to choose from. Now, Internet service comes in many shapes and sizes. The difficulty is in choosing from all the available alternatives.

Basically, there are two types of Internet services available for the casual user: independent service providers and commercial online services, such as CompuServe and The Microsoft Network. The sections that follow discuss each type of service in more detail. Since The Microsoft Network is so new, and you have that handy little icon sitting on your desktop, I'll address it separately as well.

Q&A ***Do I need to buy anything special to connect to an independent service provider or commercial online service?***

Are you a Windows 95 or Windows NT user? The only thing you'll need is a modem; everything else is included with Windows 95. You can get by with a 14400bps (bits per second) modem, but if you're fixing to buy a modem, consider purchasing a 28.8K modem. They're available for less than $200 and you'll be much happier with the results. Windows 3.1 user? In addition to a modem, you'll need software from your Internet service provider to help you connect to the Internet.

Before you move on, though, take a look at Table 2.1. It summarizes some of the issues you may confront when choosing an Internet service. A thumbs-down indicates that a type of service isn't necessarily the best choice if you're concerned about that particular issue. A thumbs-up indicates that a type of service probably is a good choice, given that particular issue. Keep in mind, however, that Table 2.1 is a generalization of different types of services. Within each type of service, you'll probably find exceptions that defy the way I've ranked them.

Table 2.1   Internet services at a glance

Issue	Commercial	MSN	Independent
Configuration	👎	👍	👍
Expense	👎	👎	👍
Open phone lines	👍	👍	👎
Support	👍	👍	👎
Speed	👎	👍	👍

Issue	Commercial	MSN	Independent
Flexibility	👎	👎	👍
National Access	👍	👍	👎
Stability	👍	👍	👎

TIP **I'm predisposed to recommend that you use an independent** service provider. This type of connection is typically faster and cheaper than most of the alternatives. It also allows you to use your own choice of client programs. In particular, the World Wide Web is a tastier treat if experienced with the fastest connection possible.

Many people use other commercial online services

Once upon a time, the only way to get access to the Internet was through a university or the government. Service providers cropped up and made it a bit easier to get online. You couldn't access the Internet, however, through services such as CompuServe. Things have changed, though. CompuServe, America Online, and Prodigy all have rather complete access to the World Wide Web and UseNet newsgroups. They're adding support for other stuff, too.

Internet access through commercial online services is still pretty weak. The connections are slower than you'll find with an independent service provider because you generally have to use their specialized software to access Internet resources, and you aren't necessarily connected directly to the Internet. These services aren't as flexible as independent service providers, either, because you're stuck with the software they provide. You can't download a better e-mail client, for example, and use it with your online service. Here's what some of the commercial online services have to offer:

- **CompuServe**   CompuServe has been around for what seems like forever. It's very close to breaking down the differences between independent service providers and commercial online services. CompuServe gives you full access to the Internet; not just through its own specialized software like the other services, but through real Internet connections. You can use any Web browser you want with CompuServe, as well as any client programs you want. Its closest competition is The Microsoft Network.

- **America Online**   America Online is today's most popular online service. Many people are happy with it, while others find its Internet service particularly slow. You can't choose which client programs you want to use with America Online, so you're stuck with what they provide—for now. America Online does plan to make its service available with non-proprietary tools such as Internet Explorer, soon. If you're looking for a quick and easy way to get on the Internet, though, you might consider their offerings, which include the World Wide Web, Internet e-mail, Gopher, FTP, and UseNet newsgroups.

- **Prodigy**   Prodigy is falling behind the pack with it's Internet offerings. It does support Internet e-mail, but you can't send file attachments. You can also use the Prodigy software to browse the Web and UseNet newsgroups. However, Prodigy doesn't allow you to use your own client programs, such as FTP client programs.

The biggest gripe I have with using a commercial online service is the cost. Whereas an independent service provider charges a flat monthly fee, a commercial online service charges you by the hour, in addition to a monthly fee. This can add up fast, especially if you get hooked on the World Wide Web (it'll happen, I promise). Table 2.2 compares the current pricing plans for CompuServe, America Online, and Prodigy. Just for kicks, I've added rows for independent service providers and The Microsoft Network. Note that this table includes the basic pricing plans for these services. Many of these services also offer special plans that have a higher monthly fee, but lower hourly connect charge. Call for more details.

Table 2.2   Internet pricing at a glance

Service	Monthly	Hourly	Free hours	Cost/20 hours
CompuServe	$9.95	$2.95	5	$54.20
America Online	$9.95	$2.95	5	$54.20
Prodigy	$9.95	$2.95	5	$54.20
MSN	$4.95	$2.50	3	$47.45
Independent	$20 – $30	–	–	$20 – $30

Microsoft Network is an easy alternative

If finding an independent service provider seems like a hassle, you might try using The Microsoft Network as your Internet service provider. The Microsoft Network is on every computer that is running Windows 95 (a source of great controversy, which I won't examine). If you don't have an account with another online service or independent service provider, this is definitely the quickest and easiest way to get onto the Internet.

Using Microsoft Network, you can do pretty much anything on the Internet that you can do with a service provider. Also, if you're one of those types who likes a certain amount of organization in their lives, The Microsoft Network might be the right choice. It makes sense out of the Internet by categorizing everything for you.

I recommend an independent service provider

Independent service providers are regional companies that sell connections to their network. Their network, in turn, is connected to the Internet.

The reasons for recommending an independent service provider are straight-forward. They're cheaper, faster, and more flexible. Want more details? Here you go:

- **Cheaper**   Most independent service providers charge a flat monthly fee for Internet access. If you spend much time on the Internet, you'll save loads of money by using an independent provider.

- **Faster** The connections are simply faster than most commercial online services—with few exceptions. The reason is that you're closer to the Internet. In fact, your computer is connected to the Internet instead of being connected to a service that has to get the information from the Internet for you.

- **Flexible** You can use any client programs you want with your independent service provider. Don't like the e-mail program you're using? Don't like your Web browser? Trade 'em in for different programs.

Selecting a good service provider and configuring Windows 95 to work with it can seem tricky, but it's not. Chapter 3, "Here's How to Connect to the Internet," will help you find service providers in your area and get your connection going in minutes.

 TIP **Don't talk yourself into subscribing to an e-mail-only or shell** account with an independent service provider. An e-mail-only account allows you to exchange messages with other Internet users, but that's all. A shell account is a text-only account that requires you to learn a bunch of archaic commands. You can't use a graphical Web browser with this type of account. E-mail-only and shell accounts are worthless, unless you truly don't intend to use the resources available on the Internet.

Here's How to Connect to the Internet

● **In this chapter:**

- **Where do I find a service provider?**

- **How do I compare service providers?**

- **Keep the information the provider gives you**

- **Here's how to configure Windows for the Internet**

- **How do I start and stop my Internet connection?**

Connecting to the Internet with an independent service pro-vider is the best alternative for most people. It's better, faster, and cheaper . . . . >

The best part about configuring Windows to connect to the Internet is that you only do it once and then forget about it. If you follow the instructions in this chapter, you'll be up and running in no time.

It's not hard. Really! Here's an overview of the process:

- Locate a service provider. After you subscribe, the provider will give you all the information you need to connect to its computer. More than likely, the provider will also give you software that you can use with your connection.

- Configure Windows. Windows 95 and NT users are in luck. Both operating systems come with everything you need to connect to the Internet. Windows 3.1 users will get the software they need for connecting to the Internet from their service provider.

Here's how to subscribe to a service provider

Independent service providers deserve a lot of credit for the momentum that the Internet has these days. Before they came along, the Internet wasn't easily accessible by the general public. If you weren't a student, research scientist, government employee, or an employee of a major corporation, you were probably out of luck.

So, what is a service provider? A service provider maintains large computer systems that are connected to the Internet. Service providers don't do it just for kicks, either. They sell connections on their computers to folks like you and me. Then you connect to the Internet through their computer systems.

Where do I find a provider?

The hardest part of getting ready for the Internet is definitely the task of locating a service provider. There isn't an Internet Power & Light company for each city that is responsible for all the local connections. The phone company doesn't sell Internet connections, either—but they should consider it. After you've located a provider, you can get online quickly with the help of this book and the service provider.

Many introductory books about the Internet tell you that these great lists of service providers exist that you'll find on the Internet; but, this is one of the great Internet paradoxes. You need a list of providers to connect to the Internet, but you need an Internet connection to get a list of providers. Argh. I've never been satisfied with these lists because they frequently don't reflect the best service providers in an area.

There are better ways to find a service provider. Use the following suggestions and you'll come up with the best service provider in your area:

- **Call your local computer store.** They always know the best service providers in your area. The smaller computer stores generally know more about the local scene, but computer stores such as CompUSA, Computer City, Best Buy, and Incredible Universe also can help.

- **Call your local book store.** Many bookstores have Internet demos set up near the computer books—particularly the technical book stores such as Protech Technical Books. These stores will be able to point you in the right direction.

- **Call your favorite radio station.** I have seen very few radio stations that aren't on the Internet. For that matter, many radio stations also broadcast simultaneously over the Internet. Call your favorite station and ask them for a referral.

- **Look for advertisements.** The larger service providers in each area typically advertise. You'll find advertisements on billboards, radio, and television. Also, look under Internet, Networking, or Communications in your phone book.

If you still can't find a service provider, you can ask a friend to log onto the Internet for you and check the Web page at **thelist.com** (you'll learn about the Web later). This is a list of service providers—on the Internet, of course—that is updated regularly. The best part about this list is that it contains reviews of each service, written by people who have used it. This is possibly the only list that I've seen on the Internet that accurately reflects the service providers found in each area.

How much is it going to cost?

There are generally two different types of rate plans: flat monthly and hourly. Here's the scoop:

- **Flat monthly** plans charge you a single monthly fee for all the Internet access that you can stand. This is the best possible, and the most common, type of rate plan for independent service providers. You can expect to pay between $20 and $40 a month. If they're charging more than $40, find out why. If you don't like the answer, don't sign up.

- **Hourly plans** charge you by the hour—usually a few bucks. If you see one of these, turn tail and run. I promise you that you'll be hooked on the Internet and you'll spend much more time online than you think you will. Monthly rate plans are too numerous to get stuck with an hourly plan. Besides, you won't feel comfortable exploring the Internet as much if you're strapped with an hourly bill.

A variation of both of these plans is one that charges you a low monthly fee, around $10, and then an hourly fee after a pre-set number of hours—between 20 and 120 hours. You'll usually end up doing no better than the flat monthly rate plan, though.

To give you an idea of how each type of rate plan compares, see Table 3.1. This table compares the total monthly amount of the various rate plans for a user who spends about 40 hours a month on the Internet (a very reasonable number, I might add).

Table 3.1   Use this table for your own numbers

Plan	Rate	Hours	Total
Monthly	$30/month	40	$30
Hourly	$2/hour	40	$80
Combination	$10/month $2/hour after 20 hours	40	$50

Am I getting a good deal?

Shopping for an Internet connection is kind of like shopping for a good plumber. You want to know that the price is fair, and that the services are good and available when you need them.

It's a bit inconvenient to frequently change service providers. So, make sure that you'll be happy with the provider you're considering. Ask each service provider you call the following questions, compare their answers, and the best provider will be obvious afterward:

- **Do you charge a monthly or an hourly fee?** See the previous section for more information about the different fee plans you'll find. There's no reason to settle for anything other than a monthly fee.

- **What's the fastest connection possible?** Don't settle for anything less than a 28.8K connection. Most service providers have them now, but you'll run across a few that are still using 14.4K connections. I'd be concerned about the level of service you will receive from a provider that is still using 14.4K modems.

- **Do you support PPP or just SLIP?** PPP is a faster connection protocol than SLIP (see Chapter 2, "What Do I Need to Know About the Internet?," for details). It also lets you automatically log on to the server. I'd hold out for a PPP connection, if possible.

- **How many modems and how many users do you have?** Divide the number of users by the number of modems. If the provider has 400 users and 40 modems, then it has 10 users per modem. This is reasonable. If the provider has more than 10 users on each modem, however, you'll get busy signals on a regular basis.

- **Do you provide 24-hour support?** Make sure that the service provider will be available when you need it. You'll find yourself trying to use your connection mostly at night and on the weekends. And, you will have questions and problems—guaranteed. If the provider isn't there to help, you're out of luck.

- **Do you support Windows 95?** If a service provider tells you that it doesn't support Windows 95, move on to another provider. Most providers recognize that many of their customers will be using Windows 95 and will make the extra effort to learn it themselves.

- **Do you support PAP?** PAP stands for password authentication protocol. This allows you to log on to the provider's server without retyping your username and password. If the provider doesn't support PAP, ask whether it will provide a script for the Windows 95 Dial-Up Scripter. Most providers already have a script that they can send to you.

TIP **The Windows 95 Dial-Up Scripts lets you automate your logon**
process, instead of typing your name and password all the time. You need a
script, though, which you can get from your service provider. You'll find the
Dial-Up Scripter on your Windows 95 CD-ROM in **\Admin\Apptools\Slip**.
You'll find instructions for installing it in the same folder, too.

- **Do you subscribe to ClariNet?** Decide for yourself whether this is a
  major issue. ClariNet is a great news service to which most service
  providers do subscribe. However, it's not practical to subscribe on
  your own.

- **Do you have a software disk?** Many providers will provide you with a
  disk full of software that is preconfigured for use with their server. If a
  provider doesn't have a disk, I'd be concerned about the level of support that you'll receive from this provider in the future. If you're using
  Windows 3.1 and the provider doesn't have software that you can use to
  connect to its service, find another provider.

- **What modems do you use?** If you haven't yet shelled out the money
  for a modem, ask a prospective service provider what modems it uses.
  Then, buy the exact same modem. More often than not, you'll have
  faster and more stable connections if you use the same modem as your
  provider.

Feel free to add your own questions to the list. I'm sure there are more you
could ask, but these stick out in my mind as the most important "deal
breakers."

What happens after I subscribe?

You've chosen a provider, called it, signed up, and, most importantly, you've
paid. What's next? The provider will set up your account and give you the
information you need to make the connection. This usually happens when
you place your order, but sometimes the provider has to call you back later
with the information.

TIP **If you have a fax machine available to you, ask the provider to fax**
the information. Then you won't have to try reading your own handwriting
later.

The following list shows what you can expect the provider to tell you. If the provider leaves something off, be sure to ask whether the provider means to leave it out—take nothing for granted. For your convenience, space has been provided on the inside of the back cover for you to write these down:

- **Dial-Up phone number**   The phone number that your computer calls to connect to the service provider's computer.

- **Support phone number**   The phone number for 24-hour support in case you run into any problems.

- **PPP/SLIP username and password**   The username and password that you'll use to log on to the provider's computer. This will frequently be the same as your e-mail account name and password.

- **E-mail account name and password**   The account name and password to log on to your e-mail account and collect your messages. This will frequently be the same as your PPP username and password.

- **Domain name**   Your service provider's domain name. This is the name that your provider's computer is known by on the Internet.

- **E-mail address**   The address to which people will address e-mail that they send you. My e-mail address is **jerry@honeycutt.com**, for example. Your e-mail address will usually be your user e-mail account name, located on the left side of the @ (at sign), and your provider's domain name, located on the right side of the @.

- **Mail server**   The name of the computer that you use to check your e-mail, as described in Chapter 7, "E-Mail and Mailing Lists." The provider may call this a mail host.

- **DNS server**   The domain name server is a computer that translates domain names into those four numbers (IP addresses) that you learned about in Chapter 2.

- **Alternative DNS server**   The alternative DNS service is a backup in case the first one isn't working. Some providers don't provide an alternative.

- **NNTP news server**   The name of the news server. This is the computer that your news reader will use to read UseNet newsgroups, as described in Chapter 8, "UseNet Newsgroups."

- **Assigned IP address and subnet mask**   Your permanently assigned IP address. Ninety-five percent of the time, you won't have one. A permanent IP address makes it easy for other people to connect to your computer while you're on the Internet—not necessarily the best thing to do. IP addresses have a subnet mask that identifies what type of IP address you have. This value will look like **255.0.0.0**, **255.255.0.0**, or **255.255.255.0**. Your subnet mask will almost always be **255.255.255.0**.

- **PAP or CHAP support (yes or no)**   If your provider supports PAP or CHAP, you won't need to use a script to log on to the provider's server. If it doesn't support these, ask it for a script that you can use with Dial-Up Scripter.

The service provider also may send you a disk of software to use with your new Internet account. You can use the software provided by the service provider, or you can use any of the software described in this book (in many cases, they'll be the same). If you're using Windows 3.1, make sure that the service provider gives you the software you need to connect to the Internet.

 TIP **Some of the software that your service provider gives you will be** shareware. That means you have to pay the author for the software if you like it and want to continue using it. See Chapter 12, "Get Your Software Fix Online," to learn more about shareware.

Here's how to configure Windows 95 for your provider

Windows 95 is very easy to configure for the Internet. You have to do three things. First, you need to install the Dial-Up Adapter, which lets you connect to another network—such as your Internet service provider—using your computer's modem. Next, you need to install the TCP/IP networking protocol that you learned about in Chapter 2. Last, you need to create a Dial-Up Networking connection for your service provider.

First, install the Dial-Up Adapter

Make sure you don't already have Dial-Up Networking installed on your computer. Open My Computer to find out if you can see the Dial-Up

Networking icon. If you cannot see the icon, you need to install the Dial-Up Adapter. Installing the Dial-Up Adapter is very easy. Here's how:

1 Open the Control Panel and double-click the Add/Remove Programs icon.

2 Click the Windows Setup tab, select communications from the list, and click the Details button. You should see a window that looks similar to Figure 3.1.

Fig. 3.1
If you see a check mark beside Dial-Up Networking, the Dial-Up Adapter is already installed.

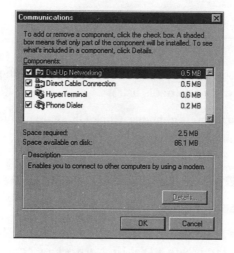

3 Click the box next to Dial-Up Networking until you see a check mark.

4 Click OK to save your changes. Click OK again, and follow the instructions that Windows 95 gives you.

Next, install TCP/IP

Installing TCP/IP on your computer isn't as formidable as it sounds. Here's how:

1 Open the Control Panel and double-click the Network icon. If you see TCP/IP in the list of networking components, it is already installed.

2 Click the Add button to display a list of the network components you can install.

3 Select Protocol from the list and click the Add button. You'll see a window that looks like Figure 3.2. This window contains a list of manufacturers on the left side and a list of protocols on the right side.

Fig. 3.2
Microsoft provides
versions of the most
popular protocols.

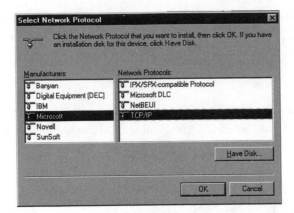

4 Select Microsoft from the Manufacturers list, and then select TCP/IP from the Network Protocols list.

5 Click OK to save your changes. Click OK again and follow the instructions that Windows 95 gives you.

Then, create a Dial–Up Networking connection

Now that you have both the Dial-Up Adapter and TCP/IP installed on your computer, you need to create a Dial-Up Networking connection for your service provider. You should now have a new folder in My Computer called Dial-Up Networking. Double-click the My Computer icon that you see on your desktop; then, double-click the Dial-Up Networking icon. Here's how to create a new connection for your service provider:

1 Double-click the Make New Connection icon you see in the Dial-Up Networking folder.

2 Type a name that you want to give to this connection in Type a name for the computer you are dialing. Click Next to continue.

3 In the space provided, type the phone number of the computer that your service provider gave you. Click Next to continue.

TIP **If you live in a metro area that has two or more area codes for the** same local calling area, and you're in a different area code than your service provider, you may have to dial with your service provider's area code.

Q&A *I live in a metro area that has two area codes for the same local calling area. I'm in one area code and my service provider is in another. I have to use my service provider's area code to dial. How do I make Dial-Up Networking dial my service provider's area code and phone number without putting a 1 in front of the number?*

When you set your dialing properties for your modem, you specified your area code. Dial-Up Networking sees that you're calling another area code and insists on putting the 1 in front of the number because it thinks you're making a long distance phone call. Here's the trick to fixing this: in the space where Dial-Up Networking asks you for your service provider's area code, put your area code instead. In the space where Dial-Up Networking asks you for your service provider's seven digit phone number, put all ten digits of its phone number, including the area code. Now, Dial-Up Networking thinks you're making a local call, but it'll dial the area code anyway because you've specified it as part of the phone number.

4 Click Finish to save your new connection in the Dial-Up Networking folder.

5 In the Dial-Up Networking folder, right-click your new connection and click Properties. This opens the property sheet for that connection.

6 Click Server Type and you'll see a dialog box similar to the one shown in Figure 3.3.

7 Select PPP:Windows 95, Windows NT 3.5, Internet from the Type of Dial-Up Server: list. Also, make sure that Enable software compression and TCP/IP are the only options selected in this window.

8 Click TCP/IP Settings and you'll see a dialog box similar to the one shown in Figure 3.4.

Fig. 3.3

Your dialog box should look exactly like this before you click OK.

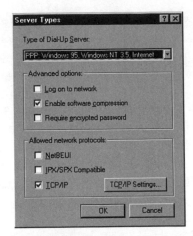

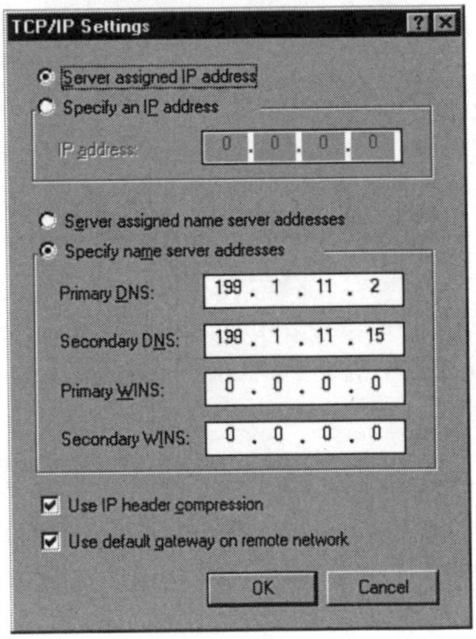

Fig. 3.4

If your service provider assigned you an IP address, select Specify an IP address and fill it in.

9 Select `Specify name server addresses` and fill in the primary and secondary domain name servers (DNS), which your service provider gave you, in the spaces provided.

10 Click OK to save your changes to the TCP/IP settings. Click OK to save your changes to the settings. Click OK one more time to save your changes to your connection.

How do I connect to a SLIP or CSLIP account?

You'll need to install SLIP and CSLIP support from your Windows 95 CD-ROM (it's not available from the diskette version of Windows 95). If you have installed Microsoft Plus!, however, it sets up SLIP and CSLIP support for you. You'll find instructions for installing SLIP support in **\Admin\Apptools\Slip** on your Windows 95 CD-ROM. Incidentally, if you follow the instructions in this file, you'll also get the Dial-Up Scripter as a bonus.

After you've installed CSLIP support, create your dial-up connection, as described in the previous steps. Open your Dial-Up Networking folder and right-click the connection. Select Properties. Change the server type by clicking Server Type and selecting SLIP or CSLIP from the Type of Dial-Up Server list. Click OK twice to save your changes.

Starting and stopping your Internet connection

All of the programs described in this book require a Winsock connection to the Internet. Your connection is configured. All you have to do is ring up your provider's computer. Here's how:

 Plain English, please!

Winsock refers to the method used by Internet programs that run on your computer to communicate with your dial-up connection to the Internet. You'll frequently see your connection to the Internet referred to as a Winsock or an **IP connection**. These are fancy buzz words that simply mean that you have a "real" connection to the Internet. **99**

1 Double-click the icon in the Dial-Up Networking folder that represents your connection. Windows 95 displays the dialog box shown in Figure 3.5.

2 Type your username and password in the fields provided. Select Save Password if you don't want to retype your password every time.

3 Click Connect and Dial-Up Networking will dial your service provider's computer. It displays a window that shows you the current status of the call.

Fig. 3.5
If you haven't used this connection before, the name and password fields will be blank.

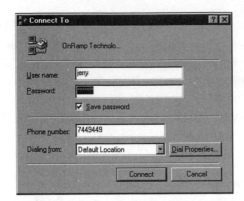

Q&A ***I choose Save Password. Regardless, every time I open my Internet connection, it asks me for it again. Why?***

Windows 95 keeps all your passwords tidy by storing them in a password list. You gain access to this password list by typing your name and password when Windows 95 first starts. This is where your connection "saves" your password. If you didn't type your name and password when Windows 95 first started (by pressing Esc when Windows 95 prompted you for your password) your connection doesn't know where to find your password list. Restart Windows 95, and log on using your password.

My computer dials the phone and the status window eventually says, "Verifying username and password." A few minutes later, Dial-Up Networking displays an error message that says "Dial-Up Networking could not negotiate a compatible set of network protocols." What's wrong?

Your independent service provider might not support PAP or CHAP. You'll need to log on to your provider's computer manually or use a script. If you can't get a script from your service provider, try logging on to the service manually. Right-click the icon representing your icon and choose Properties. Click Configure and then click the Options tab of the modem property sheet. Select Bring Up Terminal Window After Dialing, and click OK twice to save your changes.

4 If you configured your connection to log on to the server manually, Dial-Up Networking will display the Post-Dial Terminal Screen window. Log on to the server manually and click Continue.

When you're ready to disconnect from your service provider's computer, click Disconnect in the dial-up connection window.

Here's how to configure Windows NT 4.0 for your provider

Windows NT 4.0 Dial-Up Networking is a great improvement over Windows 95 Dial-Up Networking. You choose Dial-Up Networking from the Start menu and follow the instructions. That's it. Windows NT worries about installing TCP/IP and all that other stuff. Now, if you need a few more instructions than "just click ...", use these steps:

1 From the Start menu, choose Programs, Accessories, Dial-Up Networking. If the Dial-Up Networking window pops up, then you've already installed it. Otherwise, you'll see a window that tells you a bit about Dial-Up Networking.

2 Click Install to copy the Dial-Up Networking files onto your computer. If your NT CD-ROM isn't in the drive, NT will prompt you for it. After it's finished, you'll see the Add RAS Device dialog box.

3 Pick a modem from the list and click OK. Note that if you haven't yet installed your modem, NT gives you the opportunity at this point. After you pick a modem, you'll see the Remote Access Setup window, shown in Figure 3.6.

4 Click Network to choose a networking protocol. Since you're connecting to the Internet, you'll choose TCP/IP and click OK.

5 Click Continue and NT will finish copying the files it needs for Dial-Up Networking. In addition, it'll copy the TCP/IP files to your computer.

6 When it's finished, click Restart to restart Windows NT.

7 After your computer starts up, choose Programs, Accessories, Dial-Up Networking, again. You'll see a dialog box telling you that you don't have any phonebook entries.

8 Click OK to continue and you'll see the New Phonebook Entry Wizard. You use this wizard to create your Dial-Up Networking connection to your service provider.

Fig. 3.6
Click Configure to change between dial out outline, receive only, and dial out and receive.

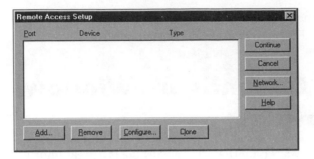

9 Type the name of your service provider and click Next. You'll see the dialog box shown in Figure 3.7, which lets you describe why you're using Dial-Up Networking.

Fig. 3.7
If you're SLIP, you must choose The non-Windows NT server...check box.

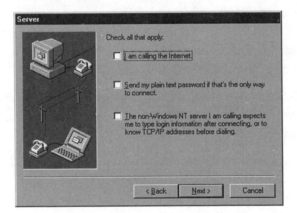

10 Check all the boxes that apply. Since you're connecting to the Internet, check I am calling the Internet. Also, select Send my plain text password if that's the only way to connect if your service provider is using a UNIX server or you're not sure what type of server it is using. Last, check the final box if you normally have to type your name and password when you log on to the Internet. Click Next to continue.

11 Type the phone number that you call to connect to the service provider and click Next to continue.

12 Select Point-to-Point Protocol if your service provider told you to connect with PPP, or select Serial Line Internet Protocol if your service provider told you to connect with SLIP. Click next to continue and you'll see a dialog box that looks like Figure 3.8.

Fig. 3.8
In most cases, one of the predefined scripts will work. Click Edit script to modify the selected script.

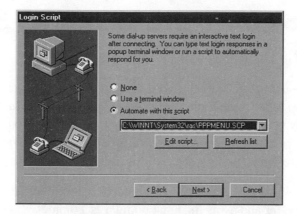

13 If you're using SLIP, or your service provider makes you type your name and password when you log on, you can use a script to automate the process. Select Automate with this script and pick a script from the list. If you're not sure which script to pick, try Generic or PPPMENU with your service provider. You can also contact your service provider and ask them to provide you a script if these don't work. Click Next to continue and you'll see the IP Address dialog box.

14 If your service provider gave you a permanent IP address, type it in the spaces that follow. Otherwise, leave this set to **0.0.0.0**. Click Next to continue and you'll see the Name Server Addresses dialog box.

15 Type your primary and secondary domain name servers in the spaces provided. Your service provider gave you these IP addresses. Errors in this dialog box are one of the most common reasons folks have trouble connecting to the Internet, so make sure that you get both IP addresses correct. Click Next to continue.

16 You're finished. Click Finish to close the wizard.

Once you have a connection, you can open the Dial-Up Networking folder in My Computer, or from the Start menu in Programs, Accessories, Dial-Up Networking. Double-click the connection icon, and click Dial to log on the Internet.

Here's how to configure Windows 3.1 for your provider

If you're using Windows 3.1, your service provider probably gave you a disk with the software on it that you need to connect to the Internet. In fact, they probably preconfigured it for you so that all you have to do is install the disk and you're off. Make sure that you ask your service provider for instructions on how to install and configure the software they give you.

A good number of programs are available for connecting to the Internet. However, far and away the most popular is Trumpet WinSock. This is probably what your service provider gave you. You'll find instructions for installing and configuring the particular Trumpet WinSock your service provider gave you in INSTALL.DOC or INSTALL.TXT. You'll find these two files on the disk your provider gave you or, if your provider gave you a ZIP file, inside the ZIP file.

Installing the Trumpet WinSock package

Installing the Trumpet WinSock package is simply a matter of copying the files that make up the software into a directory on your computer system. If you received the Trumpet WinSock as a ZIP file, unzip this archive into a directory on your system, such as C:\TRUMPET. Otherwise, copy the files into C:\TRUMPET.

After you copy the Trumpet WinSock files into a directory on your system, add this directory to your PATH by editing your AUTOEXEC.BAT file. For example, the new PATH statement may look like this:

```
PATH C:\TRUMPET;C:\DOS;C:\WINDOWS;
```

The file INSTALL.DOC (which is in Word for Windows format—you can use the file INSTALL.TXT if you do not have this software) gives complete instructions for installing and configuring the Trumpet WinSock package for various systems.

Configuring the Trumpet WinSock package

To configure the Trumpet WinSock package, you must run the program TCPMAN.EXE from the Trumpet WinSock package. You can run this program from the Windows File Manager or you can open the File menu and choose Run in the Program Manager.

The first time you run the TCPMAN.EXE program, it displays a window that contains various fields you first must set to use the Trumpet WinSock package. Here is how to configure it:

1 Select either Internal SLIP or Internal PPP, depending on the type of service from your Internet provider.

2 Fill in the IP address, netmask, gateway address, name server, and domain suffix, as provided by your Internet service provider.

3 Fill in the communications port (the port your modem is on), and the baud that your modem supports. You can usually determine these settings from your modem documentation.

After you fill in these basic options, the Trumpet WinSock program displays the status and operation window, which shows the status of your connection. After the basic configuration is done, open the Dialer menu and choose Manual Login to manually connect to your service provider. This allows you to test your connection and run network software.

After you test your connection to your service provider, you can edit the dialing scripts by opening the Dialer menu and choosing Edit Scripts. Full instructions on what you need to do when editing these scripts is provided in the Trumpet WinSock documentation.

HELP! It Doesn't Work

● In this chapter:

● What do I do if my modem doesn't work?

● My modem works, but I still can't connect

● My browser and other client programs don't work

Don't panic. This chapter shows you how to fix your connection. . . . .

I'm on dangerous turf here. Diagnosing or troubleshooting problems with an Internet connection isn't an easy thing to do. Especially without knowing much about your configuration, what hardware you're using, what software you've installed, or how you're connecting to your service provider.

I'm going to give it a shot, anyway. The suggestions in this chapter should solve most of the problems that you'll encounter. If you're still having problems, however, contact your service provider (or nerd down the street). They can usually help you fix most problems pretty fast.

I've divided this chapter into three main sections. If your modem just doesn't seem to work, start with "My modem doesn't work." If you hear your modem dialing when you try to connect, but you never seem to get a good connection, start with "I can't log on to my service provider." If you connect with your service provider just fine, but your client programs don't seem to work well, go to "My client programs don't work."

Don't feel bad

No matter how bad you think your problems are, or how stupid you think you are, you know that it could get a lot worse. Doubt me? These are purportedly "true" stories of support calls that have landed on a variety of support desks over time:

- A fellow called the support desk because his computer's cup holder wasn't working any more. The technician had the presence of mind to ask the poor fellow if the cup holder had a label that said "4X" on it. "Yup," the fellow said. It was his CD-ROM drive.

- An elderly women called the support desk frustrated because the program told her to "Press any key." She couldn't find the "Any" key anywhere on her keyboard (an oldie but goodie).

- A man called the support desk of my Internet service provider, complaining that he had stomped all over his mouse, but the darn mouse pointer just wouldn't budge. He thought the mouse was a foot peddle.

- After subscribing to service with my Internet service provider, a woman called the support desk because her connection wouldn't work. The support technician finally understood what he was up against when she asked if she needed a modem and a phone line for her connection to work.

My modem doesn't work

You're not going to get very far if your modem isn't working. Modems are a lot simpler than they used to be. There are really only two things you have to worry about. First, make sure that your cable connections are correct, as I describe in "Check your cables." Then, make sure you've configured Windows correctly, as described in "Check your modem configuration."

You may have heard things about modem setup strings, flow control, and error correction. Don't worry about these. They have no bearing on whether or not you can dial a telephone number with your modem. Your service provider may have some suggestions for tuning your modem that you can deal with later.

 TIP **If you can use your modem to connect to other online services,** such as CompuServe or America Online, your modem is probably not the problem.

Check your cables

Have you ever noticed how it's always the simple solutions that people tend to overlook—like checking your cables. I have to admit that on more than one occasion I've had my computer torn apart on the kitchen floor, only to find that I didn't correctly attach a cable to the computer.

You don't have to repeat my occasional idiocy. Check your cables. Here's the connections you should check:

- Make sure that your modem is connected to the wall outlet. As well, make sure that you've plugged the cable into the correct plug. Most modems have two plugs: wall (or line) and phone. You want to connect to the wall outlet with the plug labeled "wall."

- If you have an external modem, check to see if the front of the modem is lit up. Make sure that you've plugged the modem's power cord into a wall socket, and that you've plugged the power cord into the modem. Oh, yeah, turn on the modem. You don't have to worry about these details with internal modems.

- If you have an external modem, make sure that you've connected your modem to your computer with an appropriate serial cable. As well, your computer probably has more than one serial port: COM1 and COM2.

Make sure that you're connecting the cable to the correct port. If in doubt, try it both ways to see if it works.

 Plain English, please!

A **serial cable** is a cable that connects your modem to the back of your computer. A **serial port** is the connection on the back of the computer. Each serial port is numbered: 1, 2, 3, etc. **COM1** is the first serial port, **COM2** is the second, and so on. These days, serial ports are usually labeled on the back of your computer with an icon that contains a series of zeros and ones, like this: 010101. **"**

NOTE   **Internal modems can create a whole new set of problems. You** don't have to worry about the power or serial cables, but you do have to make sure that you configure Windows with the same settings as the modem. Check your modem's manual to make sure you've installed it correctly.

Check your modem configuration

Serial port configuration problems are common for Windows 3.1 users because Windows 3.1 doesn't automatically configure your ports correctly. Windows 95 users have it a bit easier here. For the most part, Windows 95 will configure your serial port without much intervention. If you're using Windows 3.1, on the other hand, make sure that you check your serial port's configuration. Check that the port's IRQ (interrupt request) and I/O address match your serial port's actual configuration. Also, make sure that you don't have devices on both COM1 and COM3 that you want to use at the same time. For example, don't connect a mouse to COM1 and your modem to COM3 because this creates a hardware conflict. Likewise, don't connect competing devices on COM2 and COM4.

 TIP   **If you're not exactly sure what an IRQ or I/O address is, don't try** to reconfigure your hardware. Advanced users often have trouble getting these settings exactly right, so don't expect to figure this out your first time. Call a support technician to help you.

I can't log on to my service provider

Ever hear of limbo? Oblivion? That's what it's like to be able to connect your modem to your service provider's modem, but not be able to log on to its network. Your modem is obviously working because you hear it dial and connect. You can't get past that logon, though. Ouch!

This section contains some things you should check. These suggestions represent a large number of the problems most people encounter. Check this list to see which section you should start with:

- If your modem dials, but the other computer doesn't ever answer the phone, see "Double-check the phone number."

- If the other computer answers, but you get an error that says the dialer can't log you on or can't negotiate a compatible set of protocols, see "Check your networking configuration."

- If the other computer answers, but you never seem to get past the message that tells you the dialer is logging on to the network, see "Set up a script or log on manually." In cases like this, your dialer may also appear to just hang up.

- If the network doesn't validate your user name and password, but you're absolutely sure you typed them correctly, see "Check your user name and password."

TIP Ask your service provider to watch you log on. I don't mean come to your house and look over your shoulder, either. Your service provider can see what happens when you try to log on to their network. They can usually tell you within minutes exactly what's going wrong.

Double-check the phone number

Make sure that you're dialing the correct phone number. Verify the phone number with your service provider if necessary. If you're not completely sure that you're dialing the correct number, lift the handset of your phone and dial it manually. Does a computer answer? If you hear a high pitch squeal when the other end picks up, you're probably dialing the right number. If you hear "hello," you've probably ticked off some poor old lady for the last three hours.

Check your networking configuration

If you're using Windows 95 or NT, make sure that you correctly installed Dial-Up Networking. That means you also correctly installed TCP/IP and the Dial-Up Adapter on your computer. To refresh your memory, go back and take a look at Chapter 3, "Here's How to Connect to the Internet."

If you're using Windows 3.1, you're probably using Trumpet Winsock. You don't have to install TCP/IP or Dial-Up Networking separately, as you do in Windows 95. However, you should make sure that you configured it as your service provider instructed you.

Set up a script or log on manually

If your Internet service provider doesn't support PAP or CHAP (see Chapter 3), you may need to create a script that logs you on to its network automatically. Otherwise, your service provider's computer is sitting there, waiting for you to type a password, and your dialer is sitting there, waiting for the other computer to start a PAP session. Chapter 3 shows you how to install Dial-Up Scripting for Windows 95. If you're using Windows 3.1, your dialer probably has built-in scripting.

You can also log on to your service provider manually. That is, when its computer asks for your user name and password, you type them in on the keyboard. This is a drag, but it's a real quick way to fix the problem if you're not sure how to create a script. Again, Chapter 3 shows you how to log on to your service provider manually if you're using Windows 95.

 TIP **Don't waste your time writing a script. If you find that you do** need a script to log on to your service provider's network, get the script from them. I guarantee you that they've already answered this question enough times to have created a script that they can give you.

Check your user name and password

I hope this one doesn't offend you, but make sure that you're logging on to your service provider correctly. As well, you may be typing the correct letters, but using the wrong case. Your user name and password are probably case sensitive. My user name is **jerry**, for example. **Jerry** won't get me online.

My client programs don't work

These types of problems are the easiest to fix. Your modem works. You can connect to your service provider. At least you have something to work with.

Follow this list to the appropriate sections:

- If you have a Ping utility available (Windows 95 users do), try pinging **mcp.com**. Do you get an error that says Bad IP Address? If so, try pinging **206.246.150.10**. If it works, see "Check your DNS settings."

- If you don't have a Ping utility handy, try opening **www.mcp.com** in your Web browser (see Chapter 6, "The World Wide Web," if you're not sure what opening something in your Web browser means). If that doesn't work, open **206.246.150.10** in your Web browser. If that does work, see "Check your DNS settings."

- If you can check your mail, but you can't read the news (or visa-versa), see "Call your service provider."

Check your DNS settings

A few months back, I called my Internet service provider, ranting and raving about how poor the service was. "I'm going to find me another provider," I said. "One that works more than 50 percent of the time" (never mind the fact that it works more than 95 percent of the time). The support technician very politely asked me if my DNS was configured properly. "You're darn right it is; I know what I'm doing," was my reply. I hung up. A few moments later, I thought I'd check my DNS, just to prove him wrong, and sure enough, I configured it wrong. Don't you just hate when that happens?

Moral of the story? Check your DNS settings. This is almost always the cause of problems when you can log on to your service provider OK, but you can't seem to get your mail or go to a Web site by name. To check your DNS settings, right-click your Dial-Up Networking connection icon (the one you use to dial your service provider), and choose Properties. Then, click the Server Type button, click the TCP/IP Settings button to display the TCP/IP Settings dialog box, and verify the IP addresses of your primary and secondary DNS servers. Change them if you need to, then click OK to save your changes.

Call your service provider

While problems getting online are not usually on your service provider's end, they do occasionally run into trouble. For example, if you're pretty sure that your software is configured correctly (mail host, news server, etc.), and you can read the news from the mail server, but you can't check your mail, your service provider's mail server is probably down. Likewise, if you can check your mail, but you can't read the news, your service provider's news server is probably down.

If this is the case, there is nothing you can do about it. And, as much fun as it may be to yell at your service provider, it happens to all service providers. In this rare case, the pasture is definitely not greener on the other side.

From the mouths of support folk

I recently called my Internet service provider, OnRamp Technologies in Dallas, Tx, and asked them what were the most common problems their new users encountered. Their experience may help you fix your problem much faster. Take a look:

- All of their customers don't necessarily understand that they have to dial into the network before they can do anything on the Internet. A large number of support calls are resolved by telling the customer to connect using Trumpet Winsock or Windows 95 Dial-Up Networking.

- A surprising number of calls relate to the user's modem not being plugged in correctly or the modem failing due to faulty hardware or cables.

- They get calls from a lot of users who can get connected, but not for very long. They're always getting disconnected. The culprit? Either the customer left the connection idle for too long and Dial-Up Networking, or the service provider, disconnected them, or the phone lines were bad. For bad phone lines, my service provider gives this tip: if you call the phone company because a bad phone line is causing problems with your connection, tell them that you use the phone line for a fax machine—they're not as likely to give you the run around. Also, you might ask the phone company to provide a phone line better suited for computers and faxes.

- So, what's the biggest problem new users encounter? Getting the numbers right. When you sign up with an Internet service provider, they give you the IP address for a domain name server (as well as addresses for the mail server, etc). They spend a huge amount of time helping people get these numbers right.

Part II: Getting to Know Your Tools

5

Choose Your Favorite Tools

● In this chapter:

- ● Get the tools from your service provider

- ● Short of that, buy them from the computer store

- ● Online, you can get Microsoft and Netscape tools

- ● You can also try your hand at shareware tools

- ● My Web site makes it very easy to download it all

One of the biggest challenges for some folks is getting all the tools together for the Internet. Do it all, here. . . . . ❯

The Internet is one of the world's great paradoxes. You have to have Internet-enabled programs to get onto the Internet; yet, most of the Internet-enabled programs are on the Internet. A classic chicken and egg plot (I personally believe that the Colonel came first). As George Eliot said, "Play not with paradoxes." No problem, we won't.

This chapter shows you how to get all the software you need before you get yourself on the Internet. Then it shows you how to get more goodies once you can connect to the Internet. Kind of a baby-steps-first approach to getting the tools you need for the Internet. By the time you finish this chapter, you'll have everything you need.

Hammers and chisels and browsers, oh my

I hate it when my wife tells me to go to the store and "buy some groceries." Groceries? Dr. Pepper and M&Ms, I presume. So, I'm not going to tell you to go "get some Internet tools." I'll at least give you a shopping list, like this:

Mail Client   You can't get along without a mail client. It's the work horse. You use it to exchange messages with other folks on the Internet.

Newsreader   A UseNet newsreader is another "must have" Internet tool. It lets you exchange messages with other people in a forum-like or bulletin board environment.

Web Browser   You must have a Web browser. It'll be your most used tool. You use this Internet tool to look at Web pages, which contain a variety of content, from informative to interactive.

 TIP   **If you download Microsoft Internet Explorer or Netscape Navigator, you don't really need anything else to enjoy the Internet.**

There is a variety of other Internet programs you may want to get, later. They aren't essential, however, because you can do most everything with a Web browser, mail client, and UseNet newsreader. The list of optional programs includes:

IRC Client This, and other chat programs, lets you talk to other users, using your keyboard. This is a great way to while away the hours. This would be one of the first programs I'd go after.

FTP Client This handy tool lets you download files directly from an FTP server. However, you can do the same thing through your Web browser.

Gopher Client Gopher clients let you browse servers that are very similar to Web servers, except that their content is organized like an outline. Gopher is dying a slow death, though, so I wouldn't make this a high priority. You can also do this with your Web browser.

Telnet Client This Internet tool lets you connect to other computers on the Internet and use them as if your computer were a terminal.

 This book doesn't give you explicit instructions for using each of the many Internet tools. Most of the tools available today come with rather complete, easy-to-use, online help that provides step-by-step instructions for accomplishing specific tasks. I've devoted this book to helping you learn how to apply those tools to the Internet. If you need more details about using the variety of tools available, see *Using the Internet with Windows 95* or *Special Edition Using the Internet*.

Getting the tools—pre-Internet

In order to get started on the Internet, you need to collect a few basic tools. You need software to dial-up your service provider, for example. You need a basic Web browser. At the very least, you need a utility that you can use to download other tools from the Internet, such as an FTP.

Without an Internet connection, you really have only two primary sources for getting these tools. You can get them from your Internet service provider. You'll learn why I recommend this source in the following section. In the section after that, you'll learn about the software packages that you can buy at your corner computer store.

 You can also get most of the Internet tools you need from online services such as CompuServe and America Online.

Software from your service provider

If you're a new user, I bet you'd like to keep the initial confusion down to a minimum. Wouldn't you? The best way to do that is to rely on your Internet service provider as much as possible for the Internet software you need. In Chapter 3, I told you that you should consider only those service providers that will give you a disk of software that you can use to get online. Better service providers will even preconfigure this disk so that you don't have to mess around with domain name servers and the like.

For Windows 3.1 users, for example, my service provider has a disk available that contains Trumpet Winsock, for connecting to the Internet, and a few basic Internet tools with which to get started. They'll even preconfigure the software so that the only thing you have to do is install the disk and go. For Windows 95 users, they provide typewritten instructions that show you how to configure your computer to connect to their service. You should expect the same service from your Internet service provider.

Windows 95 and NT users: look no further

If you're using Windows 95 or Windows NT, you already have the tools you need to get onto the Internet. First of all, you learned how to connect your computer to the Internet with Dial-Up Networking in Chapter 3, "Here's How to Connect to the Internet." Second, Windows 95 and Windows NT come with a handful of useful Internet programs:

- Internet Explorer is a World Wide Web browser. You should see it on your desktop. You probably have an early version of Internet explorer, however, so you should upgrade to the most recent version, or to another browser, as soon as you're comfortable with the Internet.

- FTP is a rudimentary client that you can use to download files from FTP sites on the Internet. It's a command line oriented client, though, so you'll want to replace it as soon as you feel up to it. To run Windows 95's FTP client, press Ctrl+Esc; choose Run from the start menu, type ftp, and press Enter. When you're ready to bail out of it, just type quit and press Enter.

- Telnet is a pretty good client that you can use to connect to other computers on the Internet. I don't see any reason to replace it because it's pretty decent as far as Telnet goes. To run Windows 95's Telnet client, press Ctrl+Esc; choose Run from the start menu, type telnet, and press Enter.

You'll almost always want to replace the software you get from the service provider. However, you don't need to do it right away. Wait until you're more comfortable with the Internet. The software that the service provider gives you isn't always the best stuff available. Probably the biggest reason is that they want to fit all that stuff on a single diskette. Another reason is that they purposely choose the easiest-to-use software they can find. Once you are ready to replace the software that your service provider gave you, take a look at "Getting the tools from the Internet," later in this chapter.

TIP **Get used to downloading and installing upgrades frequently. The** Internet is moving at a very fast pace and is very competitive. Companies such as Microsoft and Netscape are cranking out new and upgraded software faster than you can keep up.

TIP **Use the heck out of your service provider's support line. You're** paying for it. Many people flit around all willy-nilly without ever calling the support line. They eventually get frustrated enough to give up on the whole thing. In most cases, the problem is easily fixed with a quick call to the service provider. Don't like the answers the support person gave you? Hang up and call back—you'll probably get a different person.

Buy software from the computer store

One year ago, the computer stores in my neck of the woods carried one or two Internet-related programs. Now, they have entire portions of their stores dedicated to Internet software: Web browsers, mail clients, authoring tools, you name it.

You'll find a good variety from which to pick. Some good. Some junk. You'll also find a variety of packages that contain a CD-ROM packed with shareware Internet programs—a good deal if you don't yet have access to the Internet. To help you sort through it all when you go to the computer store, check out the following sections, which describe a couple of my favorites.

TIP **If you want to take advantage of the latest technology on the** Web, there really are only two products you should consider: Microsoft Internet Explorer and Netscape Navigator. See "Get the best stuff from Microsoft or Netscape," later in this chapter, for more information. On the other hand, if you're just starting out, the other stuff you buy at the store is relatively inexpensive and a good way to begin. You can replace it with the better software later.

Netscape Navigator

Netscape Navigator is the market leader in Internet software. It contains the Web browser that has set most of the standards. It also contains a mail client and newsreader. You'll still need to locate some of the other software, such as a good FTP client, but that's not critical because you can use a Web browser to connect to FTP sites. If you're going to buy something at the computer store, Netscape Navigator should be your first choice.

Microsoft Internet Explorer

Internet Explorer will always be free for you to download (according to Gates, that is). But, by the time this book gets into your hands, I expect that you'll be able to buy Microsoft Internet Explorer in the computer stores. Probably dirt cheap, too. You can save yourself a lot of trouble by buying it instead of downloading it.

Quarterdeck InternetSuite

InternetSuite contains a Web browser, mail client, UseNet newsreader, FTP client, and Telnet client. It also includes Connect and Play, which helps you quickly set up an Internet account and get online.

Spry Internet in a Box

Spry Internet in a Box contains a Web browser, mail client, UseNet newsreader, FTP client, Telnet client, and Gopher client. This package also lets you use your CompuServe account to access the Internet. Membership information is included in the box.

Getting the tools from the Internet

If you're already connected to the Internet, you don't need to mess with your Internet service provider or the computer store. You have access to the best sources of Internet software known to mankind. You just need to know how to get at them.

The easiest way to get a full set of software is to go directly to Microsoft or Netscape. These companies set the standards. You can also get some pretty good software from a Winsock collection such as TuCows. Last, you can go to my Web site and nab a ZIP file that I've prepared especially for you. It contains some pretty good Internet programs to get you started.

Get the best stuff from Microsoft or Netscape

Microsoft and Netscape are pretty much in the driver's seat when it comes to setting the standards. You can ignore all the hoopla about the "browser wars." Microsoft and Netscape may bloody themselves, but neither will win the war. You will. Bottom line: You can't go wrong with either package (for what it's worth, my personal favorite is Internet Explorer).

Downloading Microsoft Internet Explorer

Internet Explorer is arguably as good as Netscape Navigator. It goes far beyond Netscape in some ways, too. ActiveX objects and VBScript are two examples. The latest version of Internet Explorer is available for Windows 95 and Windows NT users. Windows 3.1 users will never have it as good as the other folks, though, because the Windows 3.1 version of Internet Explorer will always lag far behind the rest.

 TIP **If you're using Windows 3.1, you'll fare better with Netscape** Navigator. The next section shows you how to get it.

Here's how to get your own copy of Internet Explorer:

1 Open **http://www.microsoft.com/ie/download** in your Web browser. Scroll down to the bottom of the page and you'll see something similar to Figure 5.1.

2 Pop open the drop-down list, choose your flavor of Windows, and click Next. You'll see another Web page as shown in Figure 5.2.

Fig. 5.1
Select Additional Features & Add-ons to download other cool programs that you can use with Internet Explorer.

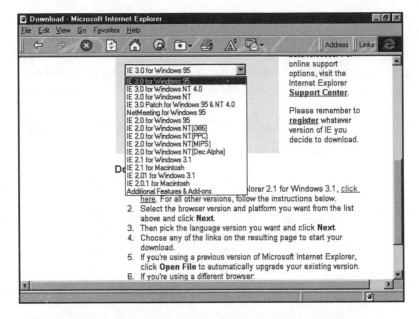

Fig. 5.2
Some of the languages are supported only by the beta product at this moment.

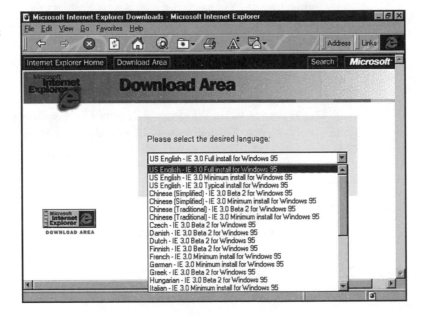

3 Choose the language and type of install you want from the drop-down list. The full install includes Internet Explorer, Internet Mail and News, the HTML layout control, and ActiveMovie.

4 Click Next, and you'll see a Web page that contains a list of download sites. Click the link text to one of the sites to start downloading the file.

Once you've downloaded the file, double-click it to install Internet Explorer and the other components. Follow the instructions that you see on the screen.

Downloading Netscape Navigator

Netscape is undoubtedly the market leader when it comes to the Web. Navigator is the godfather of Web browsers. This isn't any more evident than when you take a look at most of the Web sites on the Internet. A large number of them say that they're optimized for Netscape Navigator. That means that they take advantage of certain features in Netscape to give you a more interesting experience.

Netscape is easy to download. Here's how:

1 Open **http://www.netscape.com/comprod/mirror/ client_download.html** in your Web browser. Scroll down about half way, and you'll see something similar to Figure 5.3.

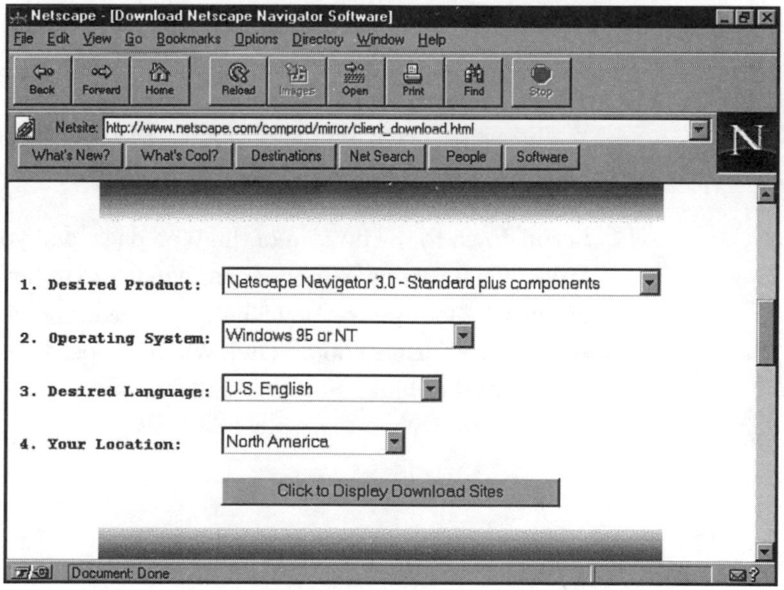

Fig. 5.3
You can download a variety of optional components from this Web page, too.

2 Choose the product you want to download, your platform, language, and location from the lists you see on the Web page.

3 Click the bar labled `Click to Display Download Sites`, and you'll see a list of download sites at the bottom of the Web page. Click the link next to the site that is closest to you. If you get an error when you click a link, try a different link as that site is probably very busy.

Download all the clients you need from TuCows

TuCows is a very popular site for freeware and shareware Internet programs. You can read about TuCows in detail in Chapter 12, "Get Your Software Fix Online." The best thing about TuCows is that you don't have to look much further to get all of the Internet programs you need. You can even download Microsoft Internet Explorer and Netscape Navigator from this site. Here's how:

1 Open **http://www.tucows.com** in your Web browser. About midway down the Web page, you see a list of **mirror sites**. Click the mirror site closest to you to go to that site.

66 *Plain English, please!*

A mirror site is an exact duplicate of the primary site. Many popular Internet sites mirror themselves on other servers because demand for their content is so high that a single server just won't do. 99

2 Scroll down to the bottom of the Web page, and you'll see a bunch of links: Win 3.x Apps, Win 95 Apps, Win 3.x Utils, and Win 95 Utils. Click either Win 3.x Apps or Win 95 Apps, depending on your platform. Windows NT users should click Win 95 Apps. As a result, you'll see a Web page that looks similar to Figure 5.4.

Fig. 5.4
Click any icon to see a list of programs that fit that category. Use your browser's Back button to return here.

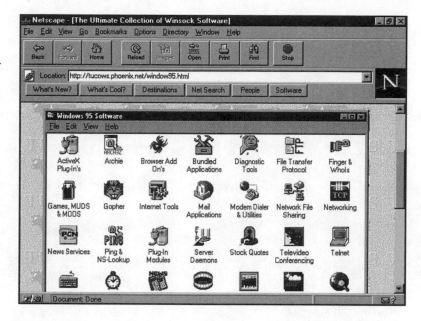

3 The following list shows you the categories of software that I recommend you download from this site (my favorites in parentheses). For each item in the list, click the matching TuCows icon, pick one of the products, and click its link to download it. You can return to the list of categories by clicking your browser's Back button.

- Mail Applications (Internet Mail)
- UseNet Newsreaders (Internet News)
- World Wide Web Browsers (Internet Explorer)

Nab all the software you need from my Web site

If you just don't want to go gallivanting all over the Internet looking for the software you need, check out my Web site. You can find more information about it in Appendix B, "Check Out the Author's Web Page." You'll find a nifty little compressed file waiting for you that contains the Internet programs you need most. Simply point your browser at **http://rampages.onramp.net/ ~jerry** and follow the instructions you see on the Web page.

Once you've downloaded the file to your computer, copy it into its own folder and double-click it to expand its contents. As a result, you'll see a file called README.TXT that describes what to do with the remains.

You can't beat this: I'll e-mail some software

Well, I won't; but a little-known service that lets you access an FTP site through e-mail will (not sure about file attachments? See Chapter 7, "E-Mail and Mailing Lists"). Here's the story:

1 Create a new e-mail and address it to **ftpmail@sunsite.unc.edu**.

2 In the body of the message, type these lines:

```
FTP ftp.mcp.com
USER anonymous
cd pub/que/internet
```

```
get software.exe
quit
```

3 Fire off your message.

A short while later, you'll receive a mail message that contains SOFTWARE.EXE as an attachment. Save this file in its own folder and double-click it to expand its contents. You'll see a file called README.TXT that describes the contents of the file.

6

The World Wide Web

In this chapter:

- **What is the World Wide Web?**

- **The Web works a lot like on-line help**

- **Do I need to know HTTP, HTML, and the like?**

- **How do I point my browser at something?**

- **How does my browser handle multimedia?**

- **The Web has pictures, sounds, and videos**

The World Wide Web is the most happening thing on the Internet . . . .

Watch the money. Where does it go? Figuring that out is a way of life for those overworked souls on Wall Street. But, it's sage advice for Internet surfers like us, too. If you want to know what the hottest thing on the Internet will be, look at where the investment dollars are going. They're going to the World Wide Web (*the Web*).

And look at what all that money has bought. The Web has grown up from a simple **hypertext** system to full-blown **hypermedia,** with graphics, sound, videos, and distributed applications. The nerd-herd has made it possible to shop and place orders online. They've made it possible to find just the right information on the Web. And they've made it possible to present interesting information in a compelling way to millions of people. The next time you see a nerd, give him or her a wink.

 Plain English, please!

> **Hypertext** is a method of linking related documents together. The author uses it to guide you to related information by providing links to other documents. You jump from one document to another by clicking the link. A document about the Internet, for example, might contain a link to another document about the Web. Add a splash of graphics, sound, and video to get **hypermedia**. **"**

The Web may be all you ever need

The Web is the only part of the Internet, other than e-mail, that most people will ever see. They'll never see a **Gopher** menu, and they probably don't need to anyway. They'll never know the joys of reading **WAIS** (pronounced *ways*) output, either. Because of the attention paid to the Web, however, everyone will be exposed to it eventually. So, prepare yourself for the inevitable—read on to learn the Web basics.

The World Wide Web for newbies

Web sites are organized similarly to Windows 95 online help. The first page of help, called Contents, shows what topics are available in the help file. If you double-click any of the topics, you'll see the help screen for that topic.

Likewise, most Web sites have an opening screen called a **home page**. From the home page, you can go to other **Web pages** at the site, or anywhere in the world—just by clicking a link.

 Plain English, please!

> A **Web page** is like many documents you have on your computer. You don't load a Web page from your computer, you load it from a Web server. A **Web site** is another name for a particular Web server. It's a computer that's connected to the Internet so you can access the Web pages it contains. **99**

Every Web page has text, pictures, and links, just like online help. However, Web pages can be much more complex. A link on a Web page can also download a file, display a picture, play a sound, or play a video. The number of things that a link on a Web page can do is practically unlimited. The next section shows some of the things that you'll find on a typical Web page.

There are other WAIS to use the Internet

The World Wide Web is only one way to find information on the Internet. Two others, **WAIS** and **Gopher**, help you find things by using different methods. Here's how they work:

- **WAIS** (Wide Area Information Servers) is a system for retrieving information from databases scattered all over the globe. You can't surf WAIS like you can the Web. Instead, you search the WAIS libraries for the stuff that you want by giving a WAIS program a list of keywords. It returns a listing (often very hard to understand) of the documents it found in the libraries.

- **Gopher** tries to reduce the Internet to a bunch of menus. After digging through a

Gopher menu, you'll eventually find items that will display a file, send you to another Gopher menu, or start some other kind of Internet service. Gopher really is a useful way to scour the Internet. However, because of all the attention the Web is getting, Gopher is falling by the wayside.

So, what happened to Gopher and WAIS in this book? I've followed the money. There are more people trying to learn the Web for the first time than there are people who care to learn WAIS and Gopher. And as always, I try to be helpful. So, I've focused more attention on teaching you the Web, at the expense of WAIS and Gopher.

What's on a Web page

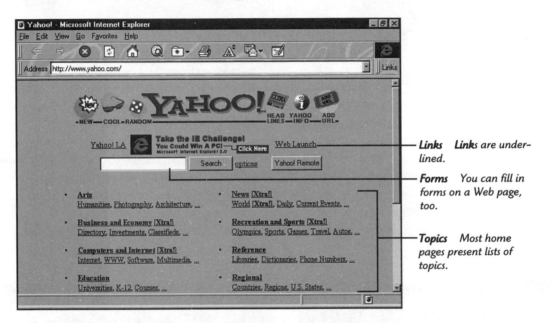

Links *Links are under-lined.*

Forms *You can fill in forms on a Web page, too.*

Topics *Most home pages present lists of topics.*

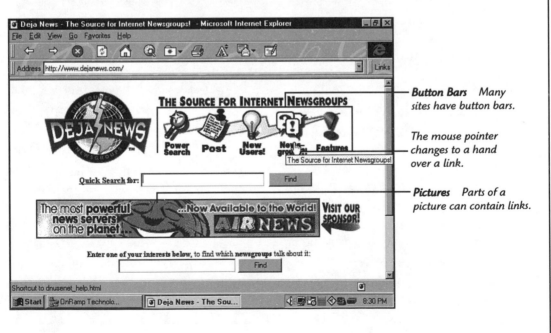

Button Bars *Many sites have button bars.*

The mouse pointer changes to a hand over a link.

Pictures *Parts of a picture can contain links.*

What will I find on the Web?

I'm on dangerous turf here. Why? Because there are so many types of things to find on the Web, I can't possibly list them all. But here it goes:

- I find myself spending a lot of time just having **fun** on the Web. The Web is full of totally useless, but entertaining, Web sites such as a bathroom wall where people scribble their comments, and a magic 8 ball that will answer all your questions.

- Show me a magazine on the newsstand and I can point you to its home page on the Web. Most **magazines**, **news dailies**, and **news shows** have a presence on the Web. Time-Warner, Ziff-Davis, and CNN are good examples of mass media on the Web.

- **Multimedia** is really taking off on the Web. You'll find movies, sounds, and gorgeous pictures all over the place. For a good look at multimedia on the Web, keep reading this chapter and you come to "Multimedia on the Web."

- Most computer companies provide **product support** and information on the Web. Microsoft, Hewlett Packard, Compaq, IBM, and Symantec are all fine examples. You can get free software at some of these sites, too.

- Students the world over can use the Web to **research** a variety of topics, including literature, math, chemistry, and philosophy. Many schools, such as Indiana University, provide helpful information for students.

- There are a variety of useful **services** available on the Web, too. You can look up the status of your FedEx or UPS shipment, search for a friend, get the latest weather for your area, or look up the 800 number of a business.

For everything that has been listed here, you'll find 50 other types of interesting and useful information. If you want to see what's available yourself, **point** your **Web browser** to **www.yahoo.com**. Yahoo! is one of the most complete indexes of information available on the Web. It organizes the index into categories, which makes for easy browsing. Figure 6.1 shows you some of the categories available on the Yahoo! home page.

66 *Plain English, please!*

A **Web browser** is a program, which you run on your computer, that knows how to load and display Web pages. It's also known as a Web client program. You'll learn how to get the two most popular Web browsers, Microsoft Internet Explorer and Netscape Navigator, in Chapter 5, "Choose Your Favorite Tools." **Pointing** your Web browser at a Web page means telling your browser which Web page you want to look at next. **99**

Fig. 6.1

Start at the top and work your way down by clicking a category until you find a Web page that interests you.

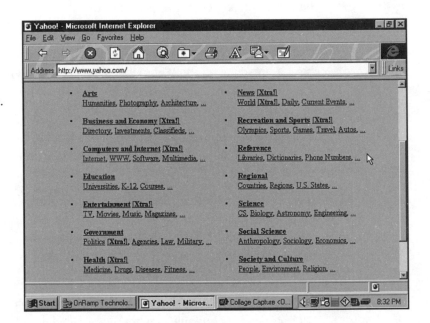

Oh, what a tangled Web we weave

Why do they call it the *World Wide Web*? As the name implies, it's global. You won't always know to what part of the world you're connecting. You can start out reading a Web page in Dallas and go to a Web page in Australia—all at the click of a mouse. The Web is making the world a much smaller place indeed.

What about that *Web* part? The World Wide Web is very similar to a spider's web. The spider's web is made of tiny strands of silk that come together to form a complex network. The spider walks along the strands of silk to go from point to point on the web (snaring an unsuspecting fly, I hope).

Instead of strands of silk, however, the World Wide Web is a complex network of information that is connected by hypermedia links. You're not going to walk from point to point. Instead, you're going to surf from Web page to Web page, using these hypermedia links.

Q&A *Who makes all these Web pages?*

An enormous, diverse group of people, including students, homemakers, businesses, schools, and governments. Some of them come from folks with too much time on their hands. The best part about the Web is the variety.

You need an address to get there

You're having a party, and you need to tell all those people how to find your home. You could send everyone a map, but sensibility isn't one of your virtues today. You tell them your address instead, and hope for the best.

A lot of folks on the Web are having a party too, and they'd really like you to come. The problem is that they don't have a map to give you. All they have to give you is their address. Just like your home, each Web page has an address on the Web called an **URL** (Uniform Resource Locator, commonly pronounced *earl*) that helps people find it.

Here's what Alex Saunders does on the Web

Alex Saunders is a product manager at Microsoft who works and plays hard. I first met Alex when he was associated with Microsoft Plus!. Alex shared with me how he uses the Web to do things like read the news and track his finances:

"I'm a newshound, so I surf the Web for news from all over the world. I look for the latest news on the computer industry, as well as reading newspapers from Canada (where I'm from), the UK, and all over the United States. CNN and USA TODAY are great sites for getting the latest high level news.

"I also use the Web to track my investments. Once a week I use Microsoft Money to pay all my bills, update my accounts, and update prices on mutual funds, 401K, etc. This is also over the Internet.

"I've also shopped, on occasion, over the Internet. The fuss about security and credit cards just doesn't seem justified to me. So I've bought CD's, flowers, etc. on the Web.

"I've also used the Web to plan vacations, look for information on scouting, and numerous other things."

The URL for my home page, for example, is

http://rampages.onramp.net/~jerry/index.html

Protocol   *Domain name of Web server*   *Path*   *Optional filename*

You may remember that I talked about protocols in Chapter 2, "What Do I Need to Know About the Internet?". The protocol tells the browser what type of program it's talking with and how the file is going to be transferred from the server. In this case, **http** (HyperText Transfer Protocol) is the protocol that your browser uses to get a Web page from the Web server. The **domain name** is the name of the computer as it is known on the Internet and the **file name** is the name of the Web page.

TIP   **Do you suspect that a company at a particular domain has a Web** page? Do you know a company's Web server domain but not the Web page's file name? If you type the name of a Web server such as **www.microsoft.com** without a file name, the Web server will usually return the home page.

Your browser does Gopher and FTP, too

Most browsers, including Internet Explorer, let you connect to Gopher and FTP servers. They may look a bit funny, though. To connect to the University of Illinois Gopher server, use the **gopher** protocol, like this:

     gopher://gopher.uiuc.edu

To connect to the Microsoft FTP server, use the **FTP** protocol, like this:

     ftp://ftp.microsoft.com

Your Web browser understands other types of protocols, too. It knows about **telnet** and **news**.

Do you notice the redundancy in these URLs? You typed **gopher** and **FTP** twice. If you type an URL in some browsers, such as Internet Explorer, you don't have to specify the protocol. For example, if you type **ftp.microsoft.com**, the browser will know that you're talking about the **ftp** protocol.

What happens when I load a Web page?

Client/server technology is all the buzz these days. The irony is that it's been around for decades, particularly on the Internet. The Internet is made of computers that place the orders (clients), and computers that take the orders (servers). You learned about client programs and servers in Chapter 2, but I'll describe them to you here in terms of the Web.

The easiest way to think about all this is to remember the last time you went to McDonald's. You're the client, and the high school student with an attitude is the server. You place your order and wait patiently for your food while the student processes it for you. Some time later, the student gives you a bag with a cheeseburger and fries. Then, you're out the door to eat your lunch. Likewise, your Web browser asks a Web server for an HTML file, and then waits patiently for the server to send it back. After the browser receives the file, it's done with the server. It formats and displays the Web page for you to see.

 Plain English, please!

> HyperText Markup Language, usually called **HTML**, is how Web pages are formatted. It's a language that specifies where the text and pictures are displayed; what fonts are used; what data entry fields are shown; and what links to other Web pages are defined. **99**

Using a Web browser

Throughout this book, I'll tell you to do things like "open a Web page," or "click the back button." You may not know exactly how to do these things. Read the sections that follow so that you can follow this book and, incidentally, use your browser to surf the Web like a pro.

Getting from place to place

The most direct route to a Web site (or FTP site, for that matter), is to tell your browser to open it. It doesn't get any easier than this: see the address bar (location bar in Netscape) just below your toolbar? Click once in that area and type the address of the Web page you want to open. If the Web page begins with **www**, you don't need to type the **http://** part of the address, either. For example, to open Macmillan Computer Publishing's Web site, click once in the address bar, and type **www.mcp.com**. On the other hand, you have to use the **http://** portion of the address to get to my Web site because its address doesn't begin with **www**: you find my site at **http://rampages.onramp.net/~jerry**.

You can also open a Web page by using your browser's menu. In Internet Explorer, choose File, Open from the main menu; type the address of the Web page, and click OK. In Netscape, choose File, Open Location; type the address of the Web page, and click Open. You see? Both browsers work pretty much the same way.

Half the fun of "surfing" the Web is in purposefully not going directly to where you're heading. That is, stop to smell the roses while you're heading to your destination. If you see a link to a Web site that looks really interesting, go ahead and click it. You can always get back to where you where by clicking the Back button (the button in the toolbar that points to the left). If you clicked the Back button, but want to take one more peak at that Web page again, click the Forward button (the button in the toolbar that points to the right).

Keeping track of your favorite Web pages

Every Web browser lets you keep track of your favorite Web pages. See a page you'd like to frequent? Add it to your bookmarks or favorite places. Then, you can get back to that Web site just by selecting it from the bookmarks menu. Internet Explorer calls them *favorites* and Netscape calls them *bookmarks*.

In Internet Explorer, choose Favorites from the main menu to see your favorite Web sites, and choose Favorites, Add to Favorites to add a Web page to your list of favorite Web sites. In Netscape, choose Bookmarks to see your list of bookmarks, and choose Bookmarks, Add Bookmark to add a cool Web page to your bookmarks list.

Got yourself lost? Well, go home

If you ever get yourself lost and you just don't know how to find your way to a Web site that you recognize, you can get back to your home page (the Web page that your browser loads when you first start it) at any time. Click the

Home button in the toolbar. That's all there is to it. Your browser will load the Web page that you normally start off with.

Interruptions aren't rude

Sometimes, you'll run across a Web page that just seems to take forever to open. Either it has huge graphics that don't play well with your modem, the Web site's server is slow, or maybe you're having trouble with the phone lines. Regardless, you can cut the Web page off in it's tracks and make your browser display as much of that Web page as it has already loaded. Frequently, this is enough for you to decide if you're interested in that Web page or if you just want to move on. So, how do you do it? Click the Stop button in your browser's toolbar. In Netscape's toolbar, it looks like a stop sign. In Internet Explorer's toolbar, it looks like an X with a circle around it.

Multimedia (and objects, too) on the Web

We expect multimedia. Nah, we demand it—from the computers we buy and the programs that run on them. When people get onto the Internet, however, their expectations aren't quite so high. Sure, you probably expect to see some pictures on the Web, but never movies and virtual reality.

I hate to raise your expectations, but the Web has it all. You'll find pictures, sounds, movie clips, and the popular world of virtual reality. There isn't anything that a Web developer can't create by using objects. This section shows you how to tap into all these things.

How does my browser know what to do with multimedia?

It may sound obvious, but multimedia titles are stored in files, like any other document or data file. All that's needed to play a multimedia title is the file and a program to do something with it. The multimedia titles on the Web, such as sounds, movies, and pictures, are just files that your browser downloads to your computer.

Both Internet Explorer and Netscape Navigator understand most of the common types of files that you'll find on the Web. These include pictures, sounds, and most video formats. This is a major improvement over these browsers' previous life-times, in which they required you to locate and install a handful of **helper applications** to get the job done.

Multimedia for every browser

The three most common types of multimedia titles on the Web are pictures, sounds, and videos. Most of the Web browsers, including Internet Explorer and Netscape Navigator, already have support for most of these types.

Pictures

An enormous variety of graphics are available on the Web. The easiest way to find what you're looking for is to use one of the Web search tools (described in Chapter 11, "Find Things on the Internet") with the keywords **image** or **picture**, combined with the keywords describing what you have in mind. Figure 6.2 shows an example of a picture I found using the keywords **image** and **Scotland.**

You'll also find a lot of photo albums on the Web. These are Web pages that have a thumbnail version of pictures listed so that you can view many smaller pictures at one time, which is much faster. When you find a picture in which you're interested, click it to view the entire picture. Again, the easiest way to find photo albums in which you're interested is to use one of the Web search tools with the keyword **thumbnail**, combined with the keywords describing the type of pictures for which you're looking. Figure 6.3 shows a photo album of mountain scenes that I found using the keywords **thumbnail** and **mountains**.

Why is it so slow?

Multimedia is slow on the Web and there are many reasons why:

Modem speed The most important factor is the speed of your modem. Connecting with a 28.8K modem can load files twice as fast as a 14.4K modem. Many multimedia files, such as RealAudio, won't work correctly with a modem that is slower than 14.4K.

File size Graphics files are a lot bigger than text files. Some images can be almost one megabyte in size. And videos are even bigger, with some files well over three megabytes. A three-megabyte file can take an hour or more to download from off the Internet.

Server speed The fastest modem in the world won't help you a bit if you're always waiting on the server to respond. Two things can affect the speed of a server. First, if the demand for the server is particularly high, the response time will be very low. Second, every server on the Web is not a Digital Alpha (a really fast computer). Many Web servers are on machines that just can't handle the load.

Fig. 6.2
Try searching with the keywords *Travel Image* to find other images like this.

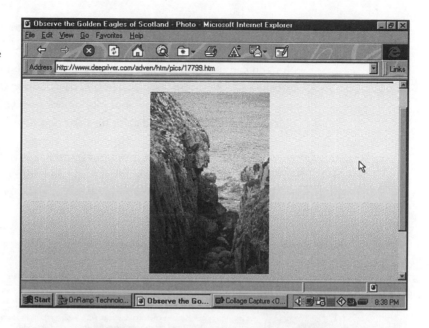

Fig. 6.3
Click any one of the pictures to see it in a larger format.

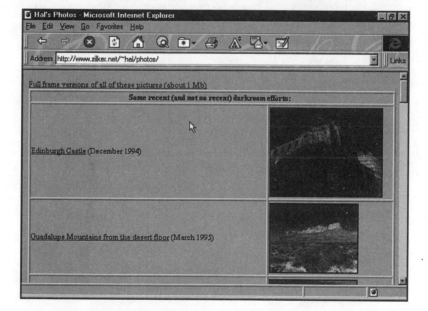

Sounds

You'll find sounds all over the Internet. You'll use them to sample a portion of music tracks, hear popular movie clips, or hear a portion of a speech.

Q&A *Do I have to have a sound card (hardware that lets you play sounds) to play sounds on the Web?*

No. You can use a PC speaker driver. Point your Web browser at **ftp:// gatekeeper.dec.com/pub/micro/pc/win3/sounds/spkqq.ziplink** to download a program that'll let you play sounds from your PC's speaker. Note that you can get sound cards for much less than $100 these days.

Many sites, such as the Enya site shown in Figure 6.4, give you the choice of the audio format you want. If you want to hear the audio immediately, select RealAudio. If you want high-quality sound, however, select one of the other formats.

Fig. 6.4
Select one of the titles and you'll be treated to entire tracks from Enya.

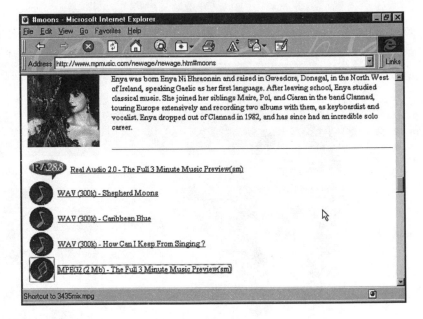

Videos

There are a few popular video formats found on the Web. MPEG, AVI, and QuickTime are the most common. Internet Explorer and Netscape support all of them.

AVI stands for Audio Video Interleave. This is the most popular video format for Windows because it comes with Windows 95—free. Although it is not the most popular format on the Internet, if you search the Web for **AVI** and **clip**, you'll find a lot of AVI movies on the Internet. Figure 6.5 shows a still shot of such a video clip. You can find MPEG and QuickTime movies by using the **MPEG** and **MOV** keywords, respectively.

Fig. 6.5
Here's Jay Leno playing Iron Jay.

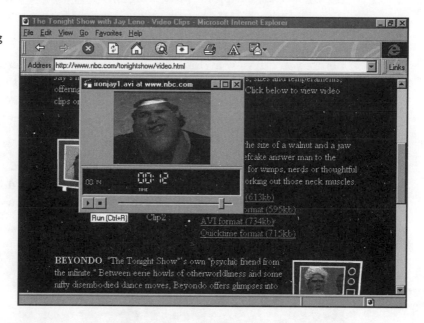

A movie of any length requires a large file size. And, if you're trying to view a movie during peak hours, the server may not be able to handle your request very quickly. So, be prepared to take a break while you're downloading the movie onto your hard drive. You can speed up the process by viewing movies during the off-peak hours for that server.

 Q&A ***All of these videos have to be downloaded before I can watch them. Where can I find video on demand?***

Video on demand is not yet a practical reality on the Internet. However, there is a lot of effort going into making it possible. For example, point your browser to **www.xingtech.com** to get more information about this topic.

Beyond the basics, it's VRML

There is a lot of exciting technology emerging on the Web. VRML (Virtual Reality Modeling Language) is at the top of my list. You've probably not given the two-dimensional aspect of the Web much thought. It's similar to a piece of paper (the one with all the doodling) sitting on your desk. Flat.

HTML is a standard for representing two-dimensional documents on the Web. Likewise, **VRML** is an emerging standard for modeling three-dimensional objects on the Web.

Before you can view a VRML file, you need a viewer. Microsoft's VRML viewer is available at **http://www.microsoft.com/ie/ie3/vrml.htm**. Netscape's VRML viewer is available at **http://www.netscape.com/ comprod/products/navigator/version_2.0/plugins/ 3d_and_animation.html**.

To play a VRML file on the Web, click the link. You'll find a lot of good VRML samples at **www.virtpark.com/theme/cgi-bin/serchrnd.html.** Click one of the links on this page to play a VRML file. Figure 6.6 shows you what a VRML file looks like in Microsoft's VRML viewer.

Fig. 6.6
View the images in this Web page from different angles.

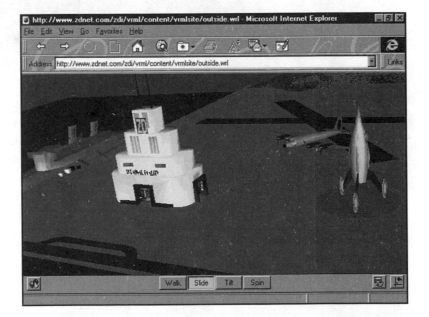

Audio on demand is here—RealAudio

If you're into instant audio gratification, RealAudio is the best way to listen to sounds on the Web. You can listen to music, prerecorded Web radio broadcasts, and other audio files, as they are sent to your computer. Contrast this to waiting until the file is completely downloaded before playing it. For example, I tried downloading a 1MB sound file from the Web and gave up after waiting an hour. However, when I clicked a RealAudio file, which was about the same size, it started playing within a few seconds.

Such power doesn't come free. The sound quality of RealAudio is comparable to AM radio. It's a bit fuzzy and you'll hear gaps in the audio. This is budding technology that will improve with time. So, if you're looking for digital music quality sound, you're better off downloading a .WAV file and playing it on your computer.

On the other hand, RealAudio isn't intended to provide digital audio. Rather, it's intended to allow you to sample sounds or listen to information instead of reading it on a Web page. In fact, some Web sites rely heavily on RealAudio to get their message across. You'll also find a lot of weekly Web radio shows popping up all over the Web. You can listen to broadcasts, such as sports and commentary, that would otherwise be unavailable to you.

Both Microsoft's browser and Netscape's browser come with the required RealAudio software. You don't have to install a thing. Click a RealAudio link and the player pops up, as shown in Figure 6.7, and starts playing the file.

Fig. 6.7
This is the RealAudio player. You can move the slider back and forth to adjust your position in the title— just like your CD-ROM player.

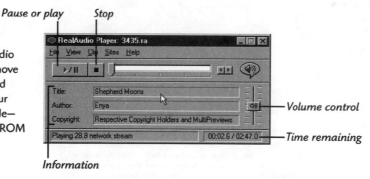

TIP **After you've started playing a RealAudio file, you can move on** to other Web pages to continue exploring while listening to the file. In fact, you can close Internet Explorer and the RealAudio file will continue to play.

Use Acrobat to view virtual paper documents on the Web

Another one of those exciting bits of multimedia technology is Adobe Acrobat. Acrobat lets you look at all those .PDF files that you see creeping around the Web. These files are documents that have the look and feel of paper. Some of them even look as sharp as the finest magazine advertisements.

You can format Web pages pretty much any way you like, right? So, why would you need the Acrobat reader? Well, a lot of organizations, especially business and government, use .PDF files to distribute information so that it's well presented and easy to read. The IRS, for example, distributes tax forms in .PDF format. As another example, many businesses make their brochures available in .PDF format.

It's a must-have. To get your own Acrobat reader, point your Web browser at **www.adobe.com/Acrobat/Acrobat0.html**. This page also has a lot of great examples of .PDF files for you to check out, as shown in Figure 6.8.

Fig. 6.8
Adobe Acrobat has integrated support for the World Wide Web.

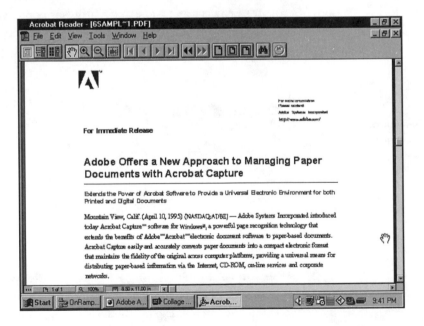

ActiveX objects are small programs that a Web developer can insert into a Web page. When you view that Web page, your browser tries to download and install any objects it finds on the page. Your browser may ask you if it's OK to do that. For the most part, you shouldn't feel funny about downloading and installing objects from reputable sites. On the other hand, if you frequent some of the less scrupulous Web sites, be careful about letting your Web browser install just any ActiveX object you run across. They could do harm to your computer. See Chapter 16, "How Do I Protect Myself and My Computer," for more information about protecting your computer from harmful viruses.

E-Mail and Mailing Lists

● In this chapter:

● **Why do I need e-mail?**

● **Internet e-mail works just like the Post Office**

● **How do I exchange files with e-mail?**

● **Mailing lists help you stay up-to-date**

No more stamps! E-mail is a quick, reliable, and inexpensive way to send your messages around the world . . . . >

You're not limited to communicating by postal service or telephones anymore. Got something to say? Drop it in an e-mail. Your addressee will get it in minutes—not days. You don't have to worry about busy signals, either.

In this chapter, you'll learn all about e-mail, including how to send e-mail and files with your favorite mail client, which you learned how to get in Chapter 5, "Choose Your Favorite Tools." You'll also learn how to take advantage of mailing lists.

Internet e-mail works just like the Post Office

I bet that you haven't given much thought to your postal service (sometimes called **snail mail** by folks on the Internet). How does a letter get from Dallas to Denver? Well, it goes something like this:

1 Your postal carrier picks up the letter in Dallas and takes it to the Post Office, where it's sorted and placed on a truck.

2 The truck delivers it to another Post Office, where it's sorted and placed on another truck.

3 Step 2 is repeated over and over until your mail eventually reaches the Post Office in Denver. Then, a postal carrier delivers your letter to the recipient.

Internet e-mail works in much the same way. Your e-mail program puts your message in a **mail-header** (the envelope) and places it on the network, using SMTP. Then your e-mail is passed from network to network (the Post Offices) using **mail gateways** (the trucks). After your e-mail arrives at the correct network, it's delivered to the recipient's mailbox by a **mail agent** (the postal carrier). The recipient retrieves the message from the network using POP3.

 Plain English, please!

An e-mail client uses two different protocols to talk with a mail server: one to send messages and one to retrieve messages. SMTP (Simple Mail Transfer

Protocol) is used to send messages, and POP3 (Post Office Protocol version 3) is used to receive messages.

This is interesting information, but it really doesn't matter how your e-mail gets to its destination. If you address it correctly, it works. Just as you never thought much about the postal service, it's also safe to take Internet e-mail for granted. Leave the details up to the nerds.

TIP **Just like the postal service, virtually every mail server on the** Internet has a **postmaster**. If your mail is returned from a mail server, send the postmaster a message and ask to have the account verified. For example, if an e-mail to **daffy@disney.com** is returned, send an e-mail to **postmaster@disney.com** and ask the postmaster to verify Daffy Duck's e-mail identification. Postmasters are very busy and don't have to provide this service, however, so you should be very polite and keep your requests small.

E-mail addresses: It's all in the @

The way an Internet e-mail address looks is the same for anyone on the Internet. Take a look at my e-mail address—and drop me a note if you like:

jerry@honeycutt.com

Did you notice the **@** symbol in the middle of the address? This symbol separates the address into two halves: the username on the left and the domain name on the right. The Internet doesn't care much about the username. It pretty much sticks with delivering the e-mail to the computer named on the right side of the address. Then the computer delivers the e-mail to the mailbox identified on the left side of the address.

❝ *Plain English, please!*

A **domain name** is the unique name given to a specific computer on the Internet. Domain names are regulated by InterNIC. See Chapter 2, "What Do I Need to Know About the Internet?," to learn more about domain names and domain name servers. ❞

They're connected directly to the Internet? Send 'em e-mail, anyway

Internet mail is only half the story. Far more people have mailboxes than have Internet mail: CompuServe, America Online, Prodigy, Microsoft

Network, Bix, and MCIMail users are examples. And you can send e-mail to pretty much all of them—if you know how to address the e-mail correctly. You can't always send file attachments to users on these other networks, however. Check with the person you're e-mailing to find out whether he or she can get files through Internet mail.

Addressing e-mail to CompuServe users is easy. Their ID is in the form of two sets of numbers separated by a comma, for example: 76477,2751. Replace the comma with a period and attach **@compuserve.com** to the end of the address to send an e-mail to that CompuServe user. Using the previous address, the Internet address would be **76477.2751@compuserve.com**.

 TIP **Got a friend on NIFTY SERVE or FIDONET? You can get the** complete details about sending e-mail to other networks, and sending e-mail from other networks, by pointing your Web browser (see Chapter 6, "The World Wide Web," if this is Greek to you) to **http:// www.cwc.lsu.edu/people/shoppe/mailguide.htm**.

Sending an Internet e-mail to America Online and Microsoft Network users is even easier. For America Online users, append **@aol.com** to the end of their America Online ID. For example, **honeycutt@aol.com** would be my address at America Online, if I had an account there. For the Microsoft Network, append **@msn.com** to the end of the user's Microsoft Network ID, such as **honeycutt@msn.com**. Table 7.1 shows the domain names for various other networks or services. To address an e-mail to a user on one of these, append (add) the user's ID to the end of the domain name you see in the table.

Table 7.1 Addresses for common networks and services

Network	Domain
America Online	aol.com
Applelink	applelin.com
ATTmail	attmail.com
BIX	bix.com
CompuServe	compuserve.com
Delphi	delphi.com

Network	Domain
eWorld	**online.apple.com**
Genie	**genie.geis.com**
MCI Mail	**mcimail.com**
Microsoft Network	**msn.com**
Prodigy	**prodigy.com**

Using an Internet mail client

You'll find a lot of good, free mail clients on the Internet. See Chapter 5, "Choose Your Favorite Tools," to learn how to find one that suits your needs. You can also buy a variety of mail clients, such as Eudora, from your corner computer superstore.

All of these mail clients work basically the same. You can create new messages, receive and read new messages, and you can even attach files to messages or receive files. The sections that follow describe some of the more common tasks you can do with e-mail.

Are my e-mail messages secure?

The short answer is no. An e-mail is sent as plain, readable text. In the previous section, you learned how your e-mail bounces from network to network until it finally reaches its destination. Anyone who really wants to and has the time to waste, can read your e-mail (including your management, if you use Internet mail at work).

Before you get too concerned about e-mail security, understand that you're most likely just to have a coworker or spouse snooping around your e-mail. Or, you could send a message to the wrong address and have the details about last night's date posted by the water cooler.

Regardless, the messages most people send are pretty benign. It really doesn't matter if anyone else reads them. Don't put anything in an e-mail that you'd regret, though. There's always a chance that someone will forward your e-mail to a person who you'd rather not have reading it.

Compose a message

To send a message, you have to compose one first—just like whipping out the stationery and writing a letter to your mother. Most mail clients have a New or Compose button in their toolbar. These features are also accessible from the pull-down menus. Click that button or menu option and the mail client pops open a window in which you can compose your message. They all have basically the same parts:

To:　　　　Type the mail addresses of the people to whom you're sending the mail. Some mail clients require that you separate each address with a comma. Others require a space or a semicolon (;).

CC:　　　　Type the mail addresses of the people you want to get a copy of your message.

Subject:　　Type a very brief description of the message you're sending. This helps the recipient tell what the message is about when they're looking through all of their new mail.

Message:　　Your mail client provides a much bigger area for you to type the body of your message. You can put any text in this area that you want.

After you have composed your message, click the Send button. In most mail clients, this does not actually *send* your message to the intended recipient, but, instead, puts your message in the Outbox. In other words, this doesn't actually send your message over the Internet. You have to connect to the mail server and transmit your messages to do that, which you learn about in the next section.

Send and receive messages

All of your new messages are sitting in your Outbox, just waiting to go. Likewise, you may have mail waiting for you on the mail server, but you can't read it until you download it to your computer. Your mail client will have a menu option that connects to the mail server, sends any messages in your Outbox to the mail server, and downloads any messages the server has waiting for you into your Inbox.

For example, in Netscape Mail, you choose File, Get New Mail to receive new mail, or File, Send Messages in Outbox from the main menu to send your mail. In Microsoft Mail and Microsoft Exchange, you choose Mail, Send, and Receive from the main menu. If you have any mail waiting for you on the server, you'll see it in your Inbox at this point.

Read your new mail

Reading your mail is easy once you have downloaded it into your Inbox. Browse the list to find a message that you want to read and double-click it. This works in most mail clients. The mail client will open the message in a new window. As well, some mail clients let you preview a message in part of the main window if you just click once on the message. That way, you can see if it's something you want to read before you go through all the trouble of opening the message in its own window. Once you're done with the message, you can close the window to look at more messages in your list.

I want to get more out of e-mail

There's much more to e-mail than just sending and receiving messages. Just as you learned how to organize your postal mail, you need to learn how to organize your e-mail. Otherwise, you'll quickly be overwhelmed by the huge number of messages you receive.

You'll also want to use e-mail with a bit of class. Finesse. That is, you can add a few touches to your e-mail to dress it up, such as smileys (see "Tell your readers what you really mean to say" a bit later in this chapter) and signatures. You'll learn about both of these in the sections that follow.

Read your e-mail. Act on it, pass it on, or trash it

Now everyone knows your e-mail address. Right? The problem is that you're getting swamped with messages and don't quite know what to do about it. Most time-management books offer plenty of advice about what to do with your postal mail. They'll tell you to read your mail. Then, act on it, pass it on, or trash it. Their wisdom applies just as much to e-mail, too.

You'll get e-mail from a variety of sources. Friends and associates will send you notes. Some mailing lists will send you ten, twenty, or even one hundred messages each day. And most of the e-mails that you send invite a response of some sort. Within a few months, your mailbox can grow to more than

100M. That's too much space for a mailbox. It'll grow faster if you send and receive a lot of files or subscribe to a couple of mailing lists.

 TIP **Do you receive a lot of e-mail with file attachments? If you** want to keep the message, you can save drive space by deleting the attachments and saving the message.

How do you keep it all straight? Frankly, throw most of it away. After you read a message, ask yourself this very simple question:

What's the worst that could happen if I deleted this e-mail?

If you can't think of anything that you'd regret, delete the message. That'll account for about 75 percent of the messages you receive. For example, if you receive a message with the e-mail address of a friend in it, save the address to your address book and throw away the message. If you receive a message from your boss with an important file in it, save the file to your hard drive and throw the message away. Get it?

So what do you do with the other 25 percent of your e-mail? You can file it, print it, reply to it, or pass it on:

- **File it**   Save really important messages to one of your folders. Good messages to save include subscriptions from mailing lists, messages that you need to document events, and instructions that you need for future reference. It's a personal matter, really. File what you don't feel comfortable deleting.

- **Print it**   You're not limited to filing messages in your mail folders. You can print them. Then place the message in an old-fashioned file folder.

- **Reply to it**   Some e-mails require a reply. If you do reply to an e-mail, it's probably safe to delete the original because another copy will be saved in your Sent Items folder. Can't reply to all your e-mail today? Create a mail folder called "Needs Reply" and stash e-mail there until you can reply to them.

 TIP **Are you including the original contents of an e-mail in your reply?** Delete everything from the original that's not necessary. That is, leave only the bits of information that your readers will need so they can remember what they said. This polite gesture will help them download their e-mail faster.

- **Pass it on**   Don't know how to handle a particular message (or maybe you just don't want to)? Forward the e-mail to someone better suited to handle it. If you want to make sure that the matter is taken care of, create a folder called "Follow Up" and stash the message there until you've checked up on it. You can always delete it later.

Tell your readers what you really mean to say

The experts say that 60 percent of all our communication is through body language—the rest is what we say and how we say it. So, when you say something to friends, they use your body language to help them interpret what you're saying.

Think about e-mail for a moment. When recipients read your message, they can't see your body language. And they certainly don't hear the tone of your voice. They don't know whether you were smiling, frowning, or crying, when you wrote the e-mail. You're communicating less than 40 percent of the message. This is why e-mail is frequently misinterpreted. You may have meant to say something sarcastic or humorous, but the reader might not know how to take it without the visual cues.

How do you convey your feelings about what you're writing in an e-mail? Emoticons. **Emoticons** (also called **smileys**) are graphics made from keyboard characters that you can use in your e-mail to indicate how you feel about what you've written. You can indicate humor, sarcasm, anger, doubt, or just about any other emotion that you can imagine.

There are as many emoticons as there are ways to put characters together. The most common ones, however, are ":-)" and ":-(". Table 7.2 shows a bunch of emoticons to get you started :@).

Table 7.2   Emoticons (look at them sideways)

Emoticon	Description	Emoticon	Description
: (	Frown	: - ¦	Expressionless
:)	Smile	; -)	Winking

continues

Table 7.2 Continued

Emoticon	Description	Emoticon	Description
; (	Crying	; . (. .	Crying
;)	Up to no good	: ^)	Happy profile
: |	Expressionless	: ^ (	Frowning profile
: @)	Happy as a pig	| - (	Tired and grumpy
8)	Bug-eyed	| - 0	Yawning
80	Yelling	| - I	Sleeping
: - 0	Shocked	| - P	Drooling
: - D	Laughing	8 - (	Terrifed
: - P	Tongue out	8 -)	Wide-eyed
: - (	Unhappy	8 - |	Concerned
: ' - (	Crying	8 - ||	Angry
: - /	Scowling	8 - 0	Scared
: -]	Sarcasm	8 - D	Laughing

FWIW, RTFM!

It's not enough that folks can communicate more efficiently with e-mail. Someone had to come up with a way to type an e-mail faster, too. FWIW, this list of acronyms is a sample of what you'll find used in e-mail and UseNet newsgroups (see Chapter 8, "UseNet Newsgroups") all over the Net:

Acronym	What it means
BTW	By the way
FWIW	For what it's worth
IMO	In my opinion
IMHO	In my humble opinion

Acronym	What it means
LOL	Laughing out loud
OTOH	On the other hand
TIA	Thanks in advance
RTFM	Read the !#%& manual

Spice up your e-mail with a signature

Are you one of those fancy stationery types? You'll be happy to know that you can easily jazz up your e-mails with the look of your own special electronic stationery. No, it's not practical to have a pretty picture down the margin of each e-mail. But, you can add your own **signature** to each one. Here's an example:

```
Jerry Honeycutt  |        jerry@honeycutt.com
                 |              (800) 555-1212
                 | Buy Using the Internet, Now!
```

Your signature can communicate anything that you want about yourself, including your name, mailing address, phone number, e-mail address, or a particular phrase that reflects your outlook on life. It is considered good form, however, to limit your signatures to three lines (plus or minus a line or two), especially if you're using a signature on UseNet newsgroups.

How do you get your signature into your e-mail? Create a text file that contains your signature. Use Windows' Notepad; it's free. Then, save it in a convenient place such as your mail directory. You can configure most mail clients to automatically insert your signature at the end of each message. For example, in Microsoft Internet Mail, you configure the signature by choosing Mail, Options from the main menu and selecting Signature tab. You also can configure Netscape Mail to automatically insert a signature by choosing Options, Mail and News Preferences, and selecting the Identify tab. In Exchange, on the other hand, you have to manually insert the signature into your message each time you want it.

Sending and receiving files

Every time my mother sends me a letter, she invariably includes a couple of pictures, a newspaper clipping, and a few stamps that serve as a reminder that I should write more often. The pictures go in a box, the newspaper clippings go in a file somewhere, and the stamps are used to pay bills—but don't tell her!

Likewise, there's more to e-mail than just sending a note to someone. You can include all types of files, even a couple of pictures and news clippings. Forget trying to send stamps, though.

Can I send any file that's on my computer?

A file **attachment** is a file that you place in your e-mail. When the recipient gets your message, the attachment usually shows up as an icon that the recipient can copy to his or her computer, or even open right there in the message. Yes, you can send any type of file that is on your hard drive. Here are the most common files that are sent as attachments:

- **Documents**   It's very convenient to send a copy of your word processing document or spreadsheet file instead of copying it to a disk or printing it out and mailing it.

- **Programs**   Did you get a great shareware or freeware program that you'd like to share with someone? Send it to a friend as an e-mail attachment.

 Plain English, please!

Shareware programs are programs that you can download and try out free of charge for a time. The author expects you to pay for it, however, if you find it useful. **Freeware** programs are programs that you can download without ever incurring a charge. **"**

- **Multimedia**   Share your favorite picture, sound, or video with a friend. You'd do well to compress these files before sending them, though—they are big files that take a long time to send and receive if they aren't compressed. See "What is WinZip? Where do I get it?" later in this chapter.

- **Shortcuts**   You can share your favorite places on the Internet with your friends. Put a shortcut to your favorite Web page in your e-mail message.

 Is there a limit to the size of a file that I can send as an attachment?

There is a limit, but it's more of a practical one. If you try to send a file that's larger than about 1 megabyte, you'll occasionally run into problems. Why? Because you're betting against the odds. The bigger a file is, the longer it takes to transmit. The longer it takes to transmit, the more likely you are to encounter an error. You'll either end up trying to send the file again, or the recipient could end up with a bad file.

Different programs create different types of files

So, where do all these files come from? Programs, of course. Different types of files are created by different types of programs. For example, a file with the .BMP **extension** is created by Paint (a windows gadget). A .DOC file is created by Microsoft Word. Fortunately, Windows 95 makes the actual file extension less important than it used to be in Windows 3.1. All you need to know is what program you used to create the file.

Common types of files

There are many types of files created by a huge variety of programs. To help you spot a file, here's a description of some of the more popular file types.

Type	Description	Type	Description
AVI	Microsoft Video files	PPT	PowerPoint presentations
BMP	Bitmap pictures	RTF	Rich Text Format
DOC	MS Word or WordPad documents	TIF	Tagged picture files
EXE	Program files	TXT	Plain-Jane text files
GIF	CompuServe pictures	WAV	Windows sound files
HTM	Hypertext files (Web pages)	WRI	Microsoft Write files
JPG	Compressed picture files	XLS	Microsoft Excel spreadsheets
MPG	Compressed video files	ZIP	PKZIP/WinZip compressed files
PCX	Paintbrush pictures		

TIP **If you're going to send a file to someone, make sure the recipient** has a program with which to open or view it. Many times, they don't have to have the exact program because a file can sometimes be opened by more than one program. If a person doesn't actually have the program (or the correct version), programs such as Windows 95's Quick View can be used to look at a file you send. Your recipient can simply right-click a file and choose Quick View.

Quick View isn't installed by the Windows 95 Typical, Compact, or Laptop installation options. If you don't see it in your context menu, you'll need to add it by using the Add/Remove Programs icon in the Control Panel.

MIME is a standard way to send files with e-mail

With all the hubbub on the Internet—people using all sorts of e-mail programs and so many different operating systems—someone had to come up with a standard way to get a file from one person to another in one piece. Someone did, and it's called **MIME** (Multipurpose Internet Mail Extensions). MIME lets a person on a Windows computer send a message, with a picture in it, to a person on (heaven forbid) an Apple computer.

You'll use MIME behind the scenes to send files with Internet mail. Mail works strictly with text. You know: letters, numbers, punctuation marks? MIME encodes binary files such as programs and word processing documents into text so that the mail program can send it through the e-mail system. All those file types that you just learned you could send in an e-mail will be **MIME encoded** when they're sent. When the recipient gets your message, that recipient's mail program—whatever it is—will **MIME decode** the files.

CAUTION   **MIME encoding a file doesn't make the file secure. Anyone with** the appropriate decoder can MIME decode the file.

TIP **If the person to whom you're sending a file attachment doesn't** have an e-mail program that supports MIME, you can temporarily disable it for that message. Use UUENCODE (a popular alternative to MIME encoding) instead.

What is WinZip? Where do I get it?

It takes a lot of time to send large file attachments, especially multimedia files. If you're sending a lot of large files, consider compressing them. Then, after they're compressed, attach the compressed file to the e-mail.

 Plain English, please!

> You can **compress** a file to make it much smaller than it normally is. This is done by programs such as WinZip or PKZIP. You can't do much with the file while it's compressed, though. When you're ready to use the file again, you **decompress** the file to its normal size.
>
> You must be asking yourself: If I can compress a file to make it smaller, why can't someone figure out how to compress all the files on my computer so that they take less drive space? Well, they beat you to it. Programs such as Stacker and DriveSpace drive compression do just that. To learn how to use DriveSpace on your computer, read *Using Microsoft Plus!*, published by Que. **"**

WinZip is a great tool for compressing and decompressing files. A shareware version is available for you to download. Point your Web browser (see Chapter 6, "The World Wide Web") to **http://www.winzip.com**. Follow the instructions you find on this Web page to download and install WinZip. Be sure to download the version that is appropriate for your flavor of Windows.

WinZip uses a file format called ZIP, which is pretty much a standard these days. The Windows 95 version is completely integrated into Windows. It adds items to the context menu, for example, that you see when you right-click a ZIP file. It also lets you add files to a ZIP file by right-clicking them and choosing Add to Zip. Figure 7.1 shows the WinZip 95 window in action.

 TIP **Use WinZip to install shareware and freeware programs you** download. When you open a ZIP file that has an installation program in it, WinZip adds an Install button to the toolbar. Click the install button and WinZip will decompress the ZIP file into a temporary directory and run the installation program for you. When you're finished, WinZip will clean up the mess for you. Life is good!

Fig. 7.1
Right-click a file in the list to delete, extract (expand), or view it.

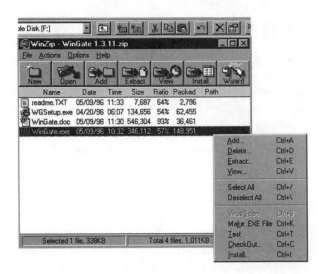

How do I send a file as an e-mail attachment?

Sending a file as an attachment to a mail message isn't much more complicated than sending a regular message. It involves a simple extra step. After you compose your mail message, attach the file through whatever means your mail client provides. In Microsoft Internet Mail and Microsoft Exchange, for example, click the Insert File button. In Netscape Mail, click the Attach button.

TIP **Do you send a lot of file attachments? Your Sent Items mail folder** contains a copy of every e-mail you've sent. You can save a lot of space by deleting file attachments from the messages in this folder or by deleting the message entirely—after all, you already have a copy on your hard drive.

What do I do with an attachment that someone else sent me?

The process of detaching a file is just as easy as attaching one. When you receive a message that has a file attachment, the mail client will indicate that it contains an attachment. Here's how to get the file after you've opened the message:

- **Zip files** You have WinZip installed, right? Double-click the attachment. WinZip opens and shows you all the files in the Zip file. Extract the files onto your hard drive so that you can use them.

- **Regular files** In most clients, you can drag an attachment from the message to a folder on your computer.

After you extract the file from the message, you can open it by double-clicking it. If you don't have a copy of the program that was used to create the file, try using something like Windows 95's Quick View. Right-click the file and choose Quick View.

 TIP **If you get a lot of attachments, your mailbox will become big** really fast. If you saved an attachment to your hard drive, delete it from the message. This will save a lot of space.

Using mailing lists

This is exciting stuff. You're on the Internet. You have Internet mail working. And you can even send a message to yourself. Other than that, however, your mailbox is pretty empty. Well, subscribe to a mailing list. You'll quickly find your mailbox full of interesting information (and some junk mail, too).

Mailing lists give you the opportunity to meet thousands of people who share your interests. If you're in the mood for a good laugh, for example, subscribe to the HumourNet mailing list. You'll get a regular dose of jokes and funny stories delivered right to your mailbox. And, if you fancy yourself a comedian, you can try out your jokes on the other list subscribers.

What is a mailing list?

A mailing list is nothing more than a special e-mail address. It's a bit unusual, though, because a person isn't usually checking the mailbox—that's done by a program called a **list server**. When a message is sent to that address, the list server forwards the message to all the people who have subscribed to that list.

Mailing lists are focused on a specific topic such as home gardening, personal finance, or computer programs. You'll even find a mailing list about mailing lists. There are thousands of other topics from which to choose. See "How do I find mailing lists?" at the end of this chapter for more details.

Q&A *Mailing lists sound a lot like UseNet newsgroups. How are they different?*

UseNet newsgroups are like bulletin boards on which you post a message for everyone else to see. The newsgroup postings, however, are not sent to the subscriber. The subscriber has to look for it. On the other hand, a mailing list sends postings directly to the subscriber. For more information about using UseNet newsgroups, see Chapter 8, "UseNet Newsgroups."

Aren't mailing lists a bit out of date now?

Not at all. A lot of information is better suited to mailing lists than to the World Wide Web or UseNet newsgroups. Regular newsletters, for example, are easily distributed to thousands of readers using a mailing list. It's convenient for you, too, because you don't have to go looking for the information.

You'll find two different types of mailing lists on the Internet: chatty lists and one-way lists. Here's what they do:

- Chatty mailing lists are like the conversations you have with friends around the water cooler. Everyone on the mailing list sees what you post, and you see everything that everyone else posts. A message you post to a list, however, takes a lot longer to reach everyone than water cooler gossip, particularly if it's a **moderated** list.

66 *Plain English, please!*

A **moderated** list is supervised by a real person. They make sure that the messages posted to the list are focused on the topic and are not too abusive. An **unmoderated** list is exactly the opposite—anything goes, and usually does. The quality of a moderated list is usually much higher because all the garbage is filtered out. 99

- One-way mailing lists are good for a lot more than just chat. They're also a great way to distribute information, such as newsletters, to a large audience. A lot of folks take advantage of this to provide some very interesting and useful information.

Subscribing to a mailing list is easy

What do you normally do when you want something from someone else? You ask them. Likewise, to subscribe to a mailing list, you send an e-mail to the

list request address asking for a subscription. That's all it takes. What you put in the e-mail request is a bit trickier, however, because it varies depending on how the list is being managed.

 Plain English, please!

The **list request address** is the e-mail address to which you send your message to ask for a subscription. The list request address is usually **listserv@*domain*** or **majordomo@*domain***.

When you send a message to the **list address** (also called a **mail exploder**), your message is forwarded to all the subscribers. The list address is usually ***listname@domain***.

Be careful not to send your subscription request to the list address or you'll receive more than a few cranky messages in return.

Follow the instructions

Anytime you see a blurb about a mailing list, you'll also find instructions for subscribing to it. For example, I lifted the following instructions from WinNews:

1 Send Internet e-mail to:
   ENEWS@MICROSOFT.NWNET.COM

2 Send the message from the account to which you want to subscribe (some people use more than one e-mail account)

3 Subject line should be blank

4 Body of message should ONLY have in the text:
   SUBSCRIBE WINNEWS

 TIP **After subscribing to a few of the chattier mailing lists, your** mailbox will be flooded with e-mail. See the earlier section of this chapter "Read your e-mail. Act on it, pass it on, or trash it," to learn how to organize your mail folders. Also, see whether the mailing list supports some sort of collage so that you'll get one e-mail that contains all the mailing list postings for that day.

Frequently, you can subscribe to a mailing list right there on the Web. When you run across a Web page like the one shown in Figure 7.2, and you want to subscribe, you simply fill in the fields with the requested information and submit the form by clicking Submit request.

Fig. 7.2
Click Submit request to send your subscription information.

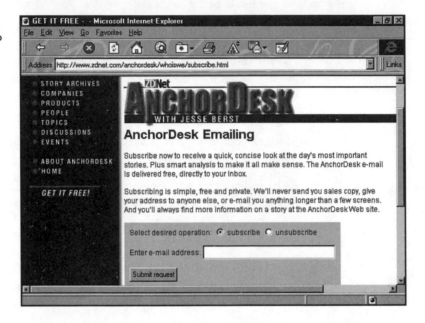

I don't have instructions. What do I do?

Mailing lists are usually managed by programs called list servers. The two most popular are **LISTSERV** and **Majordomo**. A few lists are still managed by real, live people, though. These are called **manual** lists.

So, why in the world do you care? If you know what type of list server is managing the list, all you need to know is the name of the list and the name of the machine. Here's how to subscribe to each type of list:

- **LISTSERV** Address your message to the mailing list like this:

To:	**listserv@*domain***
Subject:	(Leave this blank)
Message:	**subscribe *listname your name***

  For example:

To:	**listserv@netcom.com**
Subject:	
Message:	**subscribe this-is-true Jerry Honeycutt**

- **Majordomo** Address your message to the mailing list like this:

To:	**majordomo@***domain*
Subject:	(Leave this blank)
Message:	**subscribe** *listname*

For example:

To:	**majordomo@relay.pathfinder.com**
Subject:	
Message:	**subscribe compass**

- **Manual** Address your message to the mailing list like this:

To:	*listname*-**request@***domain*
Subject:	Subscription
Message:	**subscribe** *listname your name*

For example:

To:	**fotd-request@cs.umd.edu**
Subject:	**Subscription**
Message:	**subscribe fotd Jerry Honeycutt**

 TIP **If you don't know what type of list server is managing a particular** mailing list, assume that it's LISTSERV. If your e-mail bounces back, try Majordomo.

After you subscribe, you'll get a warm welcome

After you send your message, you'll receive a response from the list server. It will tell you the list address, where to address your administrative questions, how to unsubscribe from the list, and how to send other commands to the list server. It will also give you more information regarding what the list is about and what types of information people expect or don't expect you to post to the list—in other words, the rules.

TIP **Save the first message that you get from the list server. You'll** need this message to look up the commands you can send the server, and instructions on how to unsubscribe. It will also serve as a reminder of the lists to which you subscribe.

What do you do after you subscribe? Post a message

After you've subscribed to a list, you'll undoubtedly want to strike up a conversation with the other subscribers. First, hang out, or **lurk**, until you have a good idea about the types of things people are posting to the list. That way, you won't embarrass yourself by posting an inappropriate message to the list.

It's easy to post a message once you're ready. Send an e-mail to the list address—the one that was given to you after you subscribed. For example, to post a message to the mailing listing, send a message like this:

To:	**listname@***domain*
Subject:	A really meaningful subject line
Message:	Whatever you want to say or ask

What do you do with a message that you receive from a list? You can reply to the individual person who posted it, or you can reply to the entire list:

- **Replying to an individual**   You might not want to reply to the entire list. For example, if someone posts a message asking for help with his or her computer, send your message directly to the individual so that you don't waste everyone else's time reading a message they don't care about.

- **Replying to the list**   On the other hand, if you feel that your reply would benefit everyone on the list, reply to the list address.

Q&A *I posted a message to the list, but I don't know if it reached anyone because I didn't get a copy. Should I send the message again?*

No. It probably made it, and you'll only upset the other subscribers by sending it again. No one likes to get multiple copies of the same message in his or her mailbox. If you want to receive acknowledgments that your message made it, see "Other commands that you can use with mailing lists," a little later in this chapter.

Argh! How do I get off of this list?

If you're getting more mail from a list than you can handle, or the latest round of flame wars has you down, you'll probably want to get off the mailing list. The original response that you received from the list server included instructions for unsubscribing. If you don't have those instructions, use the following examples to see how to send your message:

- **LISTSERV**   Address your message to the mailing list like this:

  To: **listserv@*domain***
  Subject: (Leave this blank)
  Message: **signoff *listname***

Netiquette 101

Unfortunately, some Internet users are very intolerant of mistakes that new users (**newbies**) make. If you don't know the rules, how are you going to avoid hacking people off? Fortunately for you, there are some unofficial rules called **netiquette**. Here are some rules of netiquette for using mailing lists that will make your visit to the Internet more enjoyable:

- **Get the FAQ**   Before you start asking people questions, get the FAQ (a list of Frequently Asked Questions and answers). Use the LISTSERV or Majordomo **index** command to find it.

- **Don't repeat yourself**   Once or twice will be forgiven. But you'll get flamed pretty quickly if it becomes a habit.

- **Answer questions to the individual**   If a person posts a message asking a question, it's a better use of Internet resources to send a message directly to that individual's e-mail address than to the list.

- **Don't flame**   A flame is a nasty, insulting, and sometimes abusive message. They're usually the result of someone taking things too personally. Don't do it—it wastes valuable resources.

The bottom line is that you should use your good common sense: be polite and be considerate. The Internet can sometimes be an impersonal place because people find it safe to be rude over vast distances. If you do happen to make a few mistakes (it'll happen, I promise), don't worry about the flames—learn from your mistake and forge ahead. OK, lecture's over.

For example:

To:	**listserv@netcom.com**
Subject:	
Message:	**signoff this-is-true**

- **Majordomo**   Address your message to the mailing list like this:

To:	**majordomo@***domain*
Subject:	(Leave this blank)
Message:	**unsubscribe** *listname*

For example:

To:	**majordomo@relay.pathfinder.com**
Subject:	
Message:	**unsubscribe compass**

- **Manual**   Address your message to the mailing list like this:

To:	*listname***-request@***domain*
Subject:	unsubscribe *listname*
Message:	**unsubscribe** *listname your name*

For example:

To:	**fotd-request@cs.umd.edu**
Subject:	**unsubscribe fotd**
Message:	**unsubscribe fotd**

Other commands that you can use with mailing lists

You can send a list server more than just a request for a subscription. Both LISTSERV and Majordomo support additional commands. Commands for both LISTSERV and Majordomo are described in the two sections that follow.

LISTSERV commands

Table 7.3 shows more commands that you can use with a LISTSERV list. There are more, less useful, commands available. To see them all, send a message to the list request address with the word **HELP** on a line by itself. You can put more than one command in each e-mail as long as each command is on its own line.

Table 7.3   LISTSERV commands

Send this command:	To do this:
HELP	Get a list of all commands available
INDEX *listname*	Get a list of files for the list
GET *listname filename*	Get a file from the list
SET *listname* **NOMAIL**	Stop mail for a while
SET *listname* **MAIL**	Start mail again
SET *listname* **REPRO**	Send copies of your postings
SET *listname* **NOREPRO**	Don't send copies
SET *listname* **ACK**	Send acknowledgments
SET *listname* **NOACK**	Don't send acknowledgments
SIGNOFF *listname*	Unsubscribe from a list
SUBSCRIBE *listname your name*	Subscribe to a list

Majordomo commands

Table 7.4 shows more commands that you can use with a Majordomo list. As with LISTSERV, there are more, less useful, commands available. To see them all, send a message with the word **HELP** on a line by itself. You can put more than one command in each e-mail as long as each command is on its own line.

Table 7.4   Majordomo commands

Send this command:	To do this:
HELP	Get a list of all commands available
INDEX *list*	Get a list of files for the list

continues

Table 7.4 Continued

Send this command:	To do this:
GET *listname filename*	Get a file from a list
SUBSCRIBE *list first last*	Subscribe to a list
UNSUBSCRIBE *list*	Unsubscribe from a list

How do I find mailing lists?

The Web has a great shopping site for mailing lists. Point your Web browser at **www.neosoft.com/internet/paml**. This site indexes most of the public mailing lists and it is easy to navigate because you can search the mailing lists by category. Click By Subject at the bottom of the Web page, and you'll see a subject list similar to Figure 7.3.

Fig. 7.3
You'll find a mailing list for every interest on this Web page.

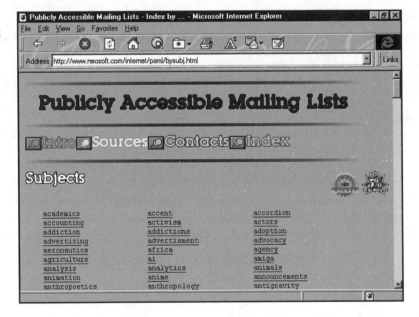

Figure 7.4 shows the instructions for subscribing to the Fruit-of-the-Day mailing list (you'll find a lot of just-for-fun, but totally useless, mailing lists). It contains a complete description of the list's purpose and subscription information.

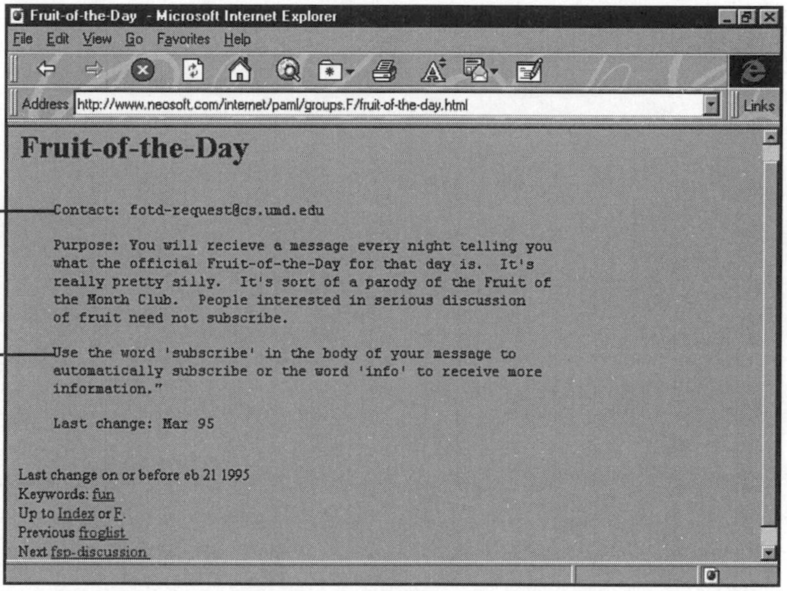

Fig. 7.4

Notice that this is a manually administered list because the address is **fotd-request@ cs.umd.edu**.

This is where you send your subscription request.

This is what you put in the body of your message.

Fruit-of-the-Day - Microsoft Internet Explorer

File   Edit   View   Go   Favorites   Help

Address http://www.neosoft.com/internet/paml/groups.F/fruit-of-the-day.html   Links

Fruit-of-the-Day

Contact: fotd-request@cs.umd.edu

Purpose: You will recieve a message every night telling you what the official Fruit-of-the-Day for that day is. It's really pretty silly. It's sort of a parody of the Fruit of the Month Club. People interested in serious discussion of fruit need not subscribe.

Use the word 'subscribe' in the body of your message to automatically subscribe or the word 'info' to receive more information."

Last change: Mar 95

Last change on or before eb 21 1995
Keywords: fun
Up to Index or F.
Previous froglist
Next fsp-discussion

UseNet Newsgroups

● **In this chapter:**

● **What are UseNet newsgroups?**

● **How do I find my way around all those newsgroups?**

● **Where do I go to learn more about newsgroups?**

● **Amidst all the noise, there's "real" news, too**

● **Search the newsgroups for something in particular**

There are millions of people all over the world looking for good conversation, advice, and even a scrappy argument. . . . .

CompuServe calls them forums. The Microsoft Network calls them BBSs (bulletin board systems). At your office, they're possibly known as cork-boards. They are all places where people come together to exchange ideas and opinions, post public notices, or look for help. The Internet has such a place, too. On the Internet, it's called UseNet newsgroups, or just **newsgroups** for short.

Newsgroups, however, are a bit more complicated than forums, BBSs, and corkboards; not in a technical sense, but in a cultural sense. Newsgroups don't have official rules that are enforced by anyone in particular. They have unofficial rules that other newsgroup readers enforce. Newsgroups also concentrate cultures from all over the world in one place—a source of a lot of conflict.

So, take a few moments to study this chapter before you dive into newsgroups head first. Make sure that you understand how newsgroups and the UseNet culture work. Then, you'll learn how to actually use one of the most dynamic parts of the Internet: Newsgroups.

CAUTION   **If you're particularly sensitive or easily offended, newsgroups may** not be right for you. Unlike the forums and BBSs on commercial online systems, no one is watching over the content of newsgroups. The material is often very offensive to some folks. You'll find plenty of nasty language and abusive remarks in some newsgroups, just like you'd expect to find in some pubs.

Newsgroups—bulletin boards for the Internet

If you've ever used a forum or BBS on a commercial online service, you're already familiar with the concept of a newsgroup. Readers **post** messages or **articles** to newsgroups for other people to read. They can also reply to articles that they read on a newsgroup. It's one way for people, like yourself, to communicate with millions of people around the world.

Newsgroups are a bit looser, however. A newsgroup doesn't necessarily have a watchdog—other than the readers themselves. As a result, the organization is a bit looser and the content of the messages is often way out of focus. The seemingly chaotic nature of newsgroups, however, produces some of the most interesting information you'll find anywhere.

 Q&A ***It sounds like there are a lot of similarities between newsgroups and mailing lists. How do I choose which one to use?*** A lot of the same information is, indeed, available in both resources. If you're concerned about spending too much time connected to the Internet (paying hourly?), consider finding a mailing list you can use. If you subscribe to a high-volume mailing list, try finding the equivalent information in a newsgroup to cut down the size of your mailbox.

Variety is the spice of, uh, UseNet

The variety of content is exactly what makes newsgroups so appealing. There are newsgroups for expressing opinions—no matter how benign or radical. There are other newsgroups for asking questions or getting help. And, best of all, there are newsgroups for those seeking companionship—whether they're looking for a soulmate or longing to find someone with a similar interest in basketweaving.

Here's a sample of some newsgroups, which will show you the diversity that you'll find on UseNet:

- **alt.tv.simpsons** contains a lot of mindless chatter about the Simpsons. D'oh!

- **comp.os.ms-windows.advocacy** is one of the hottest Windows newsgroups around. You'll find heated discussions about both Windows 3.1 and Windows 95.

- **rec.games.trading-cards.marketplace** is the place to be if you're into sports trading cards.

- **rec.humor.funny** is where to go to lighten up your day. You'll find a wide variety of humor, including contemporary jokes, old standards, and bogus news flashes.

When is a newsgroup not a UseNet newsgroup?

Not all the newsgroups available are true UseNet newsgroups. Some newsgroups are created to serve a particular region, or are so obscure that they wouldn't make it through the rigorous UseNet approval process. However, if something looks like a newsgroup, and acts like a newsgroup, it can find its way onto your news server.

Here are some examples:

- **Regional** Many regions/cities, such as Dallas and San Francisco, have their own newsgroups where people exchange dining tips, consumer advice, and other regional bits of information.

- **Alternative** The **alt** newsgroups are responsible for most of the variety on UseNet. Some of these groups have a reputation for being downright nasty (for example, pornography), but there are also groups that are dedicated to your favorite TV shows, books, or politicians.

 TIP If you have a child who will be using newsgroups, you might consider finding a service provider that makes the pornographic newsgroups, such as **alt.sex.pictures** and **alt.binaries.pictures.erotica**, unavailable.

Some UseNet newsgroups are moderated

Moderated newsgroups are a bit more civil, and the articles are typically more focused, than unmoderated newsgroups. Moderators look at every article posted to their newsgroup before making it available for everyone to read. If they judge it to be inappropriate, they nuke it.

So, what are the advantages of a moderated newsgroup? You don't have to wade through ten pounds of garbage to find one ounce of treasure. Check out some of the alternative newsgroups and you'll get the picture. Most of the alternative newsgroups are unmoderated. As such, they're a free-for-all of profanity, abusiveness, and childish bickering. The value and quality of the information that you'll find in moderated newsgroups is much higher than their unmoderated cousins.

The disadvantages, on the other hand, are just as clear. Some people believe that moderating a newsgroup is the equivalent of censorship. Instead of the group as a whole determining the content of newsgroups, a single individual determines what is fit for consumption. Another significant disadvantage is timeliness. Articles posted to moderated newsgroups can be delayed days or even weeks.

How do I participate in a newsgroup?

Remember, every Internet resource that you want to use requires a client program on your computer. Newsgroups are no exception. The program that you use to read newsgroups is called a **newsreader**.

 TIP **Don't want to wait until you learn how to use a newsreader?**
Point your Web browser to a newsgroup by typing **news:** *newsgroup* in the address bar. To check out the Simpsons, for example, type **news:alt.tv.simpsons** in the address bar.

A newsreader lets you browse the newsgroups that are available, allowing you to read and post articles along the way. Most newsreaders also have more advanced features that make using newsgroups a bit more productive. Chapter 5, "Choose Your Favorite Tools," shows you how get some of the best newsreaders available. You'll also find other ways to get at newsgroups later in this chapter.

Wading through UseNet

Sometimes, you'll feel like you're knee deep in, er, newsgroups. There are over 16,000 newsgroups available. Wading through it all to find what you want can be a daunting task. What's a new user to do?

It's all right there in front of you. There's a lot of logic to the way newsgroups are named. Once you learn it, you'll be able to pluck out a newsgroup just by how it's named. You'll also find tools to help you locate just the right newsgroup, as well as a few newsgroups that provide helpful advice and pointers to new users.

So, how do newsgroups work, anyway?

From your point of view, all the newsgroups reside on your service provider's news server. Every article posted to a newsgroup is posted to your news server. Frankly, that's all you really need to know about newsgroups.

For the terminally curious, however, there is a bit more to it. Your news server is not the only one in the world. When you post an article to it, the article is copied, using the e-mail system, to other news servers around the world. This is precisely why it can sometimes take days before other people see your article.

Organization helps you find what you want

Newsgroups are organized into a hierarchy of categories and subcategories. Take a look at the **alt.tv.simpsons** newsgroup, discussed earlier. The **top-level** category is **alt**. The subcategory is **tv**. The subcategory under that is **simpsons**. The name goes from general to specific, left to right. You'll also find other newsgroups under **alt.tv**, such as **alt.tv.friends** and **alt.tv.home-imprvment**.

 TIP **alt.tv.* means all the newsgroups available under the alt.tv** category.

There are many different top-level categories available. Table 8.1 shows some that you probably have available.

Table 8.1 Internet top-level newsgroup categories

Category	Description
alt	Alternative newsgroups
bit	BitNet LISTSERV mailing lists
biz	Advertisements for businesses
clarinet	News clipping service by subscription only
comp	Computer related topics: hardware and software
k12	Educational; kindergarten through grade 12
misc	Topics that don't fit the other categories
news	News and information about UseNet
rec	Recreational, sports, hobbies, music, games
sci	Applied sciences
soc	Social and cultural topics
talk	Discussion of more controversial topics

Q&A *I don't see all these categories you talked about. Where are they?*

Exactly which newsgroups are available on your news server is largely under the control of the administrator. Some administrators filter out regional newsgroups that don't apply to your area. They also filter out the **alt** newsgroups because of their potentially offensive content.

These categories help you nail down exactly which newsgroup you're looking for. A bit of practice helps as well. If you're looking for information about Windows 95, for example, start looking at the **comp** top-level category. You'll find an **os** category, which obviously represents operating systems, right? Under that category, you'll find an **ms-windows** category.

Other ways to find newsgroups that you'd like

Scouring the categories for a particular newsgroup may not be the most efficient way to find what you want. Here are a couple of tools that will help you find newsgroups based upon keywords that you type:

- Point your Web browser at **www.cen.uiuc.edu/cgi-bin/find-news**. This tool searches all the newsgroup names and newsgroup descriptions for a single keyword that you specify.

- Another very similar tool is at **www.nova.edu/Inter-Links/cgi-bin/news.pl**. This tool, however, allows you to give more than one keyword.

Learn the ropes: news.newusers.questions

Whenever I go some place new, I first try to locate a source of information about that place. Likewise, the first few places that you need to visit when you get to UseNet are all the newsgroups that are there to welcome you. It's not just a warm and fuzzy welcome, either. They provide useful information about what to do, what not to do, and how to get the most out of the newsgroups. Table 8.2 shows you the newsgroups that you need to check out.

Table 8.2   Newsgroups for the newbie

Newsgroup	Description
alt.answers	A good source of FAQs and information about **alt** newsgroups
alt.internet.services	This is the place to ask about Internet programs and resources
news.announce.newsgroups	Announcements about new newsgroups are made here
news.announce.newusers	Articles and FAQs for the new newsgroups user
news.newusers.questions	This is the place to ask your questions about using newsgroups

TIP   Don't post test articles to these newsgroups. Also, don't post articles asking for someone to send you an e-mail. This is a terrible waste of newsgroups that are intended to help new users learn the ropes. You'll get flamed, anyway.

Using a Newsreader

You can find a lot of free, and almost free, newsreaders on the Internet. My favorite happens to be *Internet News* from Microsoft. Netscape Navigator comes with a good newsreader, too. Other names to look for include *Free Agent* and *NewsXpress*. Chapter 5, "Choose Your Favorite Tools," shows you how to find all of these.

news.announce.newusers

The **news.announce.newusers** newsgroup contains a lot of great articles for new newsgroup users. In particular, look for the articles with the following subject lines:

- What is UseNet?

- What is UseNet? A second opinion

- Rules for posting to UseNet

- Hints on writing style for UseNet

- A primer on how to work with the UseNet community

- Emily Postnews answers your questions on "netiquette"

- How to find the right place to post (FAQ)

- Answers to UseNet FAQs

There are a few concepts that you're going to need to know in order to understand how to use a newsreader. They all work basically the same. Review the following sections to better understand how your favorite newsreader works.

Subscribe to some interesting newsgroups

As you learned, your news server can carry more than 16,000 newsgroups. You're probably interested in repeatedly visiting only a handful of these. Otherwise, it would be like a needle in a haystack: If you had to wade through 16,000 newsgroups to find those few that you're interested in, you'd quickly give up on UseNet and move on to something easier, like corkboards.

Fortunately, your newsreader lets you subscribe to the newsgroups that you frequent. Then, you can see the newsgroups to which you subscribe in a list separate from the 16,000 newsgroups. Much easier.

The process of subscribing to a newsgroup differs, depending on the newsreader. In most newsgroups, you can choose a menu command to subscribe to the newsgroup you're currently browsing. For example, in Microsoft's *Internet News*, you can choose News, Subscribe to this Group, from the main menu. Most newsreaders also let you subscribe to a newsgroup by double-clicking its name in the big list of newsgroups. You'll see some sort of icon or check mark next to the newsgroup's name that indicates you have subscribed to that group.

Browse and read the articles in those newsgroups

Once you have opened a newsgroup in your newsreader, the newsreader will download and display the headers for all the articles that are available for you to read. In some cases, your newsreader will display headers only for messages you haven't read. In other cases, your newsreader will display headers for all messages, regardless of whether you have read them.

Often, you can double-click a header to open an article in its own window. When you're done reading the article, close the window. In other cases, such as Netscape News, you simply click the header once and view the article in a portion of the main window (called a **pane**).

Plain English, please!

A **header** gives you information about the article, such as its subject, author, posting date, and size. Your newsreader downloads the header instead of the entire article. That way, you can peruse the headers and download only the articles you want to read. **"**

Post new articles to a newsgroup

You don't have to post a single article to UseNet in order to use it. You can be an observer, or **lurker**. If you're an outgoing type, however, you'll probably want to post an article sooner or later. Posting an article to a newsgroup works almost exactly like sending an e-mail message. Click New Message or the Compose button in your newsreader's toolbar, type the subject and body of your article in the spaces provided, and click the Send or Post Message button.

Cutting through all the noise—Here's the good stuff

UseNet is good for a lot more than just blathering and downloading questionable art. There's a lot of news and great information coming from a variety of sources. You'll find "real" news, current Internet events, organizational newsgroups, and regional newsgroups as well. All of which make newsgroups worth every bit of trouble.

ClariNet is all the news that's fit to read

You can be the first kid on the block with the current news. ClariNet is a news service that clips articles from sources such as the AP and Reuters news wires. They post these services to the **clari.*** newsgroups. However, these newsgroups aren't free. They sell these newsgroups on a subscription basis. You wouldn't want to pay for them, either. Many independent service providers do subscribe, however, as a part of their service.

ClariNet has more than 300 newsgroups from which to choose. My favorite ClariNet newsgroups are shown in Table 8.3. You'll come up with your own favorites in short order. One ClariNet newsgroup that you definitely need to check out is **clari.net.newusers**. It's a good introduction to all the newsgroups that ClariNet offers.

Table 8.3   Popular ClariNet newsgroups

Newsgroup	Description
clari.biz.briefs	Regular business updates
clari.local.texas	You'll find your own local news, too
clari.news.briefs	Regular national and world news updates

For your convenience, Table 8.4 describes each ClariNet news category. You'll find individual newsgroups under each category. Under the **clari.living** category, for example, you'll find **arts**, **books**, **music**, and **movies**.

Table 8.4   ClariNet news categories at a glance

Category	Description
clari.news	General news
clari.usa	National news
clari.biz	Business and financial news
clari.sports	Sports and athletic news
clari.living	Lifestyle and human interest stories
clari.world	News about other countries
clari.local	States and local areas
clari.editorial	Special syndicated features
clari.tw	Technical and scientific news
clari.net	Information about ClariNet

Net-happenings is the way to stay current

If it seems that the Internet is moving too fast to keep up with, you're right—without help, anyway. The **comp.internet.net-happenings** newsgroup helps you keep track of new events on the Internet, including the World Wide Web, mailing lists, UseNet, and so on.

The subject line of each article tells you a lot about the announcement. For example, take the following announcement:

```
WWW>Free Internet service for first 100 visitors
```

The first part tells you that the announcement is about a World Wide Web site. You'll find many other categories such as FAQ, EMAG, LISTS, and MISC. The second part is a brief description about the announcement. Most of the time, the description is enough to tell you whether you want to open the article for more information. The article itself is a few paragraphs about the announcement, with the address or subscription information near the top.

Check out the regional newsgroups

Is your geographical region represented on UseNet? A lot are. The Dallas/Fort Worth area has a couple of news groups, such as **dfw.eats**, **dfw.forsale**, and **dfw.personals**. Virtually every state has a similar newsgroup. Other states might have special needs. For example, California users might be interested in the **ca.environment.earthquakes** newsgroup.

How many ways can you skin a cat?

If browsing newsgroups with a newsreader seems like too much trouble, the tools described in this chapter might be just what you need. You'll learn to use DejaView and InReference, which let you search UseNet for specific articles.

Search the newsgroups with DejaNews

DejaNews is a Web tool that searches all the newsgroups, past and present, for terms that you specify. Point your Web browser at **www.dejanews.com.** Figure 8.1 shows you the DejaNews search Web page. To search UseNet, fill in the form, as shown in the figure, and click Find.

Fig. 8.1
Click Power Search to specify exactly which newsgroup, author, or date range to search.

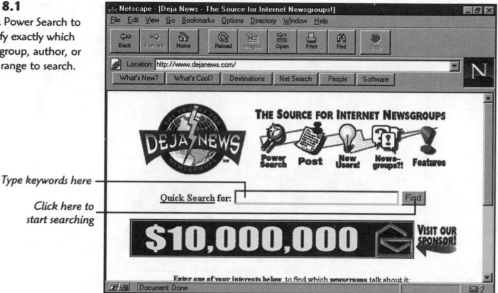

Type keywords here

Click here to start searching

DejaNews displays another Web page that contains a list of the newsgroup articles it found. You can click any of these articles to read them, or click Get Next 20 Hits to display the next page of articles. Here are a couple of other things you should know:

- You can click the author's name to see what other newsgroups they typically post to.

- You can click the subject line of an article to display that article.

TIP **Using a service such as DejaNews, you can get to newsgroups that** your service provider doesn't carry.

Let InReference do the work for you

InReference is a tool that's very similar to DejaNews. You tell InReference the keywords in which you're interested and it displays the articles that match those keywords. Like DejaNews, this is a Web tool; so point your browser at **www.reference.com**, as shown in Figure 8.2.

Fig. 8.2
Click Query Templates
to use predefined
templates for searching
through categories of
newsgroups and mail
lists.

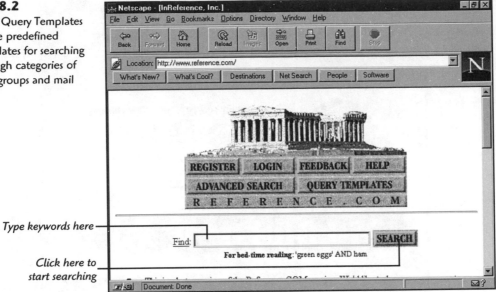

Type keywords here —

Click here to —
start searching

FTP (File Transfer Protocol)

● In this chapter:

- ● **Do you need an account on an FTP server?**

- ● **What is an anonymous FTP server?**

- ● **You already know how to get around FTP sites**

- ● **What do you do with the files you download?**

- ● **You don't have to hunt-n-click to find files**

The Internet has lots of free programs, and FTP helps you get them. . . . . **>**

The Internet is there for the picking—free files everywhere. You know they're out there. Programs, games, pictures, sounds, and more. Likewise, most of the really good Internet client programs are available on the Internet. The only problem is that you don't know how to get at them. That's where this chapter comes in. You'll learn about FTP, how to use it to nab files from the Internet, and how to find the files you want.

File Transfer Protocol (FTP) is the standard way that binary files are transferred on the Internet. And it doesn't matter whether you're using a Web browser, Gopher, or an FTP client program—they all use the same protocol. FTP doesn't require files to be encoded before they can be downloaded, unlike files downloaded from e-mail and newsgroups. FTP transfers are binary, so they're much quicker than their **UUENCODE** or **MIME** cousins.

66 *Plain English, please!*

MIME and **UUENCODE** are methods for translating a binary file into a text file so that it can be transferred in an e-mail message or a newsgroup posting. For more information, see Chapter 7, "E-Mail and Mailing Lists." 99

How do I use FTP to get files from the Internet?

As with everything else on the Internet, FTP requires both a client program and a server. The client program runs on your computer. This is the program that you use to browse through files that are available on the FTP server and to actually download files to your computer. Chapter 5, "Choose Your Favorite Tools," describes how to get WS_FTP, one of the leading FTP client programs available.

An FTP server is a computer on the Internet that has the files you want. It handles requests from the FTP client program. The client program will ask the server for lists of files that are available, for example, and when you've chosen a file to download, it will negotiate with the server to transfer the file to your computer.

Don't I need an account on an FTP server?

No. FTP would be pretty useless for average users if they had to have an account on every FTP server they wanted to access. FTP sites with files that are useful to the public allow just about anyone to log on to their servers. These FTP servers are called **anonymous FTP servers**. It sounds kind of strange, but they do exactly what the name implies. Anyone in the world can log on to the server anonymously, without an account on the server.

To log on to an anonymous FTP server, you log with the user identification **anonymous** and you use your e-mail address as the password. Using your e-mail address as the password allows the administrator to identify who logs on the FTP server. Many servers will refuse access if they don't detect a valid e-mail address given for the password. Also, if you're using your Web browser to browse an FTP site, you don't need to worry about logging on.

TIP **If you can't log on to an FTP server with the user ID anonymous,** try using the user ID **guest** or **ftp**.

Some FTP servers don't allow anonymous users, however. These are private FTP servers. Microsoft had a private FTP server, for example, which was available only to Windows 95 beta testers. Many organizations have FTP sites that are used to support their customers, or their staff, and they give out user IDs and passwords only on an as-needed basis.

Even though an FTP server allows anonymous users, there may be times when you can't log on to it. Many FTP sites restrict anonymous access to off-peak hours. They do so to make sure the server can be used for productive business purposes during the day. Most FTP sites also restrict the number of users that can log on to the FTP server at one time. Again, this keeps the FTP server from grinding to a halt when it's also used for business purposes.

Here's a secret: You already know how to use FTP

No dirty little secrets here. FTP servers are organized very much like your computer. Go ahead, open up Explorer to refresh your memory. You have folders, folders within folders, and in most folders, you'll find a variety of files. FTP servers have folders (a.k.a. directories) just as your computer does.

Most FTP servers live on UNIX computers, and its file system looks very similar to what you're used to. Because you already know how to open sub-folders, or how to return to a previous folder, you already know how to get around an FTP site.

TIP **You'll usually find the really interesting files, such as shareware** and image files, in a folder called **PUB** (public), which is off of the root folder. **PUB** usually contains other folders that intuitively are given names such as **/PUB/APPS/WIN95**.

The program you use to browse the folders and files on an FTP server is also similar to Explorer or File Manager. They don't look exactly alike, but they work pretty much the same way. In WS_FTP, shown in Figure 9.1, you open folders and drag-and-drop files just like you do in Explorer. The only differences are the way the program looks, and the fact that you have to connect to an FTP server before you can do much.

Fig. 9.1
Select your own folders and files on the left side, and the FTP server's folders and files on the right side.

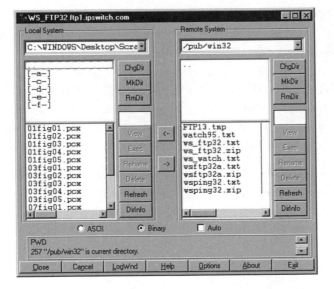

What do I do with the files I download?

Most of the files that you'll download from the Internet are compressed. There are many different types of compressed files on the Internet, but you're going after those Windows programs, right? You'll find that most Windows programs are zipped. Regardless, WinZip can handle most of the compressed files that you download from the Internet. See Chapter 7, "E-Mail and Mailing Lists," to learn how to use WinZip.

You'll also find that many files are zipped into self-extracting files. These are **EXE** files (programs you run) that automatically unzip themselves—you don't need WinZip for these files. Copy a self-extracting file to an empty folder on your computer and run the program. The program will extract the compressed files out of itself and into the empty folder. Table 9.1 lists the types of compression files that you may find on the Internet.

Table 9.1   Compression files found on the Internet

Type	Description	Supported by WinZip?
.arc	Archive, rarely used	Yes
.arj	Arj, mostly DOS files	Yes
.gz	GNU zip	No
.hqx	BinHex	No
.lzh	Most common, next to .zip	Yes
.shar	Shell archive, mostly UNIX	No
.sit	Macintosh Stuff-it	No
.tar	Tape archive, UNIX	Yes
.uu	UUENCODED	No
.z	UNIX files	No
.zip	Most common for Windows	Yes

CAUTION   **A virus can cause all sorts of havoc on your computer, including** permanently damaging files. Use your favorite virus scanning program, such as Mcafee at **ftp.mcafee.com/pub/antivirus/**, to check programs that you download from the Internet, before using them.

How do I find the file I'm looking for?

Finding files on the Internet can be as difficult as finding a document on your hard drive. Have you ever tried to locate a file on your computer that you just knew was there? You didn't know the name exactly. You just knew what was in it and that you wanted to find it. You searched. You looked in Explorer. After a lot of furious mouse-clicking, you finally found the file.

It's pretty much the same process looking for files on FTP sites; *hunt-n-click* is what I like to call it. There are a few things that make locating a file a bit easier, though, which I describe in the sections that follow.

You'll usually be given a file's location

In most cases, you'll set about looking for a file because someone told you about it. You might see a file or **anonymous FTP server** in an advertisement, newsgroup posting, or on a Web site somewhere. If you know the FTP server and location of a file, you can go right to it. Connect to the FTP server using WS_FTP, find your way to the file, and download it. You don't have to hunt-n-click.

If you do happen to see a blurb about a file on a Web page, it usually contains a shortcut that allows you to download it by using your Web browser. This is often much easier to do than loading WS_FTP, finding the file, and downloading it. Just click the shortcut and tell the Web browser where to save the file. See Chapter 6, "The World Wide Web," for an example of downloading files by using Internet Explorer.

Do you know the FTP site? Use the index

It's difficult to tell what a file is all about just by its name. Take **WG45VB.ZIP** or **JXJAG.EXE**, for example. You know absolutely nothing about what these two files represent. It would certainly help if each FTP server kept an index, in plain English, that described each file on the server.

Many FTP servers do. After initially connecting to an FTP server, you're presented with the root folder. You'll find a handful of sub-folders, such as **USER**, **BIN**, or **PUB** contained in it. Also, you'll almost always find files in the root folder called something like **ls-lR.txt**, **DIRMAP.TXT**, **INDEX.TXT**, or **README.TXT**—especially on anonymous FTP sites. These files describe the contents of the FTP server. Download and open one of these files, using

Wordpad (they're usually too large for Notepad) to see the contents of the FTP server.

TIP **If you don't know the FTP site for a particular company, try** putting **ftp.** in front of the company name, and **.com** after it. If you were looking for Microsoft's FTP site, for example, you'd use **ftp.microsoft. com** as the FTP server's name.

Know the file name? Search for it with Archie

Archie is an Internet service that locates files on the Internet for you. It works similar to Find in Windows 95. You give it a file name and it tells you where the file is. You can even use wild cards, such as **ger***, which matches both **Gerry** and **Gerald** (go figure).

You get at the Archie service using an Archie client, such as WS_Archie. The client sends your request to an Archie service which looks at its huge database of files and returns the result.

For example, if you know the file that you're looking for, or at least know a portion of the file name, you can use WS_Archie to search for it. If you know that the file name of the WS_FTP download is WSFTP-something-something, for example, but aren't sure of the last few characters, you can use WS_ARCHIE to find it. Search for **wsftp*** and Archie will return all the files it finds on the Internet that match the pattern. Chapter 5, "Choose Your Favorite Tools," describes how to get WS_Archie.

You can also use the search tools available on the Web to find files. Tools such as WebCrawler and Yahoo often index Web pages that are linked to FTP sites, and even index FTP sites themselves. For more information about using the Web search tools, see Chapter 11, "Find Things on the Internet."

10

Chat and Conferencing

● **In this chapter:**

● **Learn how to chat on IRC**

● **Make international phone calls, free**

● **Learn other ways to conference on the Internet**

If you think e-mail is too darned slow, try chatting on the Internet—instant chat gratification. . . . . ➤

F or many, chatting and conferencing are the main attractions of the Internet. Businesses like the idea of holding conferences on the Internet in order to hold down travel expenses. Ordinary folks, like you and I, enjoy using the Internet to chat with friends all over the world. For that matter, we use it to make brand new friends.

You'll learn about IRC, one of the most popular ways to chat on the Internet, in this chapter. In addition to IRC, you'll learn about other tools you can use to conference with other folks. Some tools actually let you have a spoken conversation with someone else. Other tools allow you to collaborate with your peers on a document, or share ideas on a virtual whiteboard.

Chatting on IRC

IRC (Internet Relay Chat) is the Internet equivalent of a telephone confer- ence call. You won't be talking with other people; however, you'll be chatting through your keyboard. Other people see the comments that you type on your keyboard, and you see the comments that they type on their keyboard.

IRC is particularly fun for the terminally shy individual (socially challenged). It's amazing how much freer people feel to say what's on their mind when they're hidden behind a computer keyboard. This alone makes for some very interesting discussions. If you're the type who doesn't like to participate, however, you can still have fun using IRC. There's no reason not to lurk in a chat room and watch the discussion unfold.

IRC is easy to understand

IRC might become one of the most enjoyable parts of the Internet for you. It allows you to talk to people from all over the world about any topic. Essen- tially, IRC was made for you to meet people and have some fun. But, before getting into the details of how to use IRC, you need to know how IRC started and know its major uses.

What is the purpose of IRC?

IRC is a recreational system. Because of its interactive nature, an IRC conversation is much more chaotic than the one-at-a-time, debate-style conversations you might see on UseNet newsgroups. It is possible with IRC, though, to create private, invitation-only conversations that can be as controlled and in-depth as anything that can be done over the phone—even more so in some cases because IRC is capable of transferring files and other information.

Many college students use IRC as a substitute for making long-distance telephone calls because once you have an Internet connection, using IRC is free. There is no limit to how many people can be on IRC or how many topics of conversation may be active simultaneously.

Some recreational and educational organizations hold meetings online at specified times. There are writing and philosophy groups and even an acting group that performs online. There are some business organizations that take advantage of the long-distance conferencing ability IRC provides. As with any other communication on the Internet, however, information is not necessarily secure; some companies prefer to interact within a more controlled medium.

What do I need to use IRC?

You need an Internet connection, which you already have, and an IRC client. The best IRC client is mIRC. It's a shareware program that you can get from the TuCows Web site. Chapter 5, "Choose Your Favorite Tools," shows you how to acquire a variety of Internet tools, including mIRC.

You can also use either Microsoft's or Netscape's IRC client. Microsoft Comic Chat is an interesting twist on IRC. Each person you're chatting with is represented by a comic-strip type character, as shown in Figure 10.1. As you chat, a comic strip scrolls across your screen with each person's comments in a balloon above their character's head. Netscape Chat is another decent IRC client. You can get Microsoft Comic Chat from Microsoft's Web site, as described in Chapter 5. You can get Netscape Chat from its Web site, which is also described in Chapter 5.

How Internet Relay Chat works

Internet Relay Chat relies on TCP/IP, the networking protocol upon which the Internet is based. IRC uses two of the basic components of a TCP/IP based network—servers and clients. The only part of the system you deal with directly is the client.

Fig. 10.1
If Comic Chat's comic strip characters annoy you, you can turn them off by choosing <u>V</u>iew, Plain Te<u>x</u>t from the menu.

 Q&A ***If other people can see what I type, can they also see everything else I do on my computer?***

Nope. The chat program sends only the text that you type in the window. They can no more see what you're doing than you can see what they're doing.

IRC clients

The client software allows you to connect to the IRC server, which accepts connections from many IRC clients at the same time. The various IRC servers across the Internet are interconnected—from an IRC server, you can access conferences and users connected to many other IRC servers.

IRC clients provide different levels of control over how much you can customize your IRC sessions. In all cases, the client you use greatly affects your perception of IRC. The best clients are very flexible and still remain simple to use. Some IRC clients restrict you from performing certain functions that IRC servers provide.

IRC servers

The servers are the core of the IRC system. IRC servers provide all of the supporting structure that allows Internet Relay Chat to work. The servers maintain information on the current available channels. Every time a new channel is added, the information about it has to be passed to every other IRC server. Servers also administer which users are currently connected and which options and features they have set up. All of this information is exchanged between servers as it is changed, and the technical details of how this is accomplished are quite complicated.

IRC servers are maintained by people called **IRCops**, short for IRC operators. These individuals run the servers and keep everything on IRC running properly.

After you log on to the chat server, you'll see a handful of messages displayed in the window. These messages tell you how many users are on IRC, how many chat channels are available, and other interesting, but useless, statistics. More important, you'll see messages that describe any problems with the server, and you'll see warnings about things that could get you into trouble, such as bots.

66 *Plain English, please!*

Bots are programs that automatically perform some action during an IRC chat, such as keeping other people from using your nickname. Bots are usually malicious, and always irritating. IRC operators will permanently ban you from their IRC server if you're caught using a bot. 99

There are more than one hundred IRC servers running on the Internet. When you first start your IRC client, you will probably be asked to enter the Internet address of the server to which you want to connect. If your Internet service provider maintains an IRC server of its own, it's a good idea to try that one first. Otherwise, you should pick an Internet server that exists geographically close to where you are. The reason for this is that the farther away the IRC server is from your connection, the farther messages have to travel between your client and server. The following is a short listing of some IRC servers. (There should be one in the general region in which you are located.)

Server Address	Location
irc.caltech.edu	Cal-Tech University
irc.indiana.edu	Indiana University
csa.bu.edu	Boston University
wpi.wpi.edu	Massachusetts
irc.tc.umn.edu	University of Minnesota
mothra.syr.edu	Syracuse, New York
irc.nada.kth.se	Sweden

 NOTE **When you connect to an IRC server, you will usually be asked for a** port number in addition to the Internet address. Most of the time, the port number will be 6667. So, unless it is specified to be something else, you should use this number as the default. Some clients will assume this value for the port number if you do not enter one.

There are listings of current IRC servers available on the Internet. For various reasons, IRC servers are sometimes shut down. Many of the IRC servers are set up by universities and colleges. When computing resources are scarce, these organizations take the least necessary systems off-line first. These usually include IRC, network games, and other recreational programs.

Chatting on IRC

Getting adjusted to conversations on IRC might take some time. Because everything is typed instead of spoken, the use of language and expression of opinion are different from normal conversation. Using the IRC system is often referred to as IRCing (pronounced urk-ing).

The format that IRC is based on is topic-specific channels. When you connect to IRC, you will be able to see a listing of the current active channels and the topics being discussed on them. The channel names cannot be changed once they are created. The topic of each channel is changed fairly frequently, however, and gives a better indication of what is being discussed there.

Nicknames

IRC provides a mechanism for identifying yourself by a **nickname**. Your nickname is how the people you chat with will identify the comments that you make. You can use something creative such as **Born2Surf**, or it can be a bit dull (like my nickname), and be your real first name.

Nicknames are strongly encouraged because they help add color to the text-based world of IRC. Nicknames are limited to nine characters, but you will be surprised at how creative people are with so few characters. Many people use animal and food names in combination with their own.

IRC channels

Have you ever been to a huge party with people scattered all over the house? There were people in the kitchen, in the dining room, and in the living room. There were probably different conversations going on in each room. **Chat channels** (chat rooms to you online-service types) are similar. On IRC, people go to different chat channels to talk about different topics.

Most chat channels are for social fun, such as **#niteclub** or **#simpsons**. Many other chat channels are for serious topics such as Windows 95. A lot of the channels are a bit more risqué, however. You may want to steer clear of those.

NOTE You can find help for new IRC users in channels with names similar to **#irchelp** or **#ircnewbies**.

There are thousands of chat channels from which to choose. How do you pick one? The channel name usually tells you the purpose of the channel. The channel named **#Star-trek**, for example, is dedicated to the discussion of the *Star Trek* television series and movies. That doesn't mean, however, that the discussion doesn't frequently wander off on tangents.

Some chat channels also have a current topic that is set by the **channel operator**. The operator updates the topic to reflect the current discussion. mIRC displays the topic next to the name of a channel.

Q&A *How do I know who the channel operator is?*

The channel operator's nickname always begins with the at sign (@). Note that more than one person can be a channel operator in a particular chat channel.

The Undernet

The **Undernet** is a term often used to describe the entire IRC system. The Undernet, however, is actually an IRC system separate from a standard IRC system. A few years ago, several IRC operators started to feel that the major IRC system (sometimes referred to as EFNet) was becoming overloaded with users and needed some significant improvements. There were too many IRC servers that were not interested in making major changes, so these operators went off and improved the system on their own. The result is a separate, and arguably better, IRC system called the Undernet.

To connect to the Undernet, all you have to do differently is connect to an Undernet server instead of an EFNet server. All of the Undernet IRC servers have the word Undernet in their Internet addresses. Here is a listing of several Undernet IRC servers:

Undernet Internet Address	Location
caen.fr.eu.undernet.org	Europe
ca.undernet.org	Canada
au.undernet.org	Australia
us.undernet.org	USA
pasadena.ca.us.undernet.org	West-USA
boston.ma.us.undernet.org	East-USA

The designers of the Undernet rebuilt several parts of the networking communication system on which IRC is based. They have fixed many of the annoying bugs that the EFNet IRC currently has and have made an effort to make the Undernet a friendlier place. The Undernet is, at this point, much smaller than the EFNet, but it is still large enough to carry a variety of topics of conversation.

Talk long distance—really talk, not chat

Internet Phone and similar products are innovative products that let you carry on real, live telephone conversations with other people on the Internet, and you don't put any dimes in it, either.

Now, if I told you that you can use this in your business to cut down your long-distance bills, I'd be misleading you. It's not really practical for that purpose because there aren't that many people using it yet. Also, the person you want to call has to be connected to the Internet, with an Internet phone running, before you can call them. It won't really replace AT&T in your home, either.

So, what good is it? It's a lot of fun. You'll meet a lot of interesting, sometimes strange, people on the Internet—in a more personal way. Internet Phone is also a glimpse into the future of the Internet. Read on to learn how to get an evaluation copy of an Internet phone and make your first free International call.

You need special hardware to use an Internet phone

You will be speaking on the Internet, and you will be listening on the Internet. It stands to reason, then, that you'll need a few pieces of hardware to make all this happen. It's true. Here's what they are:

Sound Card   You need a sound card installed on your computer. If you want to carry on full-duplex conversations, you either need two sound cards installed, or a sound card that supports full-duplex audio.

Microphone   In order to be heard, you have to have a microphone to record your voice. Most sound cards come with a microphone jack.

66 *Plain English, please!*

Full duplex allows you to talk and listen at the same time. If you've ever talked on a speakerphone that would cut the other party off when you made the slightest noise, you were talking on a half-duplex speakerphone. **99**

Most computers sold these days come with audio hardware already installed. If your computer doesn't have a sound card, your local computer retailer will be happy to sell you one—I'm sure.

Getting your own Internet phone

You'll find two predominant Internet phone products on the Internet. The first happens to be called Internet Phone. An evaluation copy of Internet Phone is available from VocalTec's Web site. It is truly an evaluation copy, though, because it limits you to 60 seconds of talk time. If you really like Internet Phone, you can purchase a copy online, at your computer retailer, or by phone. Instructions for purchasing Internet Phone are in the VocalTec Web page. To download the evaluation version of Internet Phone, point your Web browser at **http://www.vocaltec.com**. Follow the instructions you'll find on this Web page to download and install Internet Phone.

Quarterdeck sells a similar product called WebTalk. They don't have an evaluation copy available for you to download. However, you can get more information about it from its Web site at **http://arachnid.qdeck.com/qdeck/ products/webtalk/**.

Conferencing with more than one person

Chat tools let you communicate publicly with a large group of people, most of whom you probably don't know. On the other hand, conferencing tools let you connect with multiple people and chat, talk, sketch ideas on a virtual whiteboard, or even share documents across the Internet. For the most part, it's private, too.

Have a PowWow

One of my favorite chat tools is PowWow from Tribal Voice. It's not technically better than any of the other conferencing tools you'll learn about in a bit. It's not even particularly attractive compared to the other tools. What makes PowWow special is its total simplicity. You can do just about anything with PowWow that you can do with other conferencing tools, but you don't have to mess around with a tenth of the configuration problems that the other tools force on you. Install PowWow and you're off.

Figure 10.2 shows you what PowWow looks like during a three-person conference. As more people join the conference, PowWow divides the window into more sections. You can also use PowWow to talk to other people (using your computer's microphone and speakers), share files, or doodle on a virtual whiteboard that everyone shares.

Fig. 10.2
To learn what a button on PowWow's window does, hold your mouse pointer over it for a few seconds.

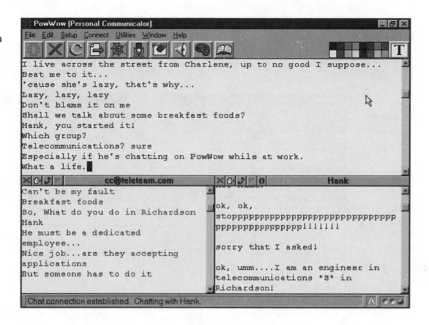

To get your own copy of PowWow, point your Web browser at **http:// www.tribal.com/powwow**. Then, click PowWow Download Page and follow the instructions you see on your screen to download and install it.

Collaboration with Microsoft NetMeeting, really

Microsoft NetMeeting does everything that programs such as PowWow, Comic Chat, and Internet Phone do. No, you can't connect to an IRC channel with it, but you can audio conference, chat, and draw on a shared whiteboard. This is a good tool for businesses to use because you don't necessarily join a "chat channel." You can connect directly to the other people in your party. Thus, you don't have to worry as much about intruders butting in on your conference. You can even use NetMeeting on your corporate network, or with a directly connected modem.

You can get NetMeeting from Microsoft's Web site. Open **http:// www.microsoft.com/netmeeting** in your Web browser. Follow the instructions you see on this Web page to download NetMeeting. Once you've downloaded the file, double-click it to install NetMeeting. Figure 10.3 shows you what NetMeeting looks like.

Share
application

Look up a person
in the directory

Fig. 10.3
You control the various
collaborative tools with
the toolbar.

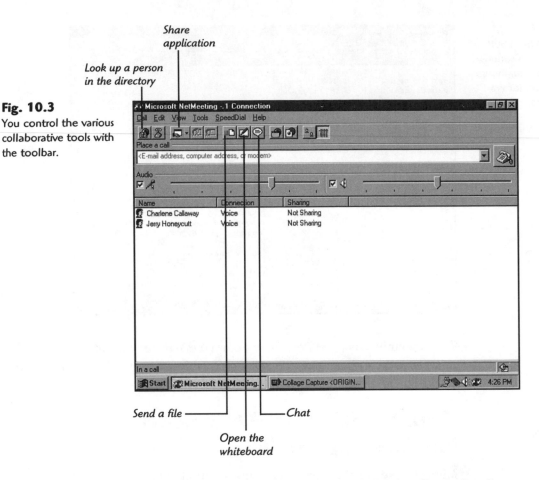

Send a file

Chat

Open the
whiteboard

Microsoft NetMeeting goes way beyond chatting. Beyond audio
conferencing, too. It lets you do real collaboration on the Internet. That is,
you can share applications with many people at once and let them work with
documents on your computer. For example, if you and a peer on the opposite coast are working on a document together, you can both pop up
NetMeeting and work on the same document at the same time. Figure 10.4
shows you an example of a collaboration between two people using
NetMeeting. The document (**Readme.txt**) is on Charlene Callaway's computer. I can control the application and edit the document, even though it's
on Charlene's computer. In fact, I see the exact same window on my screen
as she does on her screen.

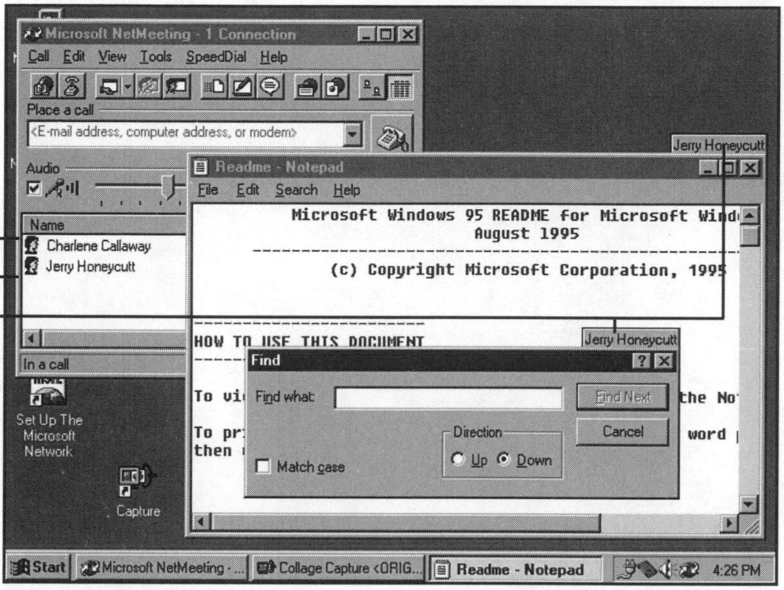

Fig. 10.4
NetMeeting is the background window; the application I'm sharing is in the foreground.

People participating in the conference

Name of person who is controlling this window

You find other conferencing tools, too

The Internet is swarming with other conferencing tools, too. Here's a list to help you find some of the best:

- Netscape CoolTalk provides about everything that Microsoft NetMeeting provides. You use it for audio conferencing, chatting, and collaboration. You can get it by opening **http://home.netscape.com/comprod/products/navigator/cooltalk/download_cooltalk.html** in your Web browser. Note that this product works with Netscape Navigator.

- You can get Quarterdeck's TALKShow by opening **http://web.futurelabs.com/home** in your Web browser.

- You can get VocalTec's Internet Conference on their home page at **http://www.vocaltec.com**.

11

Find Things on the Internet

● **In this chapter:**

● **Finding things on the Web is easy and fun**

● **Learn how to use Yahoo! and AltaVista**

● **UseNet newsgroups contain useful information, too**

● **How do I find someone's e-mail address?**

The Internet contains millions and millions of resources you can use. You have to go looking for them, though . . . . . . ⟩

I t's time to take an inventory of what you've learned so far—before we push on. You've learned how to get onto the Internet. You've downloaded and installed all the tools you need. You've learned more about those tools, too, including a Web browser, mail client, UseNet newsreader, FTP client, and chat client.

Now, you need to discover search tools. You will spend most of your time on the Internet searching: Searching for documents. Searching for people. Searching for this, that, and the other. For that matter, all of the chapters in Part III, "Using the Internet for Business and Pleasure," depend on your ability to search the Internet for information. So, pay close attention to the sections in this chapter so that you can get the most out of the Internet.

Finding documents on the Web

Have you ever visited another city—without a map? I have. And I got lost. I found, however, many great restaurants, art galleries, bookstores, and clothing stores in the process. Looking back on the whole experience, I prefer to think of it as exploring the city—not getting lost (that's what I tell my wife, anyway).

Are we really that helpless?

David Berlind, in his 7/8/96 *PC Week* column, discovered just how helpless some Internet users really are. The previous week, he had discussed a particular company and its services. As a result, he found his Internet mailbox flooded with messages from folks who had no idea how to find that company on the Internet.

He wasn't prepared for the onslaught. In his next column, he apologized to all his readers for not replying individually. As well, he dedicated that week's column to sharing a few "common-sense tricks for seeking information about a company."

Moral? You betcha. Finding a company on the Internet is akin to looking up a phone number in the phone book. It's a basic skill that you must learn. The Internet is an absolute waste of your time and money if you don't learn how to find things on the Internet. You'll get serious, productive use out of the Internet, however, if you know how to make those search tools do what you want.

The experience of "surfing" the Web is very similar except, instead of exploring a city, you'll explore a vast ethereal blob of information and ideas. You'll find art galleries and bookstores on the Web, too. You'll also find free programs, product information, reference material, and multimedia. But you'll find them all from the comfort of your own home (or, if you happen to be portable, the beaches of Rio).

You can't find everything on your own— use a tool

Jumping from Web page to Web page is an interesting way to experience the World Wide Web. You'll eventually want to find something specific, however, and you'll never find it that way. So, what do you do? Use one of the Web search tools that have evolved on the Internet.

 Plain English, please!

> A Web **search tool** is a Web page that searches the Web for other Web pages containing the keywords that you specify. Some search tools rely on the contributions of their users to find interesting pages (sometimes called **passive**), whereas others scour the Web looking for interesting pages on their own (sometimes called **active**). 💬

These tools will help you find just the Web page you're looking for. There's no limit to what you'll find. You can search for personal finance, Windows 95, pets, insurance, product support, art, free programs, and more.

Yahoo! is much more than a pretty index

Yahoo! is my all time favorite Internet search tool (shown in Figure 11.1). I'm not sure if I like it just because it has an attitude, or if Yahoo! is really that much better than everyone else. I'm never disappointed, though, because Yahoo! always points me in the right direction.

Yahoo! has two lots in life: as an index and a **spider** (spiders scour the Internet looking for documents). Internet users (such as you) submit URLs that Yahoo! indexes. When you search Yahoo!, you're actually searching that index of URLs. Now, Yahoo! is in cahoots with AltaVista, which actually searches the Internet for documents and catalogs those documents. As a result, you get the best of both worlds: an index (Yahoo!) and a spider (AltaVista).

Fig. 11.1
You'll find Yahoo! at **http://www.yahoo.com**.

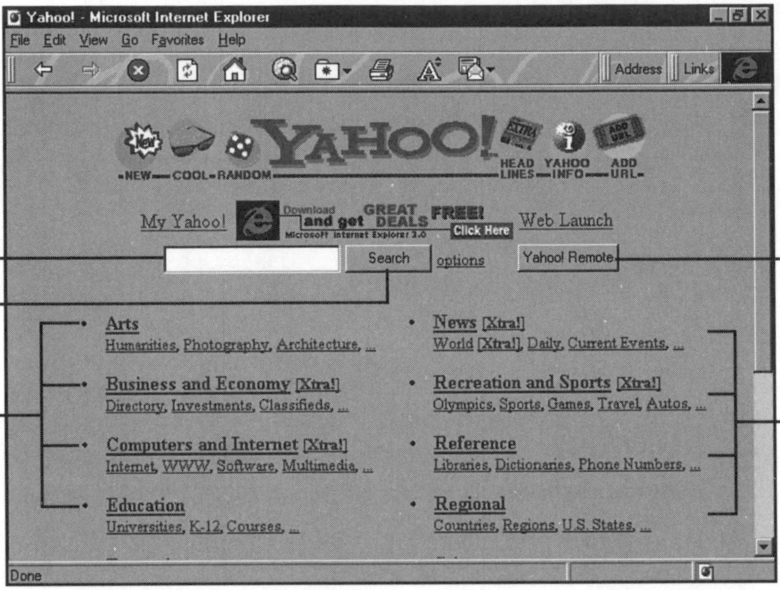
Type search keywords here
Click to start search
Main categories
Click to open the Yahoo! remote control
Hot sub-categories under the main category
Yahoo! - Microsoft Internet Explorer
Arts
Business and Economy
Computers and Internet
Education
News
Recreation and Sports
Reference
Regional

What's in a name, eh?

On the Internet, names are everything. You know about domain names, right? Microsoft's domain name is **microsoft.com**, and IBM's is **ibm.com**.

Early settlers on the Internet were smart enough to recognize the ensuing gold rush. Thus, they registered some of the hottest domain names on the Internet, anticipating that they could sell them to the companies that would want them. For example, Josh Quittner, a contributing writer for *Wired* magazine, registered the domain name **mcdonalds.com**. Brock Meeks reports in *Inter@ctive Week* that Quittner "suggested... that he might even auction off the rights to **mcdonalds.com** to the highest bidder." You should know, however, all this **mcdonalds.com** hoopla has come to a peaceful conclusion.

You can use the domain naming system to your advantage, though, even if you won't be squatting on someone else's trademark. How? You can use it to find a company's Web page on the Internet much easier. You don't even have to use the search tools. For example, if you want to look up the Web page for a little company called Intuit, add **www** to the beginning of the name and **com** to the end of the name, like this: **www.intuit.com**. Sure enough, type that URL in the address bar of your browser and, shazam, you've found Intuit's home page.

TIP **Add your own Web page to Yahoo!. Click Add URL at the top** of Yahoo!'s home page. Follow the instructions you see on the screen.

Browse Yahoo!'s catagories

Yahoo! is organized hierarchically. That means it has a few categories at the top level, such as Arts, News, and so on. Each of those categories has even more subcategories underneath it, and even more subcategories under those. After you drill down through the layers of subcategories, you eventually reach an index of links to other Web pages on the Internet. Figure 11.2 shows what the Arts category looks like after I click the Arts link in Figure 11.1.

Fig. 11.2
You can search this category for a keyword. Select Search only in Arts, type your keyword, and click Search.

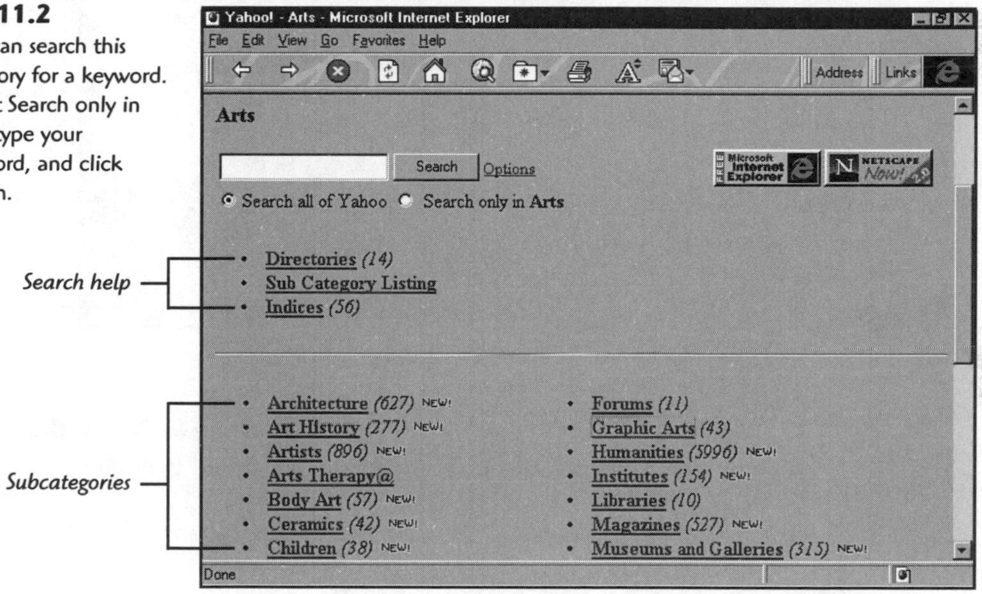

Search help —

Subcategories —

[Screenshot of Yahoo! - Arts - Microsoft Internet Explorer window showing the Arts category page with search box, "Search all of Yahoo" and "Search only in Arts" radio buttons, and links]

Arts

- Directories *(14)*
- Sub Category Listing
- Indices *(56)*

- Architecture *(627)* NEW!
- Art History *(277)* NEW!
- Artists *(896)* NEW!
- Arts Therapy@
- Body Art *(57)* NEW!
- Ceramics *(42)* NEW!
- Children *(38)* NEW!

- Forums *(11)*
- Graphic Arts *(43)*
- Humanities *(5996)* NEW!
- Institutes *(154)* NEW!
- Libraries *(10)*
- Magazines *(527)* NEW!
- Museums and Galleries *(315)* NEW!

You should know a few things about Yahoo!'s format for subcategories. First, do you see the dividing line going across the middle of the Web page? Items above that line help you further your search. You'll find links to indexes, directories, and more. In the News subcategory, for example, you'll also find links to the current day's events.

Every listing below the line is a subcategory or actual link to another Web page. The number you see next to each subcategory name tells you how many links you'll find on that subcategory's Web page. And that out-of-place-looking at-sign (@) tells you that the heading is listed in more than one place.

Click the Photography subcategory. Then, click Photographers and Personal Exhibits. You will see a Web page that looks similar to Figure 11.3. You can visit any of the sites listed on this Web page by clicking that site's link. You can also bounce back and forth between Yahoo! and a site you visit by clicking your browser's Back button.

Fig. 11.3
This Web page contains links to related categories at the top and links to specific Web sites at the bottom.

Search all of Yahoo! or this category

Links to actual Web sites

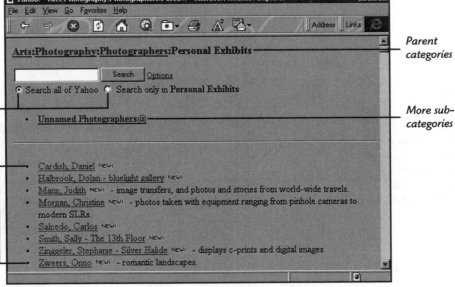

Parent categories

More sub-categories

TIP **You can jump to a parent category by clicking its link at the top of** the Web page. In Figure 11.3, you can jump back up to Photography by clicking the Photography link.

Search Yahoo! using keywords

The easiest way to use Yahoo! is to search the index using keywords you think will find the Web pages in which you're interested. For example, if you're looking for recipes, try the keywords **cooking** and **recipes**. If you're looking for information about Enya (a very talented vocalist), try the keyword **Enya**. Figure 11.1 showed you Yahoo!'s home page. To search Yahoo! using your keywords, type them in the space provided, and click Search. As a result, Yahoo! displays a search results page, as shown in Figure 11.4.

Fig. 11.4
To search AltaVista (see next section) using the same keywords, click AltaVista Web Pages.

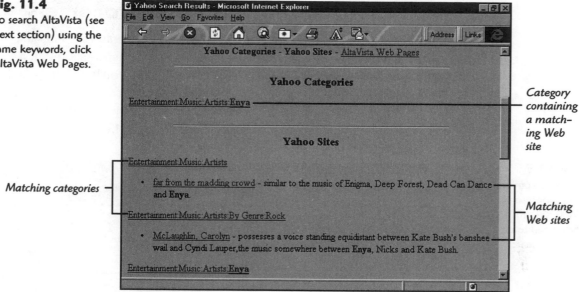

Category containing a matching Web site

Matching categories

Matching Web sites

Yahoo!'s search results return three different types of links. Here's what they are:

- Yahoo! returns categories that contain the keywords you typed. Searching for **Enya**, for example, returned `Entertainment:Music:Artists:Enya`.

- Yahoo! returns categories that contain Web sites that match the keywords you typed. If Yahoo! found a matching Web site in `Entertainment:Music:Artists`, Yahoo! would return a link to that category.

- Yahoo! returns links to Web sites that match the keywords you typed.

If you see a link to a Web site that you'd like to visit, click the link and off you go. On the other hand, you may want to browse the category in which Yahoo! found that Web site. Click the category name immediately above the link to the Web site. Once you've looked at all the Web sites on that page, you can click Next 15 Matches (located at the bottom of the Web page) to see the next batch of matching categories and Web sites.

 TIP **If Yahoo! doesn't find a match in its own indexes, it will** automatically search AltaVista for you and display the results.

AltaVista finds just the right document

Unlike Yahoo!, AltaVista isn't an index. It's a spider. It scours the Internet, looking for Web pages, and it indexes the keywords it finds. As a result, it usually returns countless many more hits than Yahoo!. You'll definitely find what you're looking for, but you'll have to wade through a lot more nonsense to do it. Figure 11.5 shows you AltaVista's home page, which you can get to by pointing your Web browser at **www.altavista.digital.com**.

Fig. 11.5
If you're comfortable with boolean operators (AND, OR, NOT), click Advanced to do a boolean search.

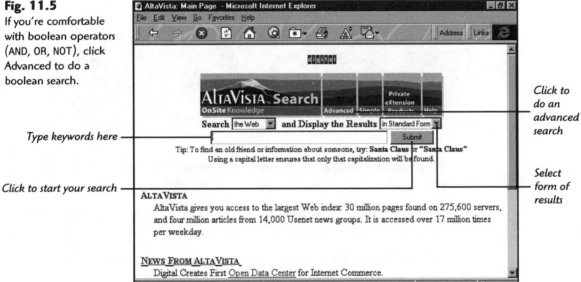

Type keywords here

Click to start your search

Click to do an advanced search

Select form of results

To search AltaVista, type your keywords in the space provided, and click Submit. You'll see a list of returns similar to Figure 11.6. If you find a link on this page that you'd like to look at, click it. Otherwise, you can look at the next page of results by clicking Next at the bottom of this Web page (you have to scroll down).

The descriptions you see aren't always useful. They usually come from the first few lines of the Web page. You can get condensed search results by selecting in Compact Form from the list at the top of AltaVista's home page. That way, you'll see a list of search results that looks like Figure 11.7.

Fig. 11.6
You can also click the link below the description to go to that Web page.

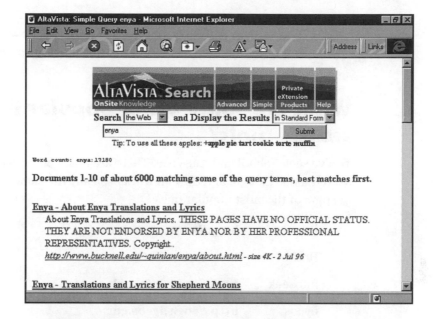

Fig. 11.7
If you didn't get the results you wanted, refine your keywords some more and click Submit.

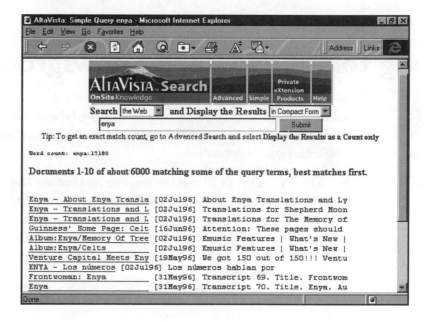

TIP You can use AltaVista to search the UseNet newsgroups, too. Select UseNet from the Search list at the top of the page.

What are some other popular Web search tools?

You've seen Yahoo! and AltaVista. There are many other very good Web search tools, though, and they all work basically the same. Here's a short list of some of the most popular ones:

Excite	**http://www.excite.com/**
HotBot	**http://www.hotbot.com/**
Infoseek	**http://www.infoseek.com/**
Lycos	**http://www.lycos.com/**
WebCrawler	**http://www.webcrawler.com/**

Finding things on UseNet newsgroups

Some of the best information you can find on the Internet is available from other users, such as yourself, who've answered questions on UseNet. You have to be careful about naively listening to all of it, but, for the most part, you'll find good information.

So, how do you get to all this information on UseNet? Deja News, that's how. Deja News is a search tool like Yahoo! and AltaVista. It doesn't search the Web, though; it searches the UseNet newsgroup postings—all the way back to March of 1995. Figure 11.8 shows you what the Deja News home page looks like. You can get to it by pointing your Web browser at **http://www.dejanews.com**.

Fig. 11.8
You can use Deja News to find specific articles or newsgroups in which people discuss a topic.

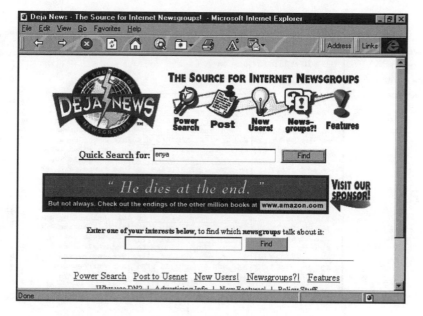

Finding related postings

The primary purpose for which you will use Deja News is to find newsgroup postings that match the keywords you specify. If you're having problems with a particular program, for example, you can search for the name of that program on UseNet to see whether anyone else has had that problem or knows of a solution.

To search Deja News, type your keywords in the space provided, and click Find. Deja News returns a list of results that looks like Figure 11.9. You can click the subject line for each message to read it, then use your browser's Back button to return to this list. Once you've looked at all the matches on this page, click Get Next 20 Hits, at the bottom of the Web page, to display another page full of matches.

Fig. 11.9
Subject lines that begin with "RE:" are the best messages to open because they contain replies to questions.

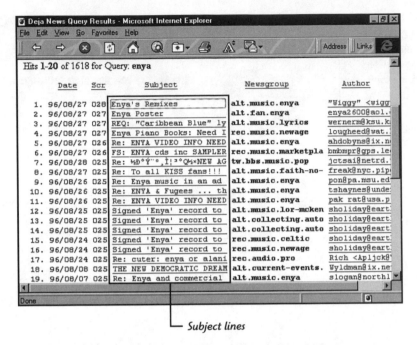

— Subject lines

Figure 11.10 shows you what an article looks like in your Web browser. You can click the subject of the article to see the entire thread. You can also click the author's name to see which newsgroups that person typically posts to. The buttons at the top of the page let you do such things as post a reply to the article or post a new article.

Finding a related newsgroup

Have you ever tried to figure out which newsgroup to visit to discuss a particular topic? You could search the UseNet descriptions, but they're not very helpful. You can just post to a newsgroup willy-nilly, but you're likely to get flamed. With way over 10,000 newsgroups available, you need a better way to find the right one.

Tada! Deja News to the rescue. You can search Deja News for a list of keywords, and it'll return the newsgroups in which those keywords are frequently used. Take a look at Figure 11.11, for example. I wanted to find which newsgroups discuss Scotland and Haggis, so I typed the keywords **scotland** and **haggis** in the bottom edit box. Then, I clicked the bottom Find button.

Fig. 11.10
You don't have to go back to the list to view the next article; click Next Article at the top, instead.

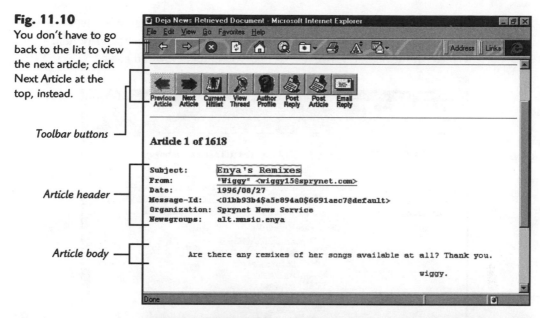

Toolbar buttons

Article header

Article body

Fig. 11.11
Make sure that you click the Find button next to the correct edit box.

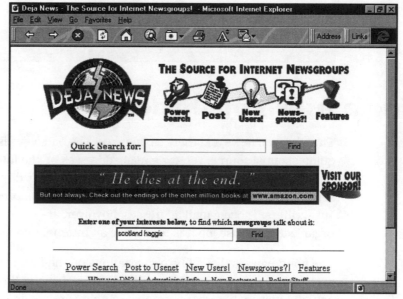

Figure 11.12 shows the results. Deja News returned a list of the newsgroups in which it found those keywords. The list is quite long, but you can see that the top two newsgroups are probably the best place to go to discuss haggis.

From here, you can click the link next to a newsgroup name to display a list of recent postings in that group. I recommend that you use your regular UseNet newsreader, however, so that you can get around easier.

Fig. 11.12
The further down the list you look, the less likely you'll want to visit that newsgroup.

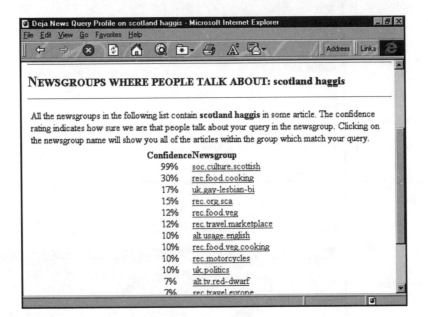

Finding a user's mail address
=============================

There's good news and there's bad news. The bad news is that there isn't a quintessential source, yet, for e-mail addresses on the Internet. Why? Like phone numbers, e-mail addresses come and go every day. Every Internet service provider is responsible for assigning e-mail addresses to its own subscribers. Those e-mail addresses, however, are not reported to a master organization whose job it is to provide an Internet phone book.

The good news is that a few organizations on the Internet have found some pretty clever ways to track e-mail addresses. Some of these **white pages** are actually university research projects. Others are commercial ventures. Read on to learn how and when to use these services to find the person for whom you're looking.

 TIP **If the white pages in this chapter don't suit your needs, point** your Web browser to **http://www.yahoo.com/Reference/White_Pages/**.

Let your computer do the walking

You'll find two basic types of white pages on the Internet. Here's what they are:

- **Active.** Active white pages get their information from Internet resources. Most typically, they look at UseNet newsgroups. For example, the MIT White Pages scans all the newsgroups, collecting e-mail addresses and related information.

- **Passive.** Passive white page services are driven by subscriber (individual or organizational) submissions. Because this is purely voluntary, you'll be lucky to find an address here.

The next few sections describe three white page services that you can use to find someone. In order of importance to the average user (like yourself), they are Four11, MIT White Pages, and InterNIC's X.500.

Four11: That's for information, isn't it?

Four11 is the best of both worlds. It actively searches the Internet for addresses and accepts individual submissions, too. That way, if users are not inclined to post to a UseNet newsgroup, they can still get their addresses listed.

Four11 contains more than one million entries in its phone book, which includes everything from the user's full name and e-mail address to their hobbies and locale. Over 100,000 of those entries are user submissions, whereas the rest are retrieved from UseNet newsgroups.

 TIP   **If you need to find the e-mail address of someone who has** changed it recently, look here. Four11 keeps two current e-mail addresses and two previous e-mail addresses for every person in its white pages.

You'll find the Four11 White Pages at **www.four11.com**. Figure 11.13 shows the Four11 search form. You can use any combination of the fields you want. For example, if you know the last name, fill it in. If you know the state where the person lives, fill it in. Note that if you fill in State, you also have to fill in Country. After you've completed the form, click the Search E-Mail button. Four11 returns a list of people that match your request.

Fig. 11.13
If your search doesn't produce results, consider using fewer keywords.

Learn about other Four11 services

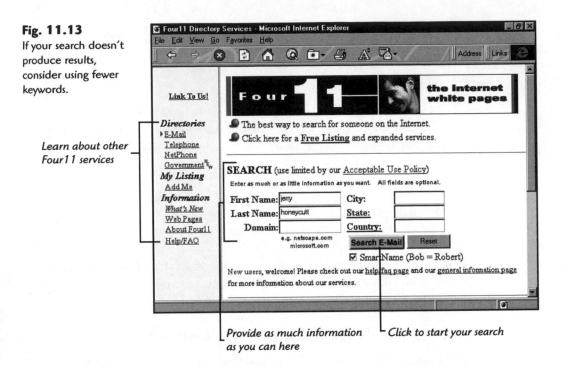

Provide as much information as you can here

Click to start your search

Figure 11.14 shows what the Four11 Search Results Web page looks like. Click one of these shortcuts to see a complete record for that individual.

Fig. 11.14
Click a shortcut, representing a person, to see vital information for that person.

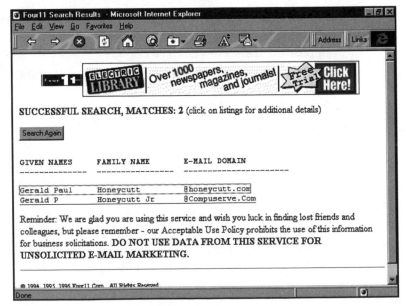

Posted to UseNet before? You'll find them at MIT

Has the user for whom you're looking ever posted to a UseNet newsgroup? If so, you'll find that person's e-mail address at MIT (assuming, of course, that they post messages using their real name). MIT scans UseNet on a regular basis and stores the e-mail addresses and related information it finds. For example, if I post a message to UseNet and use my real name, you'll find my e-mail address at MIT by searching for the words **Jerry Honeycutt**.

Using the MIT mail server is easy, too. Address an e-mail message to **mail-server@rtfm.mit.edu** and put the text **send usenet-addresses/***name* in the body of the message. To find Bill Gates' e-mail address, for example, you'd put **send usenet-addresses/Bill Gates** in the body of your message, as shown in Figure 11.15. Later (sometimes much later—be patient), you'll receive a reply from the MIT mail server that contains the list of everyone matching your request.

Fig. 11.15
Want to know the result of this search? You'll have to look for yourself.

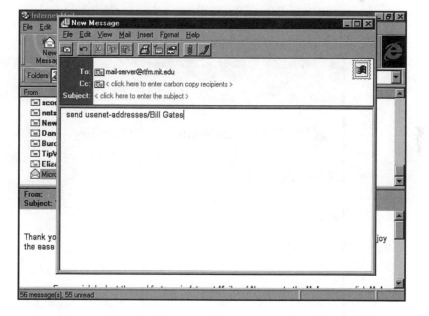

 TIP **The MIT mail server returns only the first forty matches. You'll** want to use more than one word in your search if you're getting a lot of results back and you still haven't found the right address.

Belong to a major organization? Look at X.500

Every office in every organization has them: phone lists. Most organizations print their phone list on a sheet of paper and the employees tack it to their walls. Well-to-do organizations actually print a catalog of all their employees and distribute that. Now, imagine if all these organizations added each employee's e-mail address to that phone list and made it available on a single service. You'd have a good start at a phone book, wouldn't you?

Well, the X.500 standard is a start in that direction. It does have some deficiencies, however. Only about 2,800 organizations participate worldwide. That barely scratches the surface. Also, the listings are maintained by each organization. So, they may not be up-to-date, and probably don't include all the information you would like.

Figure 11.16 shows the X.500 gateway, managed by InterNIC. To get there, point your browser to **http://ds.internic.net:8888**. Click one of the links representing a country to see a list of organizations participating in that country. Then, click one of the links for an organization to see its directory.

Fig. 11.16
Select a country from the list.

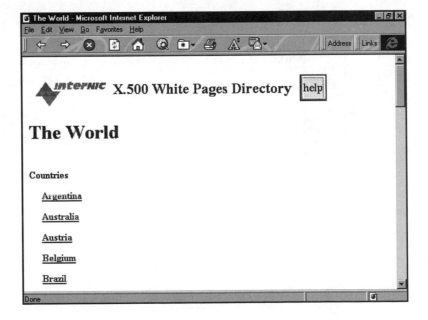

After you've arrived at an organization's directory page, type the name of the person for whom you're looking, as shown in Figure 11.17. Then, click the Do search button. If the person is in the database, you'll get all the information you could want, such as phone number, address, and, most important, e-mail address.

Fig. 11.17
This Web page contains addresses, phone numbers, and a brief description of the company.

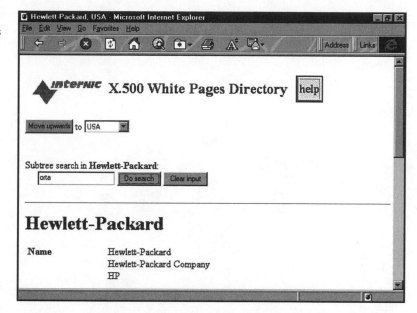

I've read about WHOIS and Finger. Are they useful?

Not really—you'll have much better luck with the services described earlier in this chapter. WHOIS maintains a database of administrators and other important Internet folks. You're not likely to find the person you're looking for there.

To use Finger, you need to know the domain name of the computer that the user you're trying to find logs on to. Not very practical if you're trying to find someone you've not spoken to (or don't want to speak to) in a while.

 TIP If you do happen to know the server a person logs on to, send the server's postmaster an e-mail asking for the user's mailbox name. Keep it brief and polite, and you'll probably get a response.

Part III: Using the Internet for Business and Pleasure

12

Get Your Software Fix Online

● **In this chapter:**

● **Learn all you want to know about shareware**

● **How do I know what I'm looking for?**

● **Here's how you locate the shareware you need**

● **Downloading shareware products is easy**

● **You can keep up-to-date on the latest releases**

The most innovative and useful programs are available on the Internet, and they're free, or close to it! . . . . ⊙

Do you need a text editor? Virus scanner? Game? How about a cool program to catalog that massive video collection you have? Don't bounce down to the corner computer store just yet. At least, not until you first check out what the Internet has to offer. Just about every type of program you can think of is available on the Internet. Some are free, while others are dirt cheap.

Yeah, right; so where do I get all these gems? The Internet, of course. You just need to know how to get at them. This chapter will help you. Not only will you learn how to find programs on the Internet, you'll also learn how to download them onto your computer and how to keep up with all the latest releases. My motto? Never pay retail.

What is freeware? Shareware?

Many programs you find on the Internet are yours for the keeping. Free. No charge. Take 'em and run. This type of software is called **freeware**. You'll find quite a few freeware programs from which to choose. Windows and Internet Utilities. Graphics. Screen savers. What have you. You won't find many freeware word-processors or spreadsheets on the Internet, though.

Shareware, on the other hand, should really be called try-it-before-you-buy-it-ware. You download a program and try it out—all free. Then, if you like the program, and you intend to keep using it, you pay the author a small registration fee. I haven't seen many commercially available products that don't have shareware alternatives, including Internet programs, word-processors, spreadsheets, games, and various utilities.

You'll find a huge variety of programs on the Internet

This chapter wouldn't be complete without a gratuitous list of freeware and shareware programs you can find on the Internet. So, here it goes:

- **Internet Tools**   The Internet is bubbling over with Internet tools such as IRC and mail clients. Web browsers, too. You can also find programs that make Windows a better environment for surfing the Internet.

- **Games**   Oh, yeah; the Internet has lots of games. You can usually find demo versions of the most popular games, such as Doom. You can also find action oriented and strategic games.

- **Screen Savers**   Are you tired of the same old Windows screen saver? The Internet has a huge variety—free. Most are pretty cheesy, but you do run across some amazing ones from time to time.

- **Applications**   You'll find a variety of traditional applications on the Internet: educational, database, spreadsheet, and word-processing programs, for example.

- **Windows Utilities**   You'll find utilities that make Windows much easier to use. Some utilities let you change your computer's settings and others make it easier to work with files. Virtually every hole in Windows has been filled, in some way, by a clever shareware programmer.

Beyond programs, you can also find a large assortment of public-domain or royalty-free artwork that you can use: clipart, icons, and sounds, just to name a few. Many of these libraries also come with programs to help you manage them.

How does shareware stack up to commercial products?

Quite often, shareware is a better alternative to purchasing a program from the computer store. You can try a program at no risk. In fact, you can try out several different programs and pick the one you like best. You don't have to worry about returning a program to the computer store, where the "customer service" clerk takes every software return as a personal affront. Don't like a program you downloaded, just delete or uninstall it from your computer.

 You can find many shareware programs at your local book or computer superstore. Look for a display rack filled with plastic envelopes that contain disks and CD-ROMs. If you're not sure, ask a sales clerk if they sell shareware programs.

As always, there's a catch. You're only buying the disk from the store. You still have to register the program with the author. This really isn't as unreasonable as it sounds. The distributor is recouping its distribution costs, but it doesn't pass any loot on to the shareware author.

Regarding quality, in some cases, shareware products are just as good as commercial products that you buy from the store. These products have just as much work put into them. They have good help files and manuals. They're easy to use, too, because a lot of effort was put into making a great user interface.

Most shareware isn't always the same quality as you'd get from a box at the store, however. It takes more effort to develop a good product than it did in years past. Whereas a single person could develop a rather complete product several years ago, it takes many people to develop a good product these days because the tools are much more complicated. The big companies, like Microsoft, can throw hundreds of developers at a product. The little guy can't do that and has to settle for limited features and limited quality.

Why do shareware authors do it?

Speaking from personal experience, I'm not exactly sure why shareware authors do it. Some shareware authors hope to strike it rich. Others use shareware as a creative outlet. It's no fun creating a masterpiece painting that no one ever sees; it's just as dull creating a program that no one ever uses.

So, if these authors want to strike it rich, or want an audience for their programs, why don't they sell them on store shelves? It takes a huge investment to put a product on a store shelf. The hidden costs are amazing. Duplication. Packaging. You have to buy shelf space from the retailer, too. And don't forget all those "experts." Most shareware programs aren't worth that kind of investment.

On the other hand, a lot of great ideas would never see the light of day if authors couldn't distribute them as shareware—they just don't have the money. Still others are risk-averse and wouldn't consider risking their life savings to launch a product. Even if an author intends to put a product on the shelf, the author should consider "test driving" the product first as shareware. If the product flies, then the author can sink some money in it.

Shareware authors are more organized than you think

Shareware authors learned long ago that there is power in numbers. They can promote each other's products, get better deals on development tools, and make payment collection easier. They also can create standards to which shareware authors and their products are held; thus, assuring you and me a certain amount of quality.

Two of the largest groups of shareware authors are the ASP (Association of Shareware Professionals) and STAR (Shareware Trade Association and Resources). I'll tell you about both in the following sections.

TIP Look for shareware products that display either the ASP or the STAR logos. You're likely to get better programs as a result.

ASP (Association of Shareware Professionals)

ASP is, by far, the most successful and longest running shareware organization. Since 1987, ASP has provided different ways for shareware authors to distribute their goods to the public. For example, members can distribute their products on the ASP CD-ROM and can include their products in the ASP catalog. Membership in ASP also provides a shareware author with a certain amount of credibility. Furthermore, ASP supports its members with deals on development tools and information that is needed to be successful in the shareware business. As you can see, it's a great deal for shareware authors.

ASP is a good deal for you, too. You can feel a certain amount of ease in buying a shareware product from an ASP member because ASP has quality standards to which members are held. You also have a place to go if you're not satisfied with the product or the support you get. It's called the **ASP Ombudsman**, which is a service that resolves disputes between users and shareware authors. Since most shareware authors value their membership in ASP, they work very hard to facilitate an agreeable outcome.

ASP has a long reach. You can access them on most online services, such as the ASP forums on CompuServe and America Online. You can also get more information about ASP on the Internet at **http://www.asp-shareware.org**. Once at the ASP Web site, click ASP Shareware Catalog to download the catalog of ASP programs.

STAR (Shareware Trade Association and Resources)

STAR is another organization, much like ASP, that promotes quality shareware products. Some of the best shareware authors, such as Nico Mak Computing, Inc. (WinZip), and Canyon Software (Drag and File), are members of STAR.

You can get more information about STAR on the Internet **http://www.shareware.org** (this isn't the same as **http://shareware.com**). You can also look in sections 11 and 12 of the UK Shareware forum on CompuServe (**Go UKSHARE**).

Shareware is easy to find on the Internet

Remember all the hype just prior to Microsoft shipping Windows 95? They used everything but a sky writer to hype its release (and I can't be certain they didn't do that). Very few people didn't know about the stores opening at midnight on August 24th to sell the first copies of Windows 95.

Shareware authors just can't put that much into their marketing efforts. ASP and STAR certainly help, but money is tight for most of these folks. Most shareware authors barely make enough from their products to pay for tools.

That means you have to go looking for their products. It's easier than it sounds because once a product catches on, people start talking about it. You can tap into those conversations to find just the right shareware product.

Find out what everyone else is talking about

As I hinted, the best way to find a shareware product that fits your needs is to discover the products other people are talking about. Certainly, there will be times when you know exactly what product you want. In that case, skip to the next section, "Best start with the shareware collections." Otherwise, stick around here a bit to learn how to locate a good shareware product to use.

Deja News is the name of a search tool that you see sprinkled here and there in this book. It searches the UseNet newsgroups for keywords that you specify, and returns messages that match those keywords. I can't think of a better way to find shareware that people are talking about. As an example, here's how I would go about finding a good genealogy program:

1 Point your Web browser to Deja News, as shown in Figure 12.1. Its URL is **http://www.dejanews.com**.

2 In the space provided for keywords, type the word **shareware,** followed by one or more keywords that describe the type of program you want—in this case **genealogy**.

Fig. 12.1
You can use the keywords **shareware** and **genealogy** to find shareware genealogy programs.

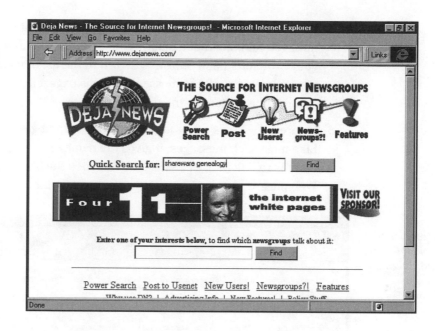

3 Click Find and Deja News returns a list similar to the one shown in Figure 12.2.

Fig. 12.2
Subject lines that begin with "RE:" are the best messages to open because they contain replies to questions.

Subject lines—

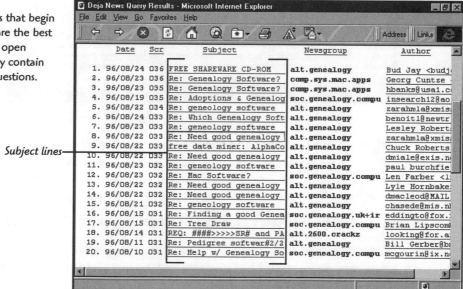

4 Click the subject line for each message to read that message's content until you find one that discusses an interesting shareware product. Use your browser's Back button to return to the list of messages. Once you've looked at all the messages on this page, click Get next 20 hits, found at the bottom of the page, to see more.

5 Figure 12.3 shows a message that I found about genealogy software. Like most such messages, it gives the name of a few products and even includes a link to a Web site. You can click the link to check out the Web page, or just make a note of the product for future searches.

Fig. 12.3
Deja News sets words that match your search term in bold characters so that you can easily identify them.

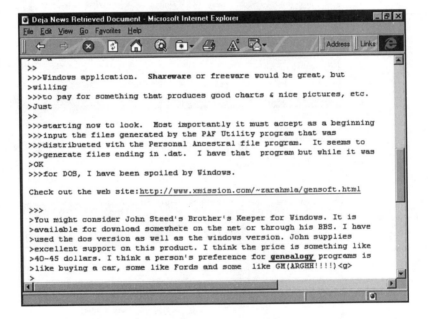

> Don't stop with the first message you find that recommends a shareware program. Read as many messages as you can tolerate so that you get a good feel for which is the best program.

TIP

Best start with the shareware collections

Shareware collections review and categorize a large number of shareware programs. Thousands. They give you an idea as to how good or how popular a program is before you download it. You can also get information up-front regarding how much the author wants for registering the product. Most collections provide a way for you to search the collection by using a variety of criteria, including number of downloads, rating, date, etc.

SHAREWARE.COM

SHAREWARE.COM is a service that C|NET provides. It catalogs thousands of freeware and shareware programs. You can search for the program by name or even by using a keyword such as **genealogy**. Here's how to use SHAREWARE.COM to find a particular type of program:

1 Point your Web browser at **http://www.shareware.com**. Figure 12.4 shows you what it looks like.

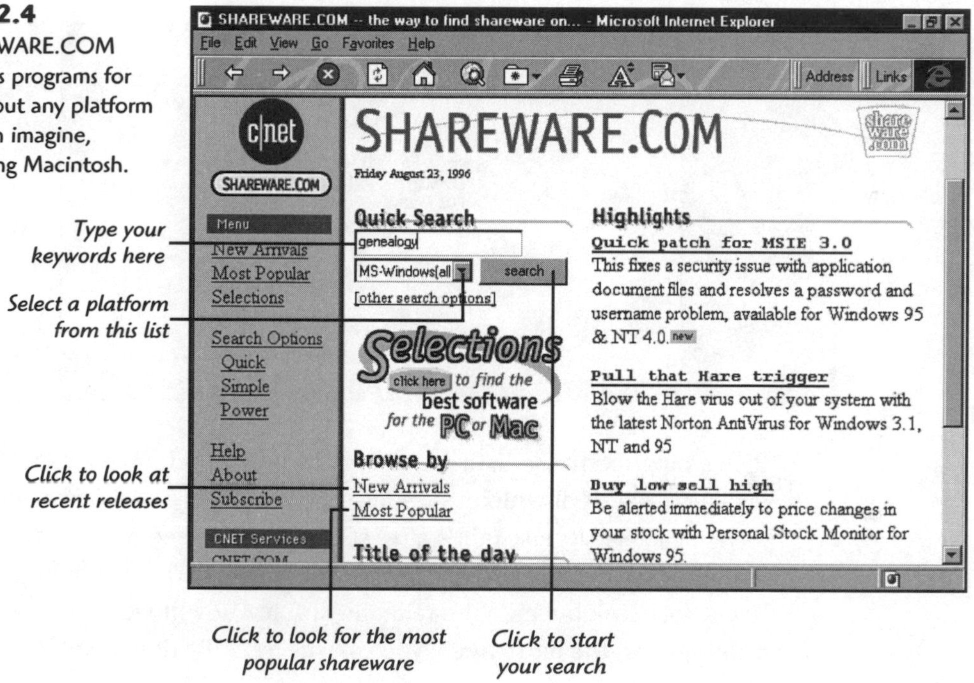

Fig. 12.4
SHAREWARE.COM catalogs programs for just about any platform you can imagine, including Macintosh.

Type your keywords here

Select a platform from this list

Click to look at recent releases

Click to look for the most popular shareware

Click to start your search

2 Type one or two keywords in the space provided. If you already know the name of a good product, type the name. Make sure that you select your platform in the drop-down list, and then click Search to start your search. Figure 12.5 shows what the search results look like after a search using the keyword **genealogy**.

TIP **Even if you're using Windows 95, I recommend that you set the** platform to MS-Windows(all) so that you get better search results. Windows 3.1 programs work just fine in Windows 95.

Fig. 12.5
The descriptions aren't always the best, so it helps to know what program you're looking for before you start.

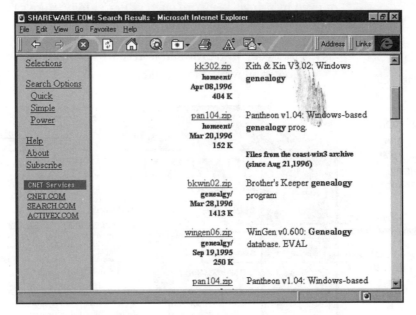

3 Pick a program in the listing and click its link. SHAREWARE.COM displays a list of download sites, as shown in Figure 12.6. It's a good idea to choose the site that's closest to you. More specifically, if you're in the states, select a site under the USA heading. The symbols to the left of each link indicate the reliability of that download site. The more little squares, the more likely you can successfully download the file from that site.

4 Click the link for one of the sites and your browser will start downloading the file. Depending on which browser you use, the browser may ask you to confirm the location in which you want to download the file, before or after it finishes.

Fig. 12.6
This list contains the filename, file size, server, and rating for each location.

Reliability ─

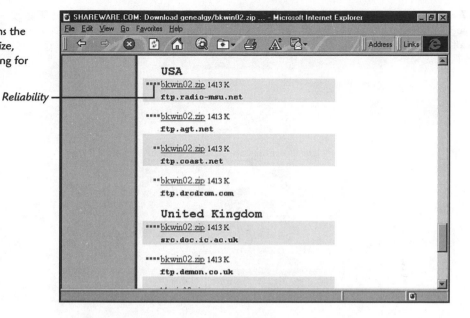

TuCows Winsock Collection

TuCows is a very popular collection of shareware. This collection is very focused on one type of shareware, though—Winsock programs (TuCows stands for The Ultimate Collection of Winsock Software). Winsock programs are basically Windows Internet programs. You know: mail, news, Web, etc. If you're looking for an Internet program, look here first:

1 Point your Web browser at **http://www.tucows.com**. You'll see a Web page that contains nothing but links to other Web pages. What's going on here, where's the shareware? TuCows has become so popular that one Web site isn't enough to handle all the demand. So, they **mirror** the primary Web site on other Web servers all over the world. That way, you can connect to the Web site that's closest to you. In my case, I'd click the Texas, USA link because I'm in Dallas. It doesn't matter which mirror site you pick, you'll see a Web page similar to the one in Figure 12.7.

2 Click the link that best suits your needs. If you're looking for Windows 95 Internet utilities, click Win 95 Utils. If you're looking for Windows 95 Internet applications, click Win 95 Apps, as shown in Figure 12.8.

Fig. 12.7
The links you see in this figure are all the way at the bottom of the Web page.

Fig. 12.8
Each icon represents a type of program.

3 Click the icon that best represents the type of program you're looking for. Need a browser? Click World Wide Web Browsers. Need more news and information (who needs that)? Click News Services. As a result, TuCows displays a Web page that contains a list of all the programs available that fit within the specified category. As an added bonus, at the top of the Web page, TuCows displays a short description of what types of programs the category includes (see Figure 12.9).

Fig. 12.9
The more cows you see at the bottom of each entry, the better the product is—at least in TuCows' opinion.

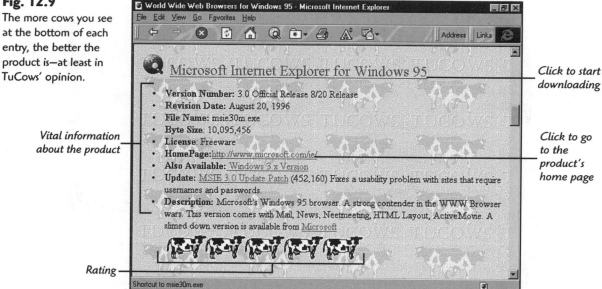

Click to start downloading

Vital information about the product

Click to go to the product's home page

Rating

4 Click the link at the top of the entry to start downloading the file. You also can click the link next to HomePage to go to that product's home page on the Internet.

ZD Net Software Library

ZD Net Software Library is one of my personal favorites. It catalogs thousands of freeware and shareware titles, just like all the other software Web sites. But, ZD Net very carefully reviews each and every title. It doesn't just slap a few stars by each program's name. ZD Net actually writes a few paragraphs about each program, describing its strong points and weak points, its price, the number of downloads to date, and more.

Point your Web browser at **http://206.66.184.152/index.html**. Figure 12.10 shows the top of the ZD Net Software Library Web page. You can click any of the links on the left side of the page to browse the software available.

Fig. 12.10
Look for announcements about new or exciting shareware programs at the top of the page.

Click these links to browse the library

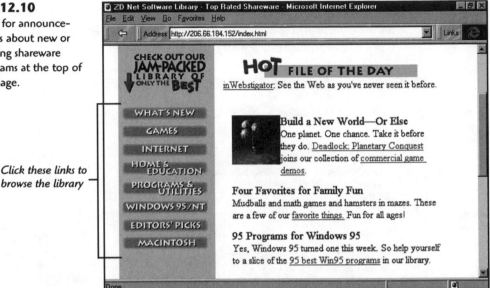

You also can go to the bottom of the page and search the library for a particular program or type of program. Here's how:

1 Go to the bottom of the Web page, as shown in Figure 12.11.

2 Type your keywords in the space provided. If you're searching for genealogy programs, type **genealogy**.

3 Click Start Search to search the library, using your keywords. ZD Net Software Library displays the listing shown in Figure 12.12.

4 Click any of the links to see the description for that program. ZD Net Software Library displays a Web page that contains a description of the product, as well as its size, cost, rating, etc.

5 Click Download to download that program. Click your browser's Back button to try a different program in the list.

Fig. 12.11
Click Power Search to
do a much more
advanced search.

Type your keywords here

Click to start your search

Fig. 12.12
Green dots in the
right-hand column
represent good
matches, yellow dots
represent so-so
matches, and red dots
represent bad matches.

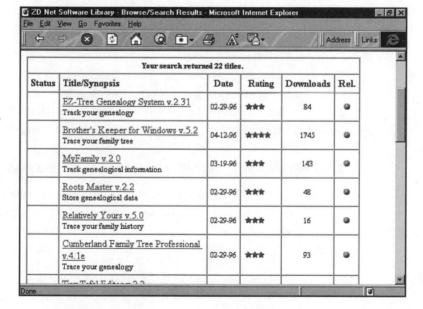

Search tools usually lead you to the author's site

You can also use most of the popular Web search tools to find shareware on
the Internet. Yahoo!. AltaVista. Excite. They all catalog Web pages. Some of
those Web pages belong to the shareware authors. Thus, these search tools

are a great way to go directly to the source and skip the collections altogether.

For example, you can use Yahoo! to find shareware programs that, you guessed it, help you track your families genealogy. Combine the keywords **shareware** and **genealogy** in the space provided and click Search. Yahoo displays a list of Web pages that contain information about shareware genealogy programs.

> **TIP** Yahoo! has a rather complete index of Web pages on the Internet that are dedicated to shareware. Point your Web browser to **http://www.yahoo.com/Computers_and_Internet/Software/Shareware** and browse to your hearts content.

Here's how to nab your favorite shareware titles

Some folks may find it a bit confusing trying to keep up with all the different ways to download files, and all the different types of files you can download. This section will help you keep it all straight.

The important thing to remember here is that you don't necessarily have a lot of decisions to make. In that regard, downloading shareware programs is easy. The author has pretty much already determined how you're going to download their program, and how you're going to install it.

Download your favorite shareware

There are two different ways you can download a shareware program from the Internet: using your Web browser or using an FTP client. Chapter 6, "The World Wide Web," describes how to use your Web browser and Chapter 9, "FTP (File Transfer Protocol)," describes how to use your FTP client.

When you find a file located on the Web that you want to download, click the link to that file, located in the browser Window. Most browsers will ask you immediately where you want to save the file. After you point to the appropriate folder (directory), the browser downloads and saves the file.

When you find a file on an FTP site that you want to download, you can use an FTP client program to download it. Note, though, that you can also use your Web browser to download a file from an FTP site. If you want to download a file called **myfile.zip** from **ftp.microfluff.com/files**, type **ftp:// ftp.microfluff.com/files/myfile.zip** in the address bar of your browser.

CAUTION If your browser asks you whether you want to open the file or save it to a disk, make real sure that you save it to a disk. Don't let the browser automatically open the file. First, it could make a mess out of your neat, clean hard drive by scattering files where you don't want them. Second, you could invite problems by unintentionally running a program that contains a computer virus. See Chapter 16, "How do I Protect Myself and My Computer?," to learn more about protecting your computer from viruses.

Installing a program you downloaded

About 99.9 percent of the time, the file you download will be an archive—usually a ZIP file or a self-extracting, self-installing file. You can use WinZip to extract a ZIP file, as described in Chapter 7, "E-Mail and Mailing Lists." Then, you can run **setup.exe** or **install.exe** after checking the files for a virus. If you don't see either of these files, the program probably doesn't have a setup program. Just copy the files into their own folder and create a shortcut in your Start menu, or a Program Item in the Program Manager.

If you downloaded an EXE file, check it for viruses first. Then, double-click the file to extract its contents. In many cases, the setup program will launch automatically and will clean up the mess when it's done. You can usually recognize one of these by its icon (see the icon in the margin). In other cases, double-clicking the EXE file just expands its contents—you still have to run **setup.exe** or **install.exe** yourself. You'll also have to clean up the mess yourself.

If you like it...if you use it...register it

Ready for the lecture? If you like a shareware product and you're using it, pay for it. That's all there is to it. Shareware products are protected under the same laws as commercial products. Failure to pay for a product that you continue to use violates the license agreement for that product.

But that's not the most important reason you should pay for shareware products that you continue to use. The biggest reason is that these poor guys and gals need to pay their bills. They spend a lot of time and money developing cool programs for people to download. The sad fact is that they rarely make any money off these programs because too few people actually register and pay for the product they use. Besides, you'll sleep better at night.

The text files that come with a shareware product provide payment instructions. You can usually pay by calling a 1-800 number, telling the operator which product you're registering, and giving the operator your credit card number. Don't worry. It's safe. I've registered many, many shareware products and have never had a bogus charge show up on my Mastercard as a result.

In return, you get a fully functioning version of the product if the shareware version is crippled (certain features disabled) in any way. In some cases, the author sends you a registration key that you input into the program in order to unlock all of its features or to keep it running past its expiration date. You sometimes get a disk and a manual, too. I saw one clever product that was absolutely free. The author was asking five dollars for a help file, though.

Here are some FTP sites to get you started

The Internet has plenty of shareware FTP sites. Here are a few to get you started:

- **The Oak Software Repository** is at **oak. oakland.edu**. This is a large site of freeware and shareware programs, sponsored by Oakland University at Rochester, Michigan. You'll find all the Windows 95 stuff in **/ pub/simtelnet/win95/**. If you're still looking for DOS and Windows 3.1 files, you'll find those at this site, too.

- **Walnut Creek** is at **ftp.cdrom.com**. I considered myself lucky to get on this FTP site. It's incredibly popular. Walnut Creek is in the business of selling CD-ROMs that are packed with freeware and shareware programs. Files from these CD-ROMs are available from the Walnut Creek FTP site, too.

- **WinSite (the FTP site formerly known as CICA)** is at **ftp.winsite.com**. This really may be the only FTP site that you need. It has the largest collection of freeware and shareware programs on the Internet. This is the Internet equivalent of CompuServe's WinShare forum (a forum on CompuServe that contains shareware Windows programs). You can also access WinSite on the Web at **http://www. winsite.com**.

Because everyone and their uncle looks for files at these FTP sites, you'll find them very crowded. At times, you won't be able to log on to the FTP server at all. Be patient; keep trying. If you give up, look at the log file to see whether they report any mirror sites that you can use.

Keep up-to-date with the latest releases

How do I keep up-to-date with the latest versions of my favorite shareware programs? Try the C|NET mailing list. It keeps you up-to-date on the latest and greatest shareware releases. It also sends you a top-ten list of the most popular shareware programs for your particular platform. You can sign-up for this mailing list by pointing your browser at **http://www.shareware.com/ SW/Subscribe**, as shown in Figure 12.13.

Fig. 12.13
You can select multiple platforms by holding down the Ctrl key as you click each platform in the list.

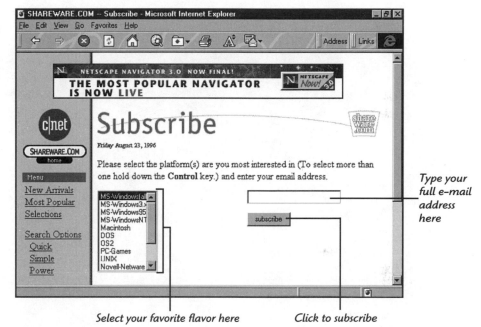

Select your favorite flavor here   Click to subscribe

Type your full e-mail address here

13

Do Your Research on the Internet

● **In this chapter:**

- **Need to look up a word? Need a quote? Look here**

- **Impress your boss with industry research**

- **Ready for a change? Use the Internet to find a job**

The Internet is the ultimate research tool. Use it . . . . **>**

The Internet has so many research tools and references on it that the mind boggles. You can access simple reference tools such as dictionaries and quotation books. You can also access countless tools that let you get real meaty information on an industry or a company. Need to get the goods on your competition? Want to impress an interviewer by getting to know their organization? Want to find a new job? You need to read this chapter.

The Internet is teeming with reference material

I'm sure my editor (my favorite person in the whole wide world) would say that not enough people use a dictionary (including me). She's probably right. More people might use things like dictionaries, thesauruses, and encyclopedias, if these bulky books were more convenient. For goodness sakes, why doesn't someone come up with a dictionary that lists words the way you're most likely to misspell them; then, it could show you the correct spelling. Kind of like a dictionary index.

That's not too far-out of an idea. The Internet does have a dictionary that suggests different words when it doesn't recognize what you typed. Besides dictionaries, the Internet also contains a variety of other reference works, such as thesauruses and famous quotations.

 TIP   **You can find more reference resources, like those in this section,** by pointing your Web browser to **http://www.yahoo.com/Reference**.

Dictionaries

You've heard of the Webster's dictionary. I'm sure of it. Did you know that there is an online version that you can use? Point your Web browser to http://gs213.sp.cs.cmu.edu/prog/webster. Then, type a word in the space provided, and click Look up definition. If the dictionary can't find the word, it'll recommend some alternative words. Quite handy if you're not exactly sure of the spelling. Figure 13.1 shows you what the result looks like.

Fig. 13.1
If you want to find a
word with similar
meaning, click
Thesaurus lookup.

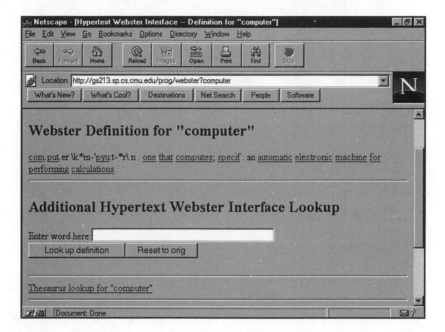

TIP You can also use wildcards to look up words. For example, you can find all the words that end in **pity** by looking up ***pity**.

Thesauruses

Like the Webster's dictionary, Roget's Thesaurus (**http://www2.thesaurus.com/thesaurus**) has a very simple user interface. Type a word in the space provided, click Now, and the thesaurus happily returns the results, as shown in Figure 13.2.

Fig. 13.2
You can also type a phrase and Roget's will provide alternative meanings.

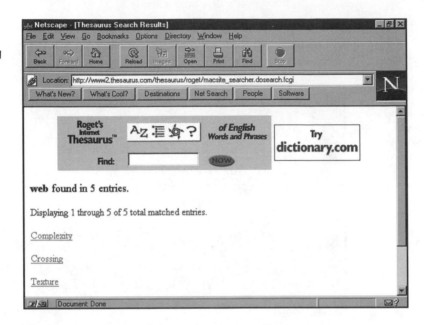

Encyclopedias

Encyclopedia Britannica is one of the best encyclopedias in the world. It just happens that you can also find it on the Internet at **http://www.eb.com**. Britannica is not a free Web site, however. You must pay a subscription to use it. Table 13.1 shows you what the subscription rates are for this service.

Table 13.1   Subscription rates for Britannica

Plan	Amount
Individual Monthly	$14.95 per month
Individual Annually	$150 per year plus $25 registration
Institutional	Dependent on size

You can try out a free trial by clicking the Free Trial link. Follow the instructions you see on the Web page, and you'll end up with a user name and password. Shortly thereafter, Britannica will mail instructions for completing the registration process. It sounds like a lot of finagling, but it's not that bad and it's really worth it.

When you log onto Britannica for the first time, you'll see a Web page that looks similar to Figure 13.3. You type a word, phrase, or question about which you want more information and Britannica returns a Web page that contains links to applicable entries. Click a link to view that entry.

Fig. 13.3
You can just type a series of keywords if you like.

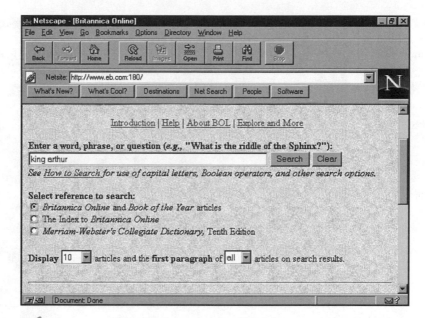

 TIP You'll see the word "index" beside some of your keywords. Click it to see a complete index of entries related to that keyword.

 NOTE Are you interested in mythology, folklore, and mysticism? Check out the Encyclopedia Mythica. You can find it by pointing your browser at **http://www.pantheon.org/myth**. It's free, too.

Quotes

I frequently speak at public events. A good source of quotations is an invaluable resource for me. Whether you speak publicly or not, you'll get a kick out of Bartlett's Familiar Quotations on the Web. Point your Web browser to **http://www.columbia.edu/acis/bartleby/bartlett**. Take a look at Figure

13.4. This resource works very much like the other reference tools you've read about so far. Type a few words to tell Barlett's what you're looking for and it'll return a Web page that contains a list of links to matching quotes. Underneath each link, you'll see the first few words of the quote.

Fig. 13.4

You can also see the contributions from a variety of people by clicking a name in the list.

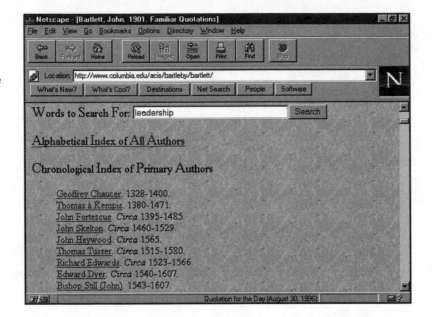

Do all your searches at Wired Source

Wired Source (shown in Figure 13.5) contains forms that work with every possible research tool on the Internet. You can search for information about news, business, politics, and more, from this site. You can also use the reference tools at this Web site such as a dictionary, ZIP code map, or patent database. Point your Web browser to **http://www.wiredsource.com**, click one of the categories in the left frame of the Web page, and follow the directions you see in the right frame to search for that type of information.

Fig. 13.5

In most cases, you can fill in the form for each search tool right there at Wired Source's Web site.

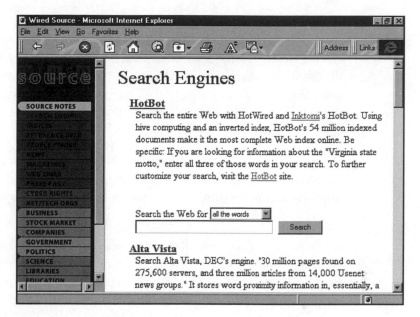

Research for work

You can't survive in the workplace anymore without the ability to do research. You have to know your own products and services. You have to know the industry in which you participate. And, you certainly want to make sure that you know the competition better than they think they know themselves.

The type and quality of information you find on the Internet depends a lot on the industry you're in. If you happen to work in one of the many computer or communications fields, you're in good shape to find all sorts of material. If you're a plumbing professional, you are just not going to find as much information. You will find some, however, so don't give up.

Search your favorite trade publications

Do you know what the predominant trade publications are in your field? You better. If you're in the computer field, for example, you probably read magazines such as *PC Week*. Virtually every industry has its own unique set of trade rags. Marketing types have *Advertising Age* and *Business Marketing*. Those insurance folks have rags such as *National Underwriter*. You get the idea.

So what's the trick to searching these publications for juicy bits of information you can use in your business? You have to find them on the Internet. The easiest way to do that is to use a search tool such as AltaVista or Yahoo!. Use the keywords **magazine**, **publication**, **journal**, or whatever is appropriate in combination with the name of the publication. If they are on the Internet, you'll find them. If they aren't yet on the Internet, I promise you that they soon will be, or they'll be gone.

For example, my favorite industry rag is *PC Week*. This is a Ziff-Davis publication. Thus, I can search using either name in combination with the keyword **magazine**. Doing so with Yahoo! yields the URL **http://www.pcweek.com**. Bingo; found my magazine.

If you look at the bottom of this Web page, you see a button that says Search. When you click it, you get a search form that looks like Figure 13.6. You can use this to search all of the magazine's past articles for keywords that you specify. Most of the online magazines you use will probably have a similar button that lets you search their archives.

Fig. 13.6

This search form works only with back issues. *PC Week* provides a different search form for the current issue.

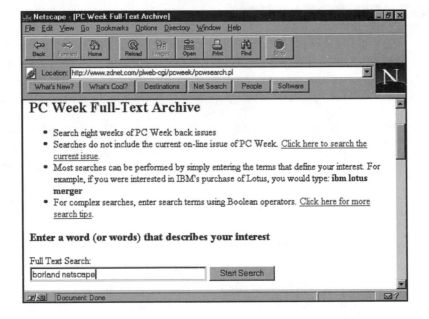

NOTE If your favorite online trade rag doesn't let you search its archives, take a look at NewsPage (see Chapter 14, "Moment by Moment News and Weather"). NewsPage contains news from a wide variety of sources—possibly yours. You can search it, too.

Search UseNet for other folks' ideas

In Chapter 11, you learned how to use Deja News (**http://www.dejanews.com**) to find newsgroup articles through the use of keywords that you provide. I'm not going to repeat all that material here, but I do want to remind you that you can tap into the knowledge that millions of other people around the world have already shared. If you want information about a competitor, for example, get online and see what other people are saying about that company. While you're there, see what they're saying about your company.

TIP Many times, you can count on someone else in the world having already done the same type of research you are doing. Ask questions on UseNet and see if anyone has any recommendations.

Get the goods on your competitors

The most obvious way you can dig up more information about your competitors is to visit their Web sites—if they have one. Are they announcing any new products or services? Do they post all of their press releases?

The information you get on a Web site doesn't always give you the competitive type of information you need, however. For that, you need to pull out all the guns. Point your browser to *Dun & Bradstreet*'s home page at **http://www.dbisna.com**. This Web page provides a lot of useful business information, but, more importantly, it lets you search its database, which contains the complete business background for millions of companies. This isn't a free service, though. Searching is free, but it costs $20 to get the report.

Down toward the bottom of the page, you'll find a Business Background Report link. Click it; then click Begin D&B's Online Access. Follow the instructions on the screen. Alternatively, you can go directly to it by pointing your browser to **https://www.dbisna.com/product/product.htm**. Figure 13.7 shows you a small section of a business report.

Fig. 13.7
Sections in the report include industry information, special events, business history, and operations.

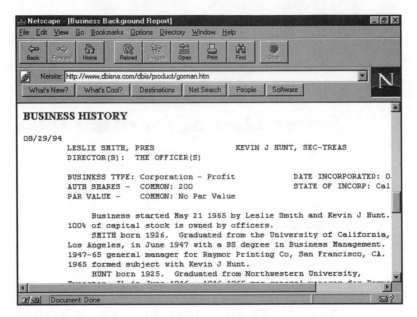

Check the FAQ (Frequently Asked Questions)

Just about every topic you can imagine has a FAQ available on the Internet. A FAQ is a list of frequently asked questions about a particular topic and the answers to those questions. For example, a FAQ about using the Internet may answer questions such as how to get online, how to download software, and how to use an e-mail program. A FAQ about golf may answer questions such as how to grip the club and how to buy the right golf ball.

Finding a FAQ about a particular topic is really easy. In your favorite search tool, use the keyword **FAQ** with words that describe the topic. For example, to find a FAQ about Mentos, use the keywords **FAQ** and **Mentos** as shown in Figure 13.8. The FAQs answer every conceivable question you might have about Mentos.

Fig. 13.8
On Yahoo!, sites marked with the sunglasses are particularly hot.

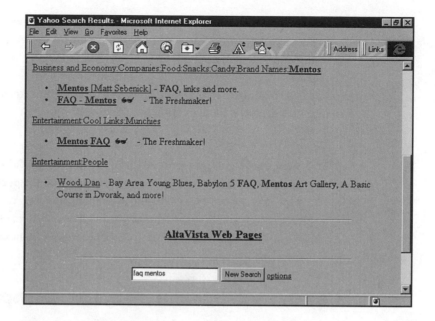

Use the Internet to find a job

Most people have undergone a job search at least once in their lives. Unless you're independently wealthy, you're no exception. Remember what it was like? Preparing your résumé. Answering ads. Finding recruiters. Taking off time from work to interview.

The Internet puts many of the resources you need to find a job right there on your desktop. You can learn how to write a good résumé, look at the job postings on the Internet, and visit with other people in your same position—as well as a variety of employment professionals.

Better learn how to write a good résumé, first

Writing a good résumé isn't easy. How much content should you include? Is more than one page OK? How should you organize it? You have a lot at stake when you write your résumé, so you want to get it just right.

The easiest way to write a good résumé is to look at a few examples. Then, blatantly copy a format that you think will work in your situation. You can find examples, as well as guidelines, of good résumés all over the Internet. The easiest way to find hundreds of samples from which to choose is to use the keywords **sample** and **résumé** with your favorite Internet search tool. These two keywords return a few hundred samples when used with AltaVista.

TIP Why don't you put your résumé on the Web? Talk to your service provider about creating your own home page. A prospective employer probably won't be searching the Web for candidates. You can point a recruiter or an employer to your résumé, however, which is often quicker than faxing it to them (you will probably impress them with your technical know-how as well).

Wanna work for a specific company?

There are two approaches to finding a job You can canvass the job market looking for anything that suits you. Or, you can find a company for whom you really want to work and find a way to get a job there. If you've decided that you really want to work for Microsoft, you need to discover what openings it has available. Then, you can send your résumé to openings that interest you.

Most corporate Web sites contain a link to a list of job openings. Figure 13.9 shows Microsoft's Employment Opportunities Web page. You might find a link to a list of openings right there on the home page. More likely, though, you'll have to search the corporation's Web site to find where it hides all those really interesting openings. If you can't search a company's Web site, try using one of the search tools with the keywords **job**, **opening**, and the company's name.

Check the local listings on UseNet

If you want to find a job in your area, you'll find thousands of listings on UseNet. In the Dallas area, for example, the **dfw.jobs** is always filled with hundreds of new postings each day. You'll probably find a similar newsgroup in your area. If you can't find one by looking at the list of newsgroup names, try finding a newsgroup with job postings in your area using Deja News, as described in Chapter 11, "Find Things on the Internet."

Fig. 13.9

You can submit your résumé to Microsoft in electronic form.

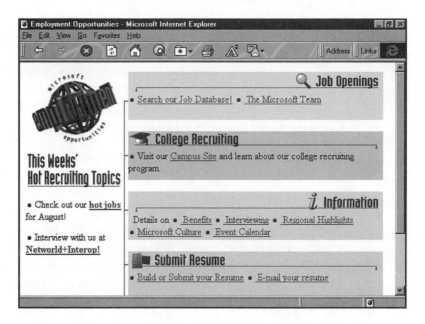

Most of the job postings come from recruiters, as shown in Figure 13.10. Thus, answering one posting can get you in the door with a recruiter that might have dozens of positions for which you're qualified. A lot of the postings in these types of newsgroups are duplicates because recruiters re-post their positions every few days. Note that most of the positions posted on UseNet are technical or computer-oriented.

Fig. 13.10

You can sort by From to keep postings from each recruiter together.

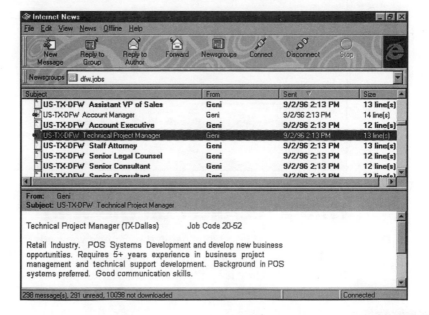

NOTE **Even though a newsgroup such as dfw.jobs is available in my area,** you might not have access to it. That's because your service provider might not subscribe to regional newsgroups that aren't in your area. Thus, UseNet isn't likely to be a good tool to find jobs in areas outside of your own.

Search the classifieds on the Web

If you don't find what you want from UseNet, you can use CareerPath.com to search the help wanted ads in most of the major metropolitan newspapers. Many employers don't advertise on the Internet (particularly non-technology companies), so this is the only way to electronically find those positions. Open **http://www.careerpath.com** in your Web browser, and click Register to sign up. Then, you'll see a Web page that looks like Figure 13.11. Select the newspapers you want to search, select the job category, provide any additional keywords, and click Search CareerPath.com to find all the matching postings.

Fig. 13.11
You can search the help wanted ads in newspapers from cities throughout the country.

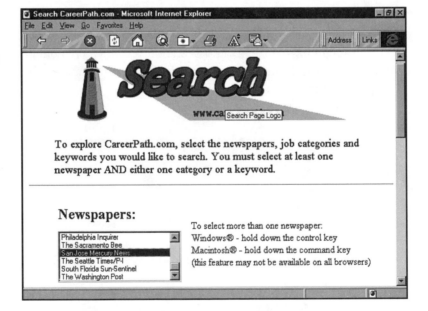

Find a recruiter on the Web

Few people find good jobs using the paper's want ads. No matter what you think of recruiters (head hunters, if you like), they're an essential tool for finding a job. They have the inside track into most of the companies in your area. Not only that, but they usually have a number of outstanding job orders from a variety of companies.

Before you contact a particular recruiter, you may want to use the Web to shop around. Check the Web sites belonging to the recruiters in your area. See if you like what they have to say. Make them sell you. Do they charge you fees? Then, call the ones you think will do the best job for you.

Using the Internet search tools to search for local recruiters isn't that easy. You can try using the keywords **career**, **job**, **placement**, **recruit** in combination with the name of the city or area in which you live. That usually doesn't return very good results, though. The best way to find the Web pages belonging to recruiters in your area is to check the Sunday paper and see if the advertisements list the company's URL. You can also use the **jobs** newsgroup. Most recruiters put the URL of their Web page inside their job postings (see "Check the local listings on UseNet," discussed earlier).

Use one of the Web's career-oriented rags

The Web has a number of really good career-minded magazines. They offer a variety of services. Some let you search for information about a prospective employer. Others let you view job postings or post your résumé for other employers to see. Here are some of the best:

- *Hoover's* (see Figure 13.12) lets you search for a company's profile or locate a company's Web site. Open **http://www.hoovers.com** in your Web browser.

- *Career Magazine* at **http://www.careermag.com** contains all sorts of useful information to help your job search. Take a look at Figure 13.13. You can get employer profiles and employment news. You can also search for job openings posted to this site.

- *CareerMosaic* is very similar to *Career Magazine*. It provides information about employers, about writing your résumé, and also provides health care information. You can use it to search for jobs overseas as well, in locations such as the United Kingdom, Japan, and Australia. Open **http://www.careermosaic.com** in your Web browser, and you'll see a Web page similar to Figure 13.14.

Fig. 13.12
Click Hoover's
Company Profiles to
search for a profile by a
company's name.

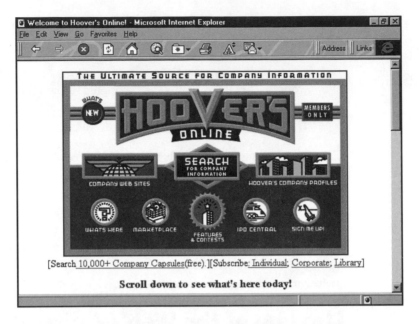

Fig. 13.13
Click Recruiter
Directory to search for
recruiters in your area.

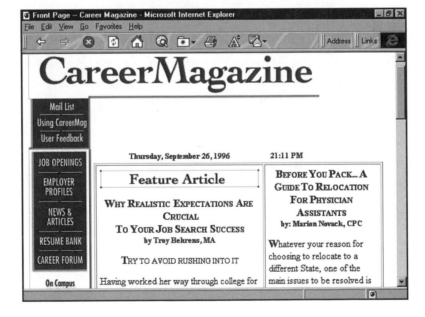

Fig. 13.14
Scroll down this Web page to see text descriptions of each link in the image map.

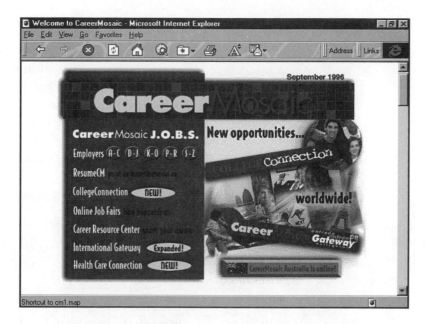

Create a support group on the Internet

Networking with the people in your profession is a basic skill you can use to help you land a job. Sometimes the best jobs can be found only by networking. They aren't advertised. No recruiter knows about them. These positions are filled by word of mouth.

Finding open positions is only one important reason you should network with the folks in your position. You can also learn ways to improve what you do. You can learn more about the industry. Find out the latest buzz. Learn which companies are doing well.

Seek out like-minded folks on UseNet

UseNet has thousands of professionally oriented newsgroups. If you're a programmer, you have it made. You have a variety of groups available for networking and learning more about your industry, such as the entire **comp** newsgroup hierarchy. UseNet also has newsgroups for lawyers, medical professionals, photographers, writers, construction contractors, and more. The easiest way to find a newsgroup in which to network is to use Deja News to locate a newsgroup for your industry, as described in Chapter 11.

Join a mailing list of folks like you

The Internet has a number of mailing lists available for networking. Some mailing lists are dedicated to keeping subscribers informed about open positions. **Jobs-mis** and **jobs-act**, for example. Other mailing lists help you refine your job hunting skills. The Publicly Accessible Mailing Lists Web site contains a handful of such lists. Open **http://www.neosoft.com/internet/ paml/bysubj-employment.html** in your Web page, and you'll see a page similar to Figure 13.15. Click one of the list names to learn how to subscribe.

Fig. 13.15
See Chapter 11, "Find Things on the Internet," to learn more about this Web site.

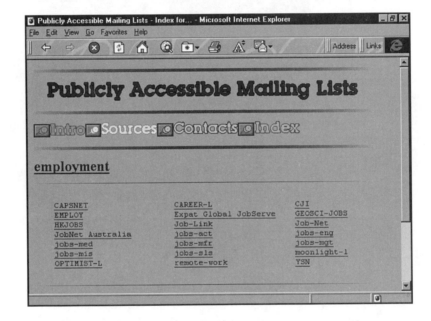

14

Moment by Moment News and Weather

● **In this chapter:**

● **Let PointCast deliver the news to your mailbox**

● **NewsPage captures stories from hundreds of sources**

● **A variety of print publications are now online**

● **The Internet search tools provide news, too**

I can't think of a better use for the Internet than staying on top of current news and industry information. . . . . >

What do you get when you combine a global communications network, a few hundred hungry news organizations, and information junkies like me? Indigestion? Nope. Internet news services. They're all over the place and, as with most new technology, the cream is rising to the top. You'll learn about those Internet news services in this chapter.

Some news organizations deliver the news directly to your desktop (PointCast). Other news organizations make you come to their site and dig through a vast pile of information (NewsPage). Still other Internet services make the news convenient by placing the day's top stories in a place that you're likely to visit anyway (Internet search tools). Oh, and don't forget all those traditional print news rags that are flocking to the Internet in droves.

Get PointCast: News delivered right to your desk

The PointCast Network is the ultimate Internet application. In a nutshell, it delivers all the news you can handle to your desktop. You don't have to look for it. No searching. No surfing. It's right there on your desktop. In addition, it replaces your normal screen saver so that you can see the current news on your screen while you're not using your computer. Here's how it works:

- After you install PointCast, you personalize it by customizing which types of news stories you want. Which companies do you want to track? Which cities do you want weather for? And so on.

- Every so often (hourly by default), PointCast connects your computer to the Internet and downloads the current batch of news to your computer. You can also update the news on demand.

- You can use the PointCast program to view the news. It has a slick interface that's easy to use. You'll learn more about it later.

- If you haven't used your computer for a while, PointCast will take over your screen, displaying bits of news. Every few minutes, it'll remove the current stories from your computer and replace them with other stories.

The best part: You don't pay diddly

You don't pay for PointCast—sponsors do. It uses the same business model that the major networks use. You get the service free as long as you're willing to put up with an onslaught of advertisements. It's really not all that bad, however, because the advertisements are usually somewhat entertaining and informative. PointCast targets the advertisements to the viewer, so you're likely to see advertisements that you would normally be interested in any-way.

How do I get my own copy of PointCast?

It's easy. Point your Web browser at **http://www.pointcast.com**, and click the Download PCN link. You'll see another Web page that contains a number of sites from which you can download the software. You'll also find instructions on the right side of this Web page that show you how to download the file pcninstl.exe. After you've downloaded the file, double-click it to start the installation. Follow the instructions you see on your screen.

 NOTE **PointCast is a Windows 3.1 program that works well with all** versions of Windows. In fact, PointCast works quite well with Windows 95 Dial-Up Networking.

Personalize PointCast

When you first install PointCast, it asks you if you want to personalize it or launch it. Go ahead and personalize PointCast so that the first batch of news you download is tailored to your needs. You can always personalize PointCast later by clicking the Personalize button in the channel viewer.

 Plain English, please!

PointCast calls each news category a **channel**. You'll see a tab for each channel in the Personalize The PointCast Network dialog box, and along the left side of the channel viewer.

You should now see a window that looks very much like Figure 14.1. This is where you pick the different types of news that you want to receive. Click each tab to customize that particular channel. When you're done, click OK to save your changes. Here are the channels that PointCast currently supports and how you customize them:

Companies	Choose the companies for which you want news and quote updates by typing their ticker symbol in the space provided and clicking <u>A</u>dd.
Weather	Choose the cities for which you want to track the weather by clicking the box next to the city's name until you see a cross through it.
Sports	Select the types of sports news you want to track by clicking the box next to the type until you see the cross.
Industries	Select the type of industry you want to track by clicking the box next to the industry until you see the cross.
Lifestyle	Select the horoscopes that you want to track by clicking the box next to the astrological sign until you see the cross. You can also show the lottery results for your state by choosing Show <u>L</u>ottery and selecting your state from the list.
Pathfinder	Select the Time-Warner publications you want to view by clicking the box next to their name until you see the cross.

Fig. 14.1

You can change the order of the channels in the channel viewer. Select a channel, and click Move <u>D</u>own or Move <u>U</u>p.

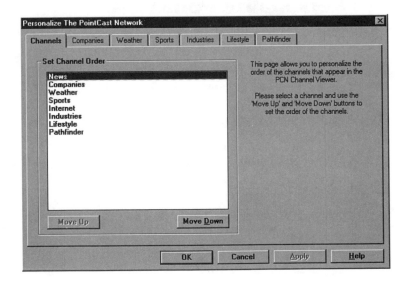

Configure your connection

When PointCast pops up for the first time, it asks you what type of connection you're using. Choose the type of connection you're using from the list. If you choose Windows 95 Dialer, PointCast asks you to pick the Dial-Up Networking connection that you want to use. If you choose one of the other options, PointCast asks you to specify the path to the WINSOCK.DLL for that dialer.

After you've configured your connection, PointCast will connect you to the Internet and download your first batch of news. This can take up to thirty minutes over a 28.8K because you have a lot of catching up to do. It's much faster over an ISDN connection, though.

Using PointCast day to day

PointCast presents the latest news in two different ways. First, PointCast acts as your screen saver so that you can see the current news while your computer isn't busy. Second, you can use the channel viewer to peruse the news as you see fit. You'll learn more about both ways of viewing PointCast in the following sections.

 NOTE   **PointCast is always adding new channels and news sources.** In fact, PointCast is scheduled to add additional channels, such as TechWire, toward the end of the year. They're also working quite hard at providing regional news that is focused toward specific markets.

The screen saver

By default, PointCast automatically installs itself as your screen saver, as shown in Figure 14.2. You will see it often because every time you let your computer sit idle for a while, PointCast will take over your screen, displaying the day's news. You can do a lot more than just look at the screen saver:

- If you see a story about which you want to read the full story, click the headline. PointCast will pop up the channel viewer with the full story.

- If you see an advertisement and you want to go to that sponsor's Web site, click the advertisement. PointCast will display that Web page in its own internal Web browser (Internet channel).

- If a screen full of news is about to scroll off of your screen, press and hold the Alt key. That freezes the screen until you release the key.

Fig. 14.2
Click any open area to close the screen saver.

Click these areas to close screen saver

Click anywhere inside to view sponsor's Web site

Click to go to that story

The channel viewer

The screen saver may be the coolest feature in PointCast, but it's not necessarily the best way to read the news. You need to use the channel viewer to get serious about that. Take a peek at Figure 14.3. This is the PointCast channel viewer. Each button along the top, left side of the channel viewer corresponds to a channel you configured in "Personalize PointCast," earlier in this chapter. You change channels by clicking the appropriate button. If there are more channels than the channel viewer can display, you can scroll the buttons up and down by clicking the up and down arrow buttons.

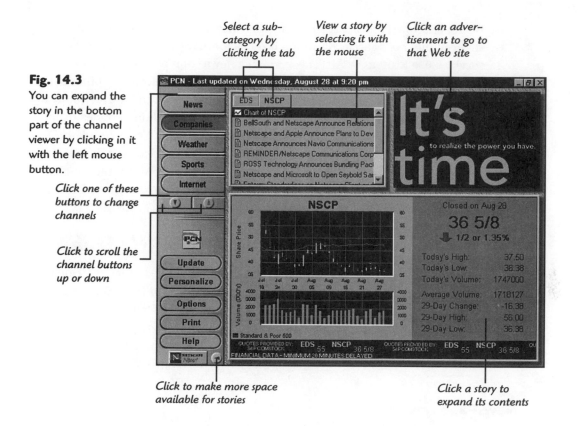

Select a sub-category by clicking the tab

View a story by selecting it with the mouse

Click an advertisement to go to that Web site

Fig. 14.3
You can expand the story in the bottom part of the channel viewer by clicking in it with the left mouse button.

Click one of these buttons to change channels

Click to scroll the channel buttons up or down

Click to make more space available for stories

Click a story to expand its contents

NewsPage consolidates hundreds of news sources

Aside from PointCast, NewsPage is my next favorite news service on the Internet. It doesn't have a viewer that you install on your computer like PointCast. It has a hierarchical group of Web pages that you view in your Web browser, instead. You point your Web browser at the top of the hierarchy, and drill your way down to the news that interests you by clicking sub-categories.

What sets NewsPage apart from the other news services on the Internet is the sheer number of sources on which it relies for news stories. Most of the news services use Reuters or AP. These are fine news sources, but they don't always provide you with enough industry-specific insight. On the other hand, NewsPage captures news from virtually every news source for every industry imaginable. For example, if you're into computers, you'll find articles from about 50 different sources, including *Computer Reseller News*, *InfoWorld*, *Information Week*, *PC Magazine*, *PC Week*, *PC/Computing*, and *WINDOWS Magazine*. NewsPage also captures hundreds of local news sources, including newspapers, for just about every major metropolitan area in the United States.

You have to register first, but it's free

Before you can get much use out of NewsPage, you have to register. Don't worry: you can get many of the articles you find there for free. NewsPage has subscription-based services, however, that give you even more information. You can easily unsubscribe if you decide you don't want to pay for the service. Table 14.1 shows you what those services are and how much they cost.

Table 14.1   NewsPage services

Service	Cost	Description
Basic	Free	Includes all of the basic news sources, such as Reuters.
Premium	$3.95/mo.	Includes all of the basic news sources, as well as all of the premium news sources, such as industry rags.
Direct	$6.95/mo.	Includes all of the basic and premium news sources. This service also sends a news summary to your mailbox each morning.

Setting yourself up on NewsPage is easy, if not a bit drawn out. Here's how:

1 Point your Web browser at **www.newspage.com** and click the Free Registration link you see in the middle of the page. As a result, your browser loads the registration form.

2 Fill in the personal information you see on the page. The fields that are set in bold characters require a response. Click Continue to move on.

TIP   **Most of the obvious user names, such as Jerry or Bob, are taken by** other users. You might as well use a combination of your first and last name (Jhoneycutt or JerryH, for example) so that you don't have to come back to this page when NewsPage discovers that your chosen user name isn't unique.

3 Choose your subscription level. You can choose Basic (it's free), Premium, or Direct, as you learned in Table 14.1. Click Continue.

4 Verify that all the information you entered is correct. If it's not, click your browser's Back button to make changes. Otherwise, click Continue, and your browser will load a nifty little survey.

5 Fill out the survey, answering as honestly as you can (wink, wink), and click Continue.

6 You're ready to go. Click the graphic that says Home Page to go to the top of the news categories.

TIP   **If you choose either Premium or Direct service, NewsPage will also** ask you for a credit card number. This is a secure transaction, so you needn't worry too much about using your card on the Internet. NewsPage will bill your credit card once each month for the price of the service, plus any pay-per-view articles that you read.

Drilling down to get the news

Now that you're registered, you can start reading the news on NewsPage. Figure 14.4 shows you the industries you find at **http://www.newspage.com**. Each of these industries contains additional categories, and each category contains additional topics. Buried about four levels deep, you'll find the actual news stories. This hierarchical organization makes it easy for you to find just the right articles.

Click one of the industries to view the categories that are available. For example, click Interactive Media & Multimedia to view the categories you see in Figure 14.5. The numbers in parentheses, to the right of each category, tell you how many topics are in the category.

Fig. 14.4
Click Hot Topics to see
the most popular
NewsPage topics.

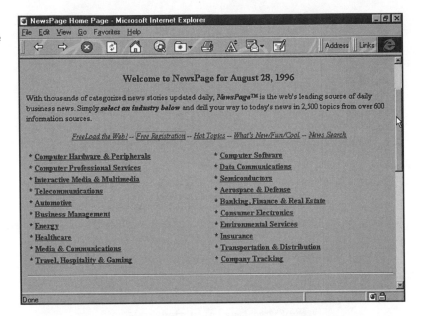

Fig. 14.5
If you're a premium
subscriber, you can
search the articles in
NewsPage by clicking
the Search button.

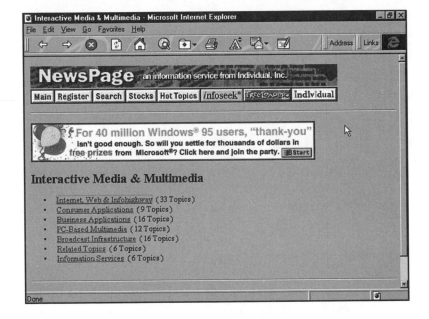

Click one of the categories to view the topics available in that category. For
example, click `Internet, Web & Infohighway` to view the Web page shown
in Figure 14.6.

Fig. 14.6
You'll typically find dozens of topics available in each category.

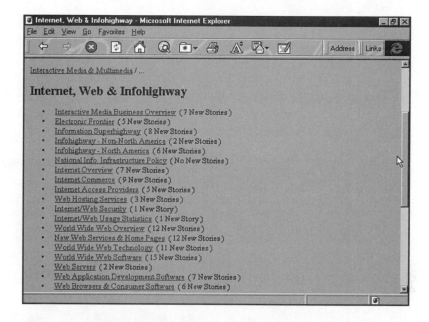

As you saw in the list of categories, the list of topics shows you how many stories are available under each topic. You click one of the topics to review the headlines and summaries for that topic, as you see in Figure 14.7.

Fig. 14.7
Click Prevous Day to see the articles posted the day before.

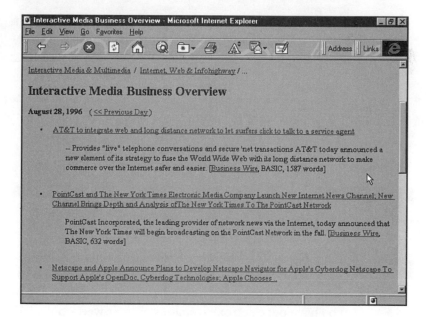

Each article in the list contains a headline you can click to look at the full story, as shown in Figure 14.8. The summary contains information about the news source, the number of words, and the subscription level needed to view the entire article. If you subscribe only to the basic service, you can still view the headlines for premium articles, but you can't view the entire story. If you do click the header for a premium article, your browser will prompt you for your user name and password.

Fig. 14.8
The Internet news services always seem to be in the news themselves.

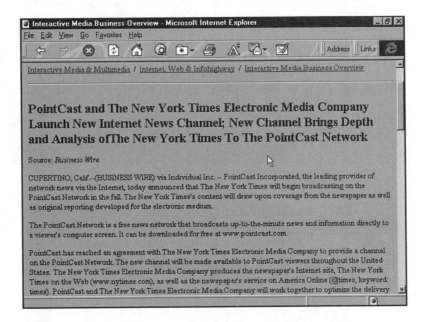

 TIP **NewsPage puts each article in more than one topic. Go to the** bottom of the article to see under which topics you'll also find this article. It's a great way to find other NewsPage topics that you may want to visit.

Newspapers, journals, and magazines galore

A number of folks predict that news journals and magazines have only five years to get their tails onto the Internet or face extinction. I can't vouch for that, but I can tell you that the Internet is teeming with news organizations who have put electronic versions of their wares online: Time-Warner (*Time*, *People*, et al.), *Newsweek*, *The Wall Street Journal*, for example. Many, many others are in the process of going online, too.

This section introduces you to a handful of outstanding journals on the Internet. You can find many more, however, by pointing your Web browser at **http://www.yahoo.com/News** (Yahoo!'s news index).

USA Today

USA Today, whose Web page is shown in Figure 14.9, was one of the first news rags to put its contents on the Internet. It didn't do this like a lot of news organizations, either; *USA Today* put pretty much all of its print content onto the Internet. Makes you wonder how they stay in business, huh? I suppose it's a bit difficult to read the online version while flying home from Timbuktu. Point your Web browser at **http://www.usatoday.com** to see for yourself.

Fig. 14.9
Click News, Sports, Money, Life, or Weather to go to the front page of that particular section.

The Wall Street Journal

The online version of *The Wall Street Journal* is every businessperson's dream. Take a look at Figure 14.10. You get complete access to all of its content—for a price, of course. The Interactive Edition also has many features that you won't find in the print edition. The first time that you point your Web browser at **http://www.wsj.com**, you'll have to subscribe. The cost is nominal, about $49 per year.

Fig. 14.10
Click Personal Journal
to customize the news
that you get each day.

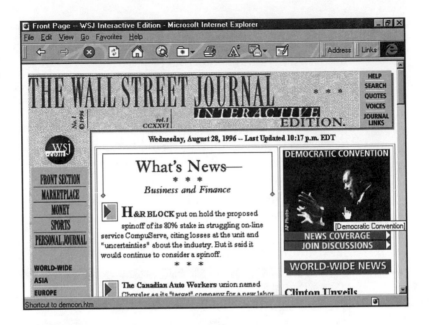

CNN Interactive

The Internet was made for CNN, or is that the other way around? CNN's Web site is a perfect complement to its daily news programs. You can find more information about current broadcasts or take a look at stories from previous broadcasts. In most cases, you'll find additional information to supplement the moment's hottest news stories. For example, when TWA flight 800 crashed into the Atlantic, CNN had maps and photographs of the crash site available on its Web site within hours. In addition, CNN usually complements each news story with RealAudio and video clips, as well as links to related sites on the Internet.

Figure 14.11 shows you what CNN's home page looks like. You can get there by pointing your Web browser at **http://www.cnn.com**. It's a completely free news service, too.

From CNN's home page, you can get to CNNfn by clicking the CNNfn link on the left side of the page. CNNfn is a Web site dedicated to the financial world. It's a great place to stay on top of the markets, learn more about investing your money, or get stock quotes. Figure 14.12 shows you what it looks like.

Fig. 14.11
CNN's Web site is updated around the clock; check in often.

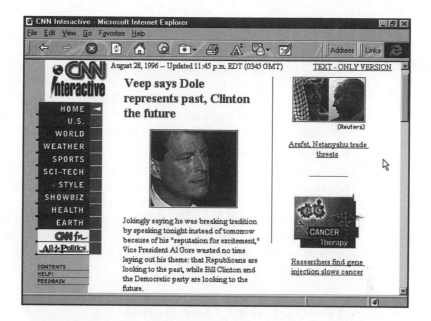

Fig. 14.12
You can get here directly by pointing your Web browser to **http://www. cnnfn.com**.

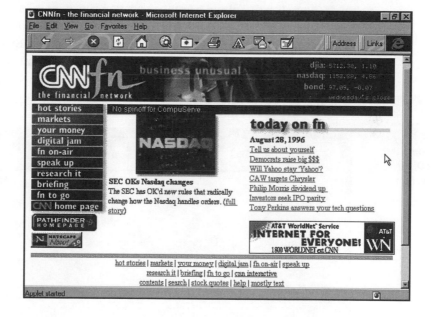

Hey, don't forget your favorite Internet indexes

Remember those Internet search tools and indexes you learned about in Chapter 11, "Find Things on the Internet"? They've wised up. They know that folks like us use those tools several times a day, and they need hits to rake in more money from their sponsors (they're in business to make money these days). One way they can make themselves more attractive is to provide a one-stop place for all sorts of information, including news.

In this section, you'll learn about the news offerings from two of the better Internet indexes: Yahoo! and Excite. As a bonus, you'll also learn how to personalize the news that Yahoo! gives you and how to put Yahoo!'s news on your Windows 95 desktop.

Yahoo! has the news

At the very top of Yahoo!'s home page, you see an icon labeled Headlines. Click this icon and you'll go to a Web page that looks somewhat similar to Figure 14.13. It's divided into several categories such as Business, Technology, and Sports. You can view the headlines for each category by clicking the Headlines link next to that category, or you can view the news summaries by clicking the Summaries link.

Fig. 14.13
If you're a computer buff, click ZD News to get the latest from Ziff-Davis.

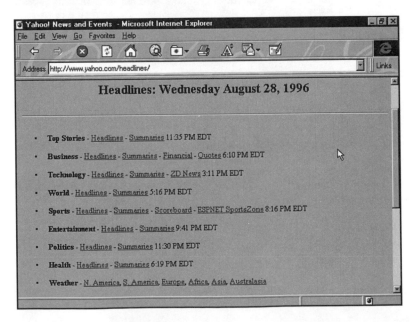

NOTE **Yahoo! gets its news from Reuters, so it's not nearly as compre-**
hensive as the news you get from a service such as NewsPage. Proximity
counts, however. It's right there on a tool that you probably use everyday;
you might as well check out the big stories of the day.

Build your own Yahoo! home page

How about a more personal touch to your news? Yahoo! has launched a new,
free service called My Yahoo!. You customize exactly what information you
want to see on your own personal version of Yahoo!. You can choose which
companies you want to track. You can choose which sports team you want to
read about. You can also customize the types of news stories you want to
receive, and which cities you want the weather for. Figure 14.14 shows you
what my personal version of My Yahoo! looks like.

Fig. 14.14
My Yahoo! is spon-
sored by advertisers,
so you pay nothing.

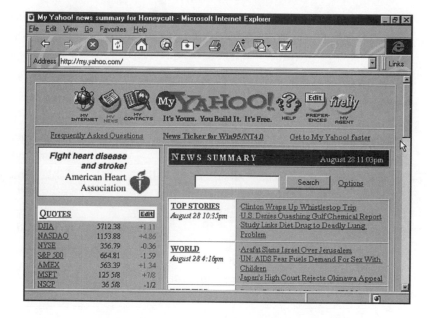

You'll need to set up a user name and password when you first point your
Web browser at **http://my.yahoo.com**. This doesn't mean that you have to
pay anything. It's just a way for Yahoo! to keep track of your preferences. In
fact, different people in your household can have their own accounts set up
with Yahoo! so that when they log on, they get their own personal view.

Click Start your own now, about midway down the Web page, to select a user name and password. Yahoo! will ask you for a name, password, birthday, and a few other tidbits of information it can use to personalize your news. Then, it will give you the opportunity to select the types of news you want on your page.

The next time you point your browser to **http://my.yahoo.com**, you'll see your personalized Web page. You don't normally have to supply your user name and password because they're stored on your computer and Yahoo! knows how to ask your browser for them. If you end up back at the Web page you saw originally, however, type your user name and password. Then, click Login.

Do you see those icons at the top of your personalized Yahoo! Web page. They let you do some pretty cool stuff. Take a look at this:

 My Internet takes you to a list of links that Yahoo! thinks you'll like, based upon how you answered the questions when you registered.

 Preferences lets you change your user profile, including your password, mail address, and so on.

 My News takes you to a Web page that contains all of the news in which you've expressed an interest.

 My Agent is cool. It guides you to additional places on the Internet that Yahoo! thinks would interest you.

 My Contacts helps you locate other people on the Internet by searching for them by name.

 Help, well, it displays help.

Fig. 14.15
You can also make the News Ticker run in *its* own window. Right-click it and choose Taskbar Dock / Undock.

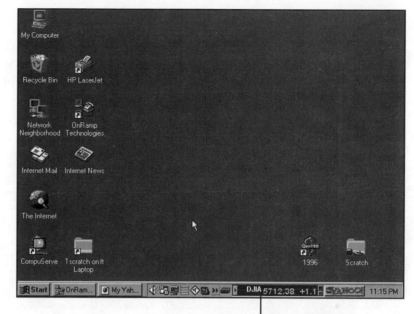

The News Ticker docked on the Task Bar

Put Yahoo! on your Windows 95 taskbar

At the top of your personal Yahoo! Web page, you see a link called News Ticker for Win95/NT4.0. This takes you to a handy product that lets you put the latest news and information right there in your Windows 95 or Windows NT task bar. If you're not sure what I'm talking about, take a look at Figure 14.15, which shows you my task bar with the News Ticker on the right side.

The News Ticker gets the news based upon how you configured My Yahoo!. Thus, if you configure My Yahoo! to watch Microsoft (MSFT) and Netscape (NSCP) stock, you'll see stock quotes for both companies scrolling across your task bar.

To download and install the Yahoo! News Ticker, click News Ticker for Win95/NT4.0 and follow the instructions you see on the next Web page. Unfortunately, Windows 3.1 users are left a bit in the cold here because Windows 3.1 doesn't have a task bar.

Excite does the news, too

Yahoo! isn't the only Internet index that does the news. Excite does it, too (see Chapter 11). From Excite's home page at **http://www.excite.com**, click Excite News. You'll see a Web page similar to Figure 14.16. Like Yahoo!, Excite uses Reuters, so it's not as comprehensive as NewsPage, but it's awfully convenient.

Fig. 14.16
Click one of the topics to see the headlines for that topic.

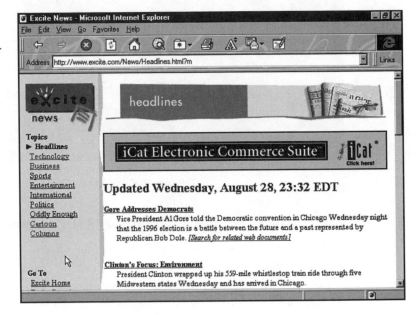

15

The Web Is Your Personal Entertainment Guide

● **In this chapter:**

- **Your computer's alter ego—a hi-tech TV guide**

- **Find the very best restaurants in the states**

- **Find out what a film is about before you go**

- **Looking for a good golf course?**

- **You can print a street level map of your community**

- **You'll find many other ways to stay out of trouble**

Bored? Wanna go do something? Use the Internet as an entertainment guide; then, get out of the house. . . . . . .

Most big cities have those entertainment guides at book stores or in front of the local pub, which you can pick up for free. They contain all sorts of information about what's going on that week. Concerts. Plays. Dining. Special events.

You can get the same types of information on the Internet. It's more convenient, though, because you don't have to run to the store to get it, and you can search for things that specifically interest you.

You don't need TV Guide; get the listings online

I canceled my subscription to *TV Guide*. Not that it's a bad magazine or anything. They do a good job. The only thing I'm after is the TV listings, though. And, well, I can get them online. So can you. TV1 is a cool Web site that contains TV listings for every network and cable channel that you can imagine. Figure 15.1 shows you TV1's home page.

Fig. 15.1
You'll find TV1 at **http:// www.tv1.com.**

Click Join Now to register and set up your preferences. When you register, you create a username and password; then, TV1 asks you a few questions such as name, locale, and mail address. It also asks for some information about your computer. Then, it lets you customize your own settings. You can choose your favorite viewing hours, TV source (cable, satellite, etc.), and the type of programming you like to watch. You can also choose which network and cable channels you want.

The next time you show up at TV1's home page, click Member Listings and log on. That'll get you to the Control Panel (see Figure 15.2), where you can change your preferences, search the listings, or view the listings in one of four different formats:

Grid	Displays a grid with the channels across the top and times down the left side.
Time	Displays the familiar TV guide type of listing with programs shown underneath their starting times.
Category	Displays all of the shows that fit within a particular category such as specials, sports, or news.
Channel	Displays all of the programs for the particular channel you choose.

Fig. 15.2
Click one of the days underneath the format you want to view.

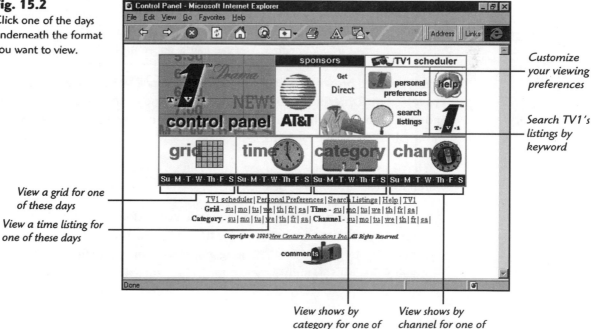

Customize your viewing preferences

Search TV1's listings by keyword

View a grid for one of these days

View a time listing for one of these days

View shows by category for one of these days

View shows by channel for one of these days

TIP **Bookmark or add the Control Panel to your Favorites so that you** don't have to go through the home page anymore.

I'm looking for a good restaurant—any advice?

It's hard to find a good place to eat in Dallas. Not that we don't have many restaurants; Dallas is absolutely overflowing with restaurants. They can't pack them in tight enough. That's the rub, though: Dallas has so many places to chow down that you can't find what you want, like a kid in a candy store.

The Internet to the rescue, again, with Zagat Dine. You use this Web service to search for specific types of restaurants in different communities across the states. For example, you can find places that serve seafood and that also have been given the highest ratings for atmosphere; or, you can find a burger joint that has been given great marks for service. You tell Zagat what you want and it'll find it for you.

NOTE **For the uninitiated, Zagat Dine comes from the Zagat Surveys.** People from every part of the states dine at different restaurants and submit surveys to Zagat. Then, Zagat rolls-up all the information about each restaurant into a summary. You can hardly go wrong.

Point your Web browser to **http://pathfinder.com/@@tY48aAcAehPfa6nc/ Travel/Zagat/Dine/index.html**. Don't want to type all that nonsense? You'll find Zagat Dine on Pathfinder at **http://pathfinder.com**. Figure 15.3 shows you what its Web page looks like.

You have two different ways to use Zagat Dine. You can browse or you can search for restaurants, like this:

- Click the name of the city in which you wish to feast. The next page shows you a list of restaurants for that city, which you can view alphabetically; by type of food, ranking, popularity, or sorted by best bargains. Figure 15.4 shows the list for Dallas, sorted by popularity.

Fig. 15.3
Zagat Dine has reviews
for most of the large
metropolitan areas.

Fig. 15.4
Click a restaurant's link
to read its review and
ratings.

- Click Find to search Zagat Dine for a restaurant. Zagat presents you with a form that asks you where you want to eat; what type of food you want; what price range you're willing to pay; and what your preferences are for quality, service, and decor. After you've completed the questions, click Submit to see a list of restaurants that match, as shown in Figure 15.5.

Fig. 15.5
They didn't have haggis, but a good steak house will do.

TIP   **Zagat has many other online services. Check out the toolbar** at the top of its Web page.

Get the goods on the movies before you buy

The Internet Movie Database at **http://us.imdb.com** is to movies what Zagat Dine is to restaurants (movies are reviewed by the public). You use it to get more information about a movie before you spend your hard earned bucks on it. At its home page, click the movie ticket to search for a particular movie. Using the form in Figure 15.6, you can search for movies based upon the movie's name, cast and crew, character names, or biographies.

Fig. 15.6
The bottom of this Web page has links to more advanced ways for searching the movie database.

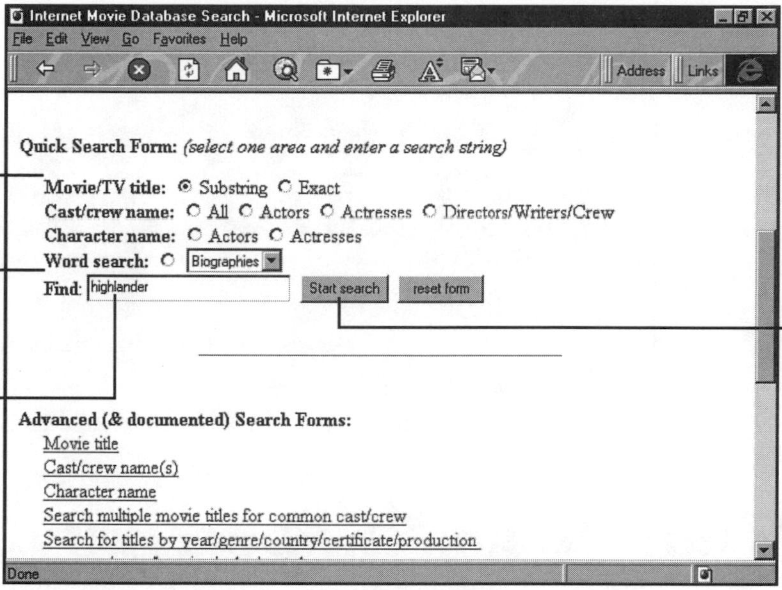

The Internet Movie Database returns a list of links to movies that match your query. Click one of the links to view all sorts of information about the movie, including its rating and a summary of the movie. While you're here, put your own two cents in by rating the movie from one to ten. The Internet Movie Database doesn't stop there, though. Check out Figure 15.7. Each of the icons in the middle of the page represent different types of information you can get about the movie. You can find out how to buy it. You can get technical stuff and trivia. Wanna hear some quotes from the movie or hear what the critics have to say about it? Staggering.

NOTE **The Internet Movie Database doesn't always provide information** about the latest movies to hit the streets. However, you can find a whole list of other sites that review current movies at Yahoo!. Point your Web browser to **http://www.yahoo.com/Entertainment/Movies_and_Films/ Reviews** and pick one of the sites, such as Mr. Cranky.

Fig. 15.7
The bottom portion of this Web page contains the names of the complete cast and crew for this movie.

Here's how to find the best golf course around

I know. Not everyone is a golfer. For those of you who do have this dreaded disease, you can use golf.com to find courses all across the states. Are you tired of putting on the same old greens or whacking your golf eggs into the same puddle of water? Find a different course. Point your browser to **http:// golf.com/course** and click the country of your choice. Then, drill down through a series of maps until you see a list of golf courses for that area. Click one of the courses to get all the details, as shown in Figure 15.8.

Fig. 15.8
Read the reviews at the
bottom of the page.

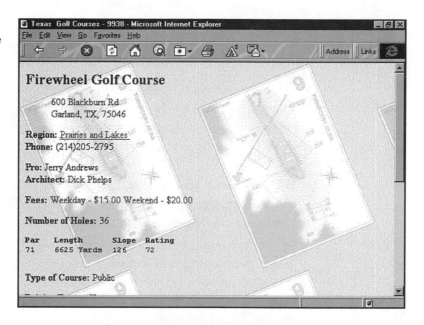

Need a map? Get street level maps from the Web

The a-number-one requirement for getting to know your community, or any other community, is to know your way around. I chatted with a fellow on PowWow a while back who has lived in the Dallas area for three years; but, he still doesn't know many of the major streets and features in the area. For that matter, I've lived in a tiny Dallas suburb called Frisco, and I barely know my way around it.

There's no excuse. Maps are easy to get. I don't mean run down to the bookstore and unload $20 bucks on one, either. Get onto the Internet, point your Web browser to MapQuest's Web site at **http://www.mapquest.com**. This is unbelievable. The first decision you have to make is which version of MapQuest you're going to use:

- Click Java Atlas to run the Java version of MapQuest. This works well with any browser that supports Java, such as Internet Explorer and Netscape.

- Click ActiveX Altas to use the ActiveX control version. This is an excellent example of ActiveX control. It's easy to use and has many of the interface features you expect in a real application.

- Click one of the countries at the top of the Web page to view the HTML version of that map. You may think that you're settling for fewer features by using this version, but this version actually has many more features than the others, such as locating points of interest.

Q&A ***When I open the ActiveX version of this map, Internet Explorer pops open a Potential Safety Violation Avoided dialog box. The map doesn't work—why?***

By default, Internet Explorer makes program security very strict. It won't let you run programs that aren't certified. You can get around this: choose View, Options from the main menu; click the Security tab; click the Safety Level button, select Medium; click OK; click OK again to save your changes. Reload the ActiveX map. You'll get a warning about the safety violation now, but you can continue by clicking Yes.

I want to use the ActiveX version of the map in Netscape. Can I?

Yup. You need to install a plug-in that is found at **http://www.ncompasslabs.com**. This plug-in lets you use ActiveX controls in Netscape Navigator.

All three versions of the map work basically the same. The example you see in Figure 15.9 is from the HTML version. The following list shows you how to do a few things with the map.

Find Place	Click Find to display a map based upon any combination of a business name, address, city, state, ZIP code, and country.
Zoom In/Out	Select Zoom In or Zoom Out. Then, click the location on the map where you want to be centered when it zooms.
Print	Click Print, and MapQuest will prepare a Web page that is especially designed for you to print. Print the page from your browser. Click the Print button in Internet Explorer, for example.

Find POIs   To locate different points of interest, select the type of thing you want to see on the map, such as dining, lodging, or shopping (my favorite). Then, click Update Map at the bottom of the page.

Customize   Click Options to customize the map with your own settings, such as size and the amount of detail.

Fig. 15.9
The MapQuest Atlas looks much better if you have a display with a resolution greater than 640 by 480.

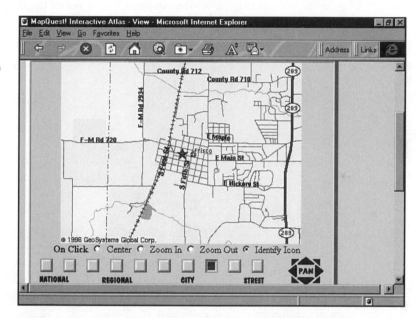

Check out these great community resources

A map will help you get around, but it won't help you find interesting things to do in your community. It won't help you find the movie theaters or museums. It won't help you find all those great stores, either. You can depend on the newspaper, but you will have to dig through an awful lot of dead trees.

On the Internet, you can find information about your community when you want it, and you can go directly to the interesting stuff, without having to wade through the classifieds first. Two resources on the Internet come to mind. First, CityView is available for many of the major metropolitan areas. The second is City.Net, which covers even more cities than CityView. Both of these Internet services are sponsored by advertisers, so they're free to you.

CityView

CityView, at **http://www.cityview.com**, is available for several areas. After you open CityView's home page, click one of these links to go to that particular city:

Atlanta

Dallas

Fort Worth

Houston

Las Vegas

Mexico City

New Orleans

San Antonio

Seattle

Figure 15.10 shows you the types of information that CityView provides for each community: dining, shopping, movies, sporting events, weather, and a whole lot more. Click any one of the links to open a Web page that will help you find information about that category. You can search many of the categories, too. For example, click Dining and you can search for restaurants by type of food or restaurant name. You can also click the map to select an area of the city in which you want to search. Pretty sharp.

Fig. 15.10
Click The Tour to take
a tour of the city.

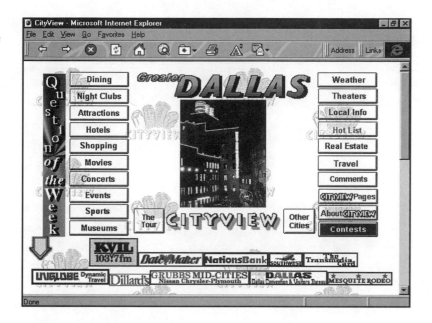

City.Net (by Excite)

City.Net covers many more cities than City View. It is a service provided by
Excite. Point your Web browser to Excite (**http://www.excite.com**), click
the City.Net link you see at the top of the page, and you'll see a Web page
similar to Figure 15.11. You can also get there by opening **http://city.net**.
From here, you can search for a city by typing its name in the space provided
and clicking Take me there. You can also click one of the cities on the right
side of the Web page.

Figure 15.12 shows the City.Net page for Dallas. You can open Web pages to
view maps, weather, dining, and a variety of other topics related to that area.
Just click the appropriate link.

TIP **Click Search to find things to do in the city.**

Fig. 15.11
City.Net also provides maps, which you can get to by clicking Maps at the top of the Web page.

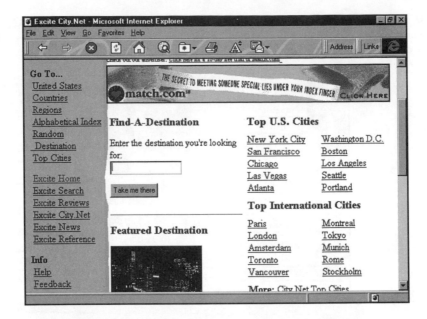

Fig. 15.12
Click one of the links in the Menu to learn more about that particular city.

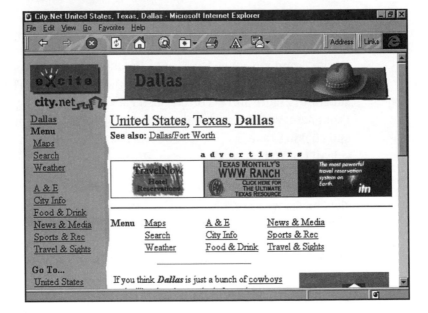

Local radio and TV stations are a great source

Show me a radio or TV station that doesn't have a Web page on the Internet, and I'll show you a company led by a dolt. You can count on your local media having all sorts of goodies on the Internet. The more in-touch stations provide community information such as upcoming charity drives, sporting events, concert information, museum events, theater, etc. The other ones at least provide the lottery numbers.

Finding the stations in your area isn't hard. Open your favorite search tool. Mine, as you've noticed, is Yahoo!. Use the keyword **radio** or **television** with the name of your city. To find the radio stations in my area, I'd use **radio** and **Dallas**, for example. Figure 15.13 shows you how fruitful that search is.

Fig. 15.13
Click a link to go to that radio station's home page.

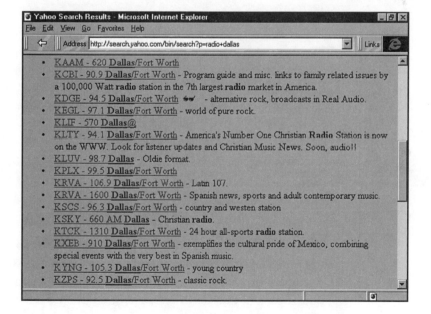

So, what does a typical radio station's Web page look like? Take a look at Figure 15.14. As you can see, it contains information about the local sports teams, weather, and concerts. Oh, yeah, the lottery, too.

Fig. 15.14
Ron Chapman of KVIL
should be proud of his
organization's Web site.

NOTE A new phenomenon is developing on the Internet. Many radio
stations are broadcasting their shows live via RealAudio. If you're not sure
what RealAudio is, go back to Chapter 6, "The World Wide Web," and take
a look. If you see the RealAudio logo on a radio station's Web page, you
can listen to their broadcasts through your computer.

Here's how to find more things to do in your area

Don't do TV? Don't eat out much? How about the movies or golf? No, huh,
well the Internet has other ways for you to find things to do in your area. You
can check out the indexes on the Internet, such as Yahoo! and Excite, or you
can take a peek at UseNet to see what other people recommend.

Check out an entertainment index

Most of the Internet indexes, like Yahoo!, contain plenty of regional information. For example, if you point your Web browser to **http://www.yahoo.com/
Regional** (don't forget the capital R), you can get at regional information in a
few different ways:

- Click Regions to look at broad geographical areas, such as the Midwest in the United States, or Europe.

- Click Countries. Then, drill your way down through progressively smaller regions in that country.

- Click U.S. States. Then, click a particular state, such as Texas, followed by a particular city. All of Yahoo!'s city indexes are listed under each state at **http://www.yahoo.com/Regional/U_S__States**. That's two underscores between the "S" and "States."

Once you've pinned down a region, you can explore the art centers, businesses, and museums for that area—among other things. Figure 15.15, for example, shows you the types of resources available for the city of Dallas. Most of the regions that Yahoo! indexes contain similar links.

Fig. 15.15
Click Entertainment to see what types of things that region or city offers to keep you out of trouble.

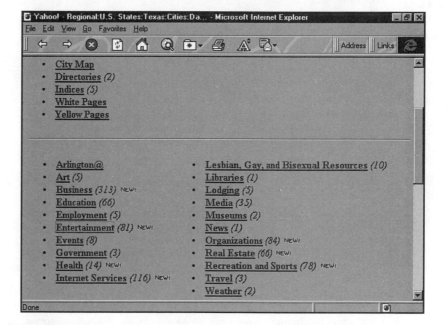

NOTE **Most of the listings for cities in Yahoo! also contain links to city** maps, white pages, and yellow pages, etc. Bookmark the city in which you live so that you can keep a tremendous resource close at hand.

Look for suggestions on UseNet

The Web is cool, but it takes a while for the information to be updated. If a new restaurant opens, or a brand new theater opens, you have to wait a while before you see anything about it on the Web. Solution? Hit the newsgroups. You'll find information about your area in the regional newsgroups. If you don't remember how newsgroups are organized, take another look at Chapter 8, "UseNet Newsgroups."

Figure 15.16 shows the newsgroups available for the Dallas/Fort Worth area. They're easy to find because they belong to the **dfw** hierarchy—a common abbreviation for the area. You see a newsgroup for dining (**dfw.eats**), classifieds (**forsale**), jobs, politics, etc. Your area probably has a similar set of newsgroup, too.

Fig. 15.16
The actual newsgroups you'll find for each area vary.

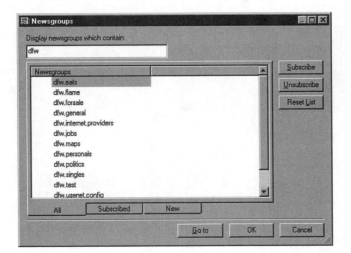

Finding those newsgroups is another question. Most news servers carry well over 10,000 groups. Going through all of them by hand is out of the question. Your best bet is to use Deja News, described in Chapter 11, "Find Things on the Internet," to see which newsgroups discuss your particular city or geographical area. For example, to find newsgroups about the San Diego area, type **San Diego** in the bottom edit box of Deja News, as shown in Figure 15.17. Then click Find. As a result, Deja News returns newsgroups such as **sdnet.forsale** and **sdnet.test**. This gives you a good indication that the newsgroup hierarchy you're looking for is **sdnet**.

Fig. 15.17
Make sure you click
the second Find
button.

 Many of the regional newsgroups aren't carried by all of the news servers. Thus, you may not find yours on Deja News. If you don't have any luck with Deja News, give your Internet service provider a shout and ask them about regional newsgroups for your area.

16

How Do I Protect Myself and My Computer?

● In this chapter:

- ● **Learn how to keep other people off your computer**

- ● **Be proactive. Don't be a victim of a virus**

- ● **Take control of the programs your browser runs**

The Internet is a wonderful place. However, you need to protect yourself from those who would do you harm . . . . . **>**

I certainly don't want to panic anyone. Most people will never run into a problem while using the Internet. You can send your credit card number over a plain Internet connection a hundred times, and, in all likelihood, no one will ever nab it. The odds are in your favor.

However, the last person you want to talk about odds with is a person who has been hit by lightning, or, in this case, bitten by a virus. The chances are slim, but they exist. Thus, you need to protect your computer from the morons on the Internet who would like to do it harm. This chapter shows you how.

Can other people access my computer when I'm online?

Yep. I'm not kidding. If you don't protect your computer, other people on the Internet can get access to the files on your hard drive. Same goes for networks. You need to protect your network from intruders. Fortunately, it's very simple to protect your computer. It takes a little know-how to protect a network, however, but I'll introduce you to the concepts so that you can drill your network administrator (have fun).

Protect your computer if you're dialing in

Windows 3.1 users really don't need to worry much. You're probably using Trumpet Winsock, and it won't let other people have access to your computer.

On the other hand, Windows 95 and NT users need to be more cautious. Networking is built into the operating system. So is file sharing. To the operating system, your Internet connection is just another network. A network that supports file sharing. You can keep people off your computer, though, by double-checking your network configuration, like this:

1 On your desktop, right-click the Network Neighborhood icon and choose Properties. You should see a dialog box that looks like Figure 16.1.

Fig. 16.1
The Network property sheet is where you configure all of your network settings.

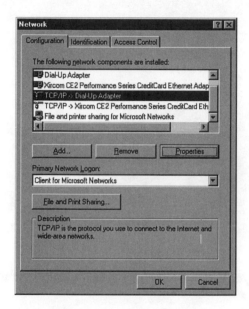

2 Look for an item in the list that says TCP/IP -> Dial-Up Adapter. Select it and click Properties.

3 Click the Bindings tab (see Figure 16.2). Do you see an item in the list that says File and printer sharing for Microsoft Networks? If not, Click Cancel a few times to get a reading of the Networking property sheet. Otherwise, move on to the next step.

4 Is there a check mark next to the item that says File and printer sharing for Microsoft Networks? If so, click the box until the check mark goes away, as shown in Figure 16.2. Note that this turns off file and printer sharing for all dial-up TCP/IP connections.

Fig. 16.2
Don't tamper with any of the other settings in this dialog box, or you may break your connection.

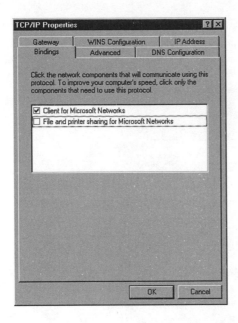

Protect your network if you are on a LAN

Protecting a network that is connected to the Internet isn't as easy as flipping a few switches. Your network administrator needs to install a program called a **firewall** on your network. A firewall is like a very picky eater who'll only put certain types of foods in his or her mouth. A network firewall allows most outgoing Internet traffic. It's more picky about incoming Internet traffic, though. It decides if a bit of data has any business at all coming into the network. If something looks like a security threat, it spits it back out.

Check with your administrator to see if your network is protected. If not, you can recommend that they look at a few trade magazines, such as *Lan Times* or *PC Week*, to find more information about evaluating Internet firewalls.

Protect yourself from viruses

I wouldn't be nearly as concerned about someone getting access to my computer as I would be about a virus getting ahold of it. Viruses are nasty. Some are pretty mundane, doing things like displaying annoying messages at a predetermined time. Other viruses are deadly to your computer, though, and are capable of wiping out your entire hard drive and all the files on it.

Most viruses spread by attaching themselves to programs. When you run the program, the virus may find other programs on your computer to infect, or it might decide to inflict its damage right then and there. When you share an infected program with a friend, you help the virus spread itself to even more areas. Given the number of programs that change hands on the Internet, and the number of floppies you exchange, you can imagine just how quickly a virus can spread.

Ooh. Sounds ominous, doesn't it? Kind of Orwellian. You can protect yourself. The sections that follow show you how.

 Viruses can't spread via e-mail or data files, such as pictures. Just won't happen. A virus is a program, like any other program. It has to execute in order to spread. This means that someone can send you an e-mail with a program that contains a virus. It also means that someone can send you a document, such as a Word or Excel file, that contains a virus-type macro.

Download programs from reputable sites

You had to know that this was coming: ABSTAIN. Don't download freeware and shareware programs onto your computer. That'll certainly take care of the virus problem, but that's not a very realistic solution. Half the fun of getting onto the Internet is downloading cool software. You double your fun when you actually try it out.

Your best protection is to download files from a reputable site. I'd be a bit wary of downloading shareware files from a newsgroup, for example, on which anyone in the world can post just about any program they like. You have no way at all of knowing whether the file contains a virus. The shareware sites that you learned about in Chapter 12, "Get Your Software Fix Online," are all pretty safe, though.

 **If you're using a computer on a company network, be thoughtful** and professional about using shareware and freeware products on your computer. Don't do it. You're putting your company at risk of catching a virus that could do serious harm to the files on the network. In fact, some companies have strict policies regarding the use of this kind of software on a networked computer.

Use a virus scanner

An essential item these days is a virus scanner. These tools do three things. First, they check your computer when you start up to make sure that it hasn't been tampered with by a virus. Second, it lurks in the background, watching for things to happen that may be caused by a virus. If it detects any questionable behavior on the part of a program, it notifies you immediately. Last, it will **inoculate** your computer if you do catch a virus. That is, it will remove the virus from your computer.

 Q&A *My Windows 95 computer has suddenly ground to a halt. I was zipping along just fine, but the next time I started my computer, everything suddenly slowed down. My animated cursors don't work anymore, either. What's wrong?*

It's very likely that you've contracted a virus. If Windows 95 thinks that the system areas on your boot drive have been tampered with, it'll start your computer in something called DOS Compatibility Mode the next time you log on. This is much slower because it uses slower disk drivers. Nab one of the virus scanners and see if you're infected. To learn more about DOS Compatibility Mode, check out a Que book called *Windows 95 Registry and Customization Handbook*.

Norton Antivirus

I use Symantec's Norton Antivirus. I can't say whether it's really better than any other antivirus scanner, I just have a long history of buying Norton-branded products. You can purchase Norton Antivirus at any computer store or at an electronics store such as Best Buy. It does a good job at preventing viruses, as well as removing them once you're infected.

Symantec provides regular updates to the program, too. New viruses are born every day. You should check Symantec's Web site regularly to get any updates for the latest flurry of viruses. Point your Web browser at **http://www.symantec.com/avcenter/index.html**, and follow the instructions you see to download the update.

McAfee

McAfee's antivirus utility is probably the most popular on the Internet and with network administrators. Whereas Symantec does business in a lot of software categories, McAfee makes network security its only business.

You can purchase McAfee in most retail computer stores, but, why do that when you can download an evaluation version for free? Open **http://www.mcafee.com** in your Web browser and click Download McAfee. At the bottom of the Web page, you'll see a link to download a personal evaluation copy. Click that link and follow the instructions you see on the next page.

Like Norton Antivirus, you can get updates for McAfee that account for the latest viral scourge. Go back to the same place from which you downloaded McAfee, and click Get that Dat. Follow the instructions you see on the next page.

ThunderBYTE

ThunderBYTE Anti-Virus is another popular utility that frequently gets better marks than McAfee in the press. You can download an evaluation copy of ThunderBYTE by opening **http://www.thunderbyte.com** in your Web browser. Then, click the Software Demos link to get your own evaluation copy. The evaluation lasts 30 days.

Protect your computer from errant programs (ActiveX)

The next big threat to your computer will be Java and ActiveX applications. In particular, ActiveX controls that your browser downloads from the Internet can do just about anything they like on your computer. On the other hand, Java applets pretty much work in a sandbox (they live inside a very controlled environment) and can't get to all of the services on your computer.

Your browser provides features to protect your computer from these badly behaved programs. You can be very extreme and totally disallow them; you can be moderate and just have the browser notify you when you download one; or, you can be completely liberal and let your browser download any old ActiveX control that it wants, without so much as a peep.

If your browser supports Java or ActiveX, it probably supports security. The examples in the following sections use Internet Explorer only because its security features are currently a bit more advanced than the other browsers. However, Netscape also supports many of the same security features.

NOTE   **After installing Internet Explorer 3.0 or greater, you may want to** download and install the patches available for it. In particular, Microsoft has made a patch available that fixes some security flaws in Internet Explorer 3.0. Open **http://www.microsoft.com/msdownload/iepatch.htm** in your Web browser to download the patch appropriate for the version of the browser that you installed.

What are publisher certificates? How do I use them?

When you install a publisher certificate in your browser, you're telling the browser that anything published by the company listed in the certificate is A-OK. The browser can trust that company. It's similar to buying shrink-wrapped software at the computer store. You know the computer store and you know the publisher. You trust them. So, you run home and install the program without worrying too much about the damage it might cause to your computer.

Certificates are given by a certifying authority and they're validated when your browser tries to download and install a program from the Internet. If the browser doesn't find a certificate for the program, it'll either dump the program into a bit bucket or ask you if you want to go ahead and install it anyway (see Figure 16.3). This is totally under your control, too, as you'll learn in the next section.

What do browsers and frogs have in common?

As I write this chapter, Internet Explorer definitely has the one-up on Netscape as far as security features go. The two browsers tend to leapfrog each other, so by the time you read this, Netscape may have the one-up on Microsoft.

You can't win. It's not practical to bounce back and forth to whichever happens to be the browser of the day. My advice? Pick a browser and stick with it. If it lags a bit behind the other, it'll catch up in short time.

Fig. 16.3
I don't know anything about this company or its Web site, so I'm not too keen on installing this control.

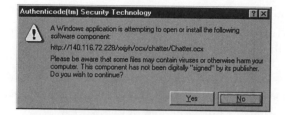

If the browser finds a certificate for the program's publisher, the browser installs the program without asking you. Note that the first time you install a digitally signed vendor's program, the browser asks you how you want to treat other programs from that same vendor, as shown in Figure 16.4.

Fig. 16.4
Hey, this is Microsoft. You can trust them because their software never has bugs.

TIP **On the Internet, you'll hear a variety of terms related to publisher** certificates, such as **Authenticode** or **code-signing**. Both are terms used to describe publisher certificates.

Site certificates identify Web sites to your browser

As the heading says, site certificates identify Web sites to your browser. That is, you know that the information you send a secure Web server is going to the intended recipient. When you log on to a secure server, it sends a certificate to your browser. The certificate provides security information about that site. Before the browser sends information to such a site, it verifies the certificate so that you know the information you're sending is definitely going to the owner of the certificate.

In Netscape, you can view the site certificates that you've installed by choosing Options, Security Preferences from the main menu. Then, click the Site Certificates tab, as shown in Figure 16.5.

Fig. 16.5
Internet Explorer also supports site certificates. Choose View, Options from the main menu; click the Security tab; and click Sites.

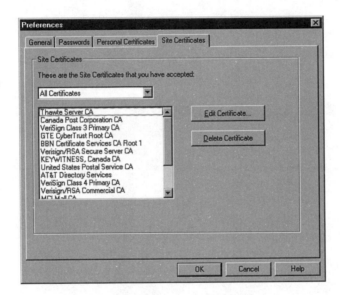

You can control what can and can't run in your browser

Internet Explorer gives you complete control over what it will do with ActiveX and Java programs that it downloads to your computer. You can instruct it to ignore those programs. You can also instruct it to go ahead and install them and, perhaps, give you a warning when it does. Take a look at these steps:

1 From Internet Explorer's main menu, choose View, Options. Then, click the Security tab. You'll see the dialog box in Figure 16.6. The part in which you're interested is the bottom area.

Fig. 16.6
The Security tab lets
you control ratings,
certificates, and the
security level for
ActiveX content.

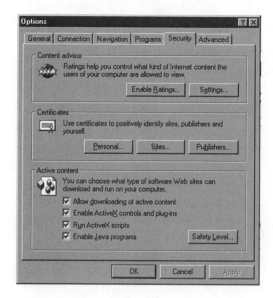

2 The four check boxes at the bottom determine what type of content
you'll let the browser run. Table 16.1 describes each of these settings.
Change these settings to suit your needs.

Table 16.1   Security settings for ActiveX content

Name	Description
Allow downloading of active content	If this setting is disabled, your browser won't even attempt to download ActiveX controls or Java programs.
Enable ActiveX controls and plug-ins	If this setting is disabled, the browser won't run ActiveX controls or Netscape plug-ins.
Run ActiveX scripts	If this setting is disabled, the browser won't run VBScript or JavaScript scripts.
Enable Java programs	If this setting is disabled, the browser won't run Java programs at all.

3 Click the Safety Level button. You'll see the dialog box in Figure 16.7.

Fig. 16.7

Don't even bother selecting None because it leaves you completely open to very badly behaved programs.

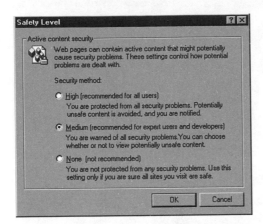

4 These three check boxes determine what the browser does when it downloads a program that could be a security problem. Select High if you want the browser to avoid any control that doesn't have a certificate, select Medium if you want the browser to give you a choice, or select None if you want the browser to install all programs no matter what.

5 Click OK to save your changes to the safety level. Then, click OK again to save your Security settings.

You can also control what Netscape will download and run. However, Netscape doesn't use publisher certificates, so you don't have as many options available. Choose Options, Network Preferences from Netscape's main menu. Then, if you don't want to download and run Java applications, click the Languages tab and de-select Enable Java. Now, if you don't want to execute JavaScript scripts, de-select Enable JavaScript. Click OK to save your changes.

17

You Can Entertain and Educate Your Children

● In this chapter:

● How do I keep my kids safe on the Internet?

● Share these "rules" with your child

● Yahooligans! is the perfect site for your kid

● Find your child a pen pal—friends for life

The Internet is a great place for your kids, you need to be careful, though . . . .

F or your kids, the Internet is a fact of life. It's not going away. They'll need to know how to use it at work and play. They'll use it to communicate with friends and associates. They'll watch movies delivered via the Internet. Voting? Shopping? Entertainment? All on the Internet. A day will come when the Internet will be as important to how we live as the telephone and the TV are now.

You need to take care of your children, though. Be careful. Even though the Internet has a lot of wonderful things for your kids, it also has a lot of dangers. In some cases, pure evil lurks on the Internet— people that want to take advantage of them. With a few precautions, though, you can make sure that your kids have a good time surfing the Internet and don't fall into any holes.

How do I keep my kids safe while they surf?

Once you've connected your computer to the Internet, you and your children can access anything and everything that is out there. I've heard all those arguments that say the Internet's more questionable side doesn't come looking for you; and, for the most part, they're right. With the exception of the perverts who look for children on the chat channels—your child has to go looking for the Internet's nastier content.

But, that type of content is entirely too easy for your child to find. All a curious curtain-climber has to do is use the appropriate (or inappropriate) choice of words with one of the Internet search tools, and, shazaam, they see links to some of the filthiest sites on the Internet. They're literally two mouse clicks and four keystrokes away from the nastiest content you can find.

This is not a good reason to keep your child off the Internet, however. They need it. Don't believe me? The schools in my area give students extra credit if they do their homework with the help of the Internet. I'm sure other schools offer similar things. The Internet has countless resources to help your child better understand their world. So, before you yank the phone line out of your kid's computer, consider the tips for making your child safe that you will see in this chapter.

Some service providers make it safe for you and your children to enjoy the Internet. A service provider in my neck of the woods lets you block access to adult sites on the Internet. They also provide custom software that lets you see anything you want on the Internet, while your children can only see a limited number of sites. It's a "social" interface, in the spirit of the failed Microsoft Bob, which lets your children explore the Internet through objects with which they are very familiar. You can probably find a similar Internet service provider in your area.

Share these rules with your children

You can teach your children some very simple rules to follow, which, if they stick to, will help them stay safe while on the Internet—not to mention protect their impressionable minds. This list of rules comes from one of my favorite Internet sites for kids: Yahooligans! (see, "Yahooligans! is made just for kids," later in this chapter). Take a look. Then, rip them out of this book and post them next to your kid's computer:

- I will not give out personal information such as my address, telephone number, parents' work address/telephone number, or the name and location of my school without my parents' permission.

- I will tell my parents right away if I come across any information that makes me feel uncomfortable.

- I will never agree to get together with someone I "Meet" online without first checking with my parents. If my parents agree to the meeting, I will be sure that it is in a public place and bring my mother or father along.

- I will never send a person my picture or anything else without first checking with my parents.

- I will not respond to any messages that are mean or in anyway make me feel uncomfortable. It is not my fault if I get a message like that. If I do I will tell my parents right away so that they can contact the service provider.

- I will talk with my parents so that we can set up rules for going online. We will decide the time of day that I can be online, the length of time I can be online, and appropriate areas for me to visit. I will not access other areas or break these rules without their permission.

You'll find other resources on the Internet that show you how to keep your kids safe. One of the better resources is Kid Safety at **http://www.uoknor.edu/oupd/kidsafe/start.htm**.

NOTE **All of the tools in this section are just that: tools. In fact, many** children are bright enough to get around most of the protections described in this chapter. Thus, they don't replace parent participation. That is, there is no substitute for knowing what your child is doing online. Talk with your child about what they can and cannot access, as well as what they have already accessed on the Internet.

Places you don't want your kids visiting

I hope this doesn't sound too restrictive to some folks, but there are definitely some places from which you should keep your kids. I'm not talking about portions of places, I mean the whole enchilada. The only exception to this advice is if you're using one of the products that filter or block out obscene content. You'll learn about those products in the next section; meanwhile, I'd keep your kids completely away from these Internet resources:

UseNet	I have yet to see a single, unmoderated newsgroup that didn't contain extreme profanity and some pretty bizarre ideas. The folks who regularly post to those newsgroups aren't always the culprits, either. Some people get their jollies by randomly flaming or posting obscene messages to newsgroups, hoping to cause a spectacle. And, don't forget, UseNet has a good number of newsgroups dedicated to pornography.
CU-SeeMe	My eyes bugged out the first time I saw what some of the CU-SeeMe users do with that tool. Kind of a virtual swinging scene. I won't go into detail here, but it's nasty and it's live.
IRC	I'm willing to bet that 80% of the IRC channels have obscene names and, more than that, contain all sorts of profanity and sexually oriented messages. Even if your child promises to stick with the handful of clean IRC channels, there is no guarantee that a person whom you wouldn't normally let your child talk with on the street won't pop in and start trouble.

Plain English, please!

CU-SeeMe is an Internet program that allows people to share real-time video of themselves with other people on the Internet. It works much like the chat or conferencing programs you learned about in Chapter 10, except that it's actually video conferencing. **"**

 See if your service provider can block bad UseNet groups. In addition, see if they provide a "clean" IRC server for your kids to use. Many service providers provide this service for users with children.

Try a product that protects your young'un

After the first media outcry about pornography and children on the Internet, a couple of resourceful companies built products to help you filter out, or block, bad content.

Two of the most notable are SurfWatch and Net Nanny, which you'll learn about in the upcoming sections. There are other products, too. They do basically the same thing: they keep your child from viewing content you'd rather they didn't see. Note that these are subscription services. They provide updates on a regular basis to account for any new adult sites on the Internet.

 All of the products I looked at are good. I feel most comfortable recommending SurfWatch to you, however, based upon the reviews I've read and their alliances with a variety of content providers and vendors.

SurfWatch

You can get more information about SurfWatch, by Spyglass, at its Web site: **http://www.surfwatch.com**. It blocks sexually explicit Web sites, FTP sites, UseNet newsgroups, Gopher sites, and IRC channels. At the bottom of the SurfWatch home page, you see links that are for the different platforms you may have. Click the link that matches your platform (SurfWatch for Windows 95, for example) to learn more.

You can order SurfWatch at the number you see on its Web page. You can also purchase SurfWatch online. Click the Online Ordering link at the bottom of its home page. You can't download it right then, however; they ship it to you instead. They even call you personally to get your credit card number.

TIP If you've recently purchased a new computer, you may already have Surf Watch. It's bundled with a variety of machines, including certain Compaq and Packard Bell lines.

NOTE You can contact the makers of SurfWatch directly by calling 1 (800) 458-6600.

Net Nanny

Net Nanny is very similar to SurfWatch. The biggest difference I've noticed is that Net Nanny works with more than just the Internet; it works with online services such as CompuServe, too. In addition, Net Nanny doesn't charge for its subscription services like SurfWatch does.

You can evaluate Net Nanny for free. Point your Web browser at **http://www.netnanny.com**. Click the Free Evaluation Copy link and follow the instructions you see on the next Web page to download it.

NOTE You can contact the makers of Net Nanny directly by calling 1 (800) 340-7177.

Use the browser's built-in rating system

Internet Explorer has a built-in rating system that is designed to help you block questionable material. Other browsers haven't added support for this rating system yet, but they soon will. And, they'll work very similar to the manner I described earlier in this chapter.

Internet Explorer supports an Internet Ratings system whereby Web publishers can voluntarily rate their own Web sites. Then, you can control which ratings you want to allow in Internet Explorer. Here's how to set it up:

1 Choose <u>V</u>iew, <u>O</u>ptions from Internet Explorer's main menu and click the Security tab.

2 Click the Enabled <u>R</u>atings button. The first time that you set up the ratings, Internet Explorer asks you for a password. This is for parental control. Type your password in the space provided and click OK. You'll then see the property sheet shown in Figure 17.1.

Fig. 17.1
Click More Info to
learn more about this
rating system.

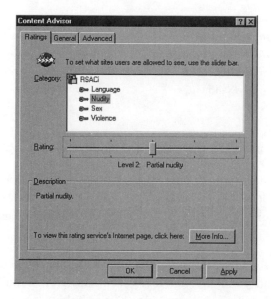

3 Choose the ratings category you want to set from Category: Language, Nudity, Sex, or Violence.

4 Move the slider to the right to allow a higher level of explicit material to be viewed for that category, or move it all the way to the left to prevent explicit material from being viewed for that category. You'll see a description of what types of material each setting allows.

5 Repeat steps 3 and 4 for each category you want to change, then click OK to save your ratings.

6 Click OK again to save the Security tab.

The next time you open the Internet Ratings property sheet, you'll be asked for your password. No one can change these ratings without the password. You can change your password by clicking the General tab in the Internet Ratings property sheet. Then, click Change Password.

 TIP **If you really want to see what your child has been looking at,** check the browsers history folder and sort by date.

These, and all other rating systems, depend on the cooperation of the Web content providers. If an adult site doesn't participate in the rating system, your child can still visit that site—even though you configured the ratings to disallow it.

Yahooligans! is made just for kids

Are you beginning to wonder if there is a site made for kids? A site that's safe? Educational? Entertaining? There really are a lot of sites like that on the Web. My favorite children's site is called Yahooligans! This site is maintained by the same folks who bring you Yahoo!.

Point your Web browser to **http://www.yahooligans.com**. It works exactly like the Yahoo! you know and love (see Chapter 11, "Find Things on the Internet"). It has links just for kids, though. Take a look at Figure 17.2 to see what I mean.

CAUTION **Don't be lulled into thinking that Yahooligans! will protect your** little one. They can still go to any other site on the Internet, unless you're blocking those sites with ratings or a product like SurfWatch.

Fig. 17.2
Your kid can search
Yahooligans! for
interesting sites just like
you can with the
regular Yahoo!

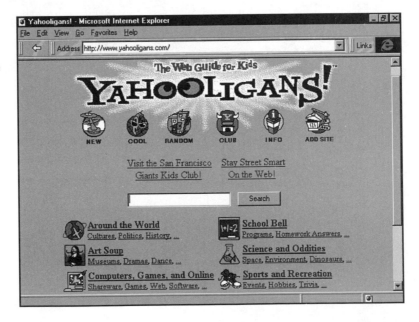

18

The Stores Are Open and They Have Things

● In this chapter:

- Don't worry about using your credit card

- You can use electronic cash, if you like

- Here's how to find a good online mall

Hang on to your wallet; you'll find all sorts of ways to spend your money on the Intenet . . . . ▸

I've never watched those silly home shopping networks that you find on cable TV. Just couldn't get into them. I'm not sure that many other folks watch them, either. I'll be the first to admit that I've gone nuts shopping on the Internet, however. Movies. Music. Clothing. Flowers. I've bought it all on the Internet.

The thing that holds most people back from shopping on the Internet is the fear of using their credit card. This chapter might dispel some of that fear. It also shows you how to find bargains in your own neck of the woods, and how to find the best places to shop on the Internet.

I'm not using my credit card on the Internet. Period

Okay. Nobody's going to force you. And if you don't feel completely comfortable using your credit card on the Internet, don't do it.

Hopefully, however, I can make you feel a little bit better about doing it (or worse about going to the gas station). Bought gas on your credit card lately? Been to the department store and charged up a whopping bill for neck-ties (nah, me neither)? How about the cash machine; did you toss that little receipt it gave you into the trash can? When you placed a call using your calling card, did you say the number out loud to the operator?

If you did any of these things recently, you're at much more risk of getting ripped off than if you used your credit card on the Internet. The odds are against getting victimized on the Internet. The amount of traffic that flows through the Internet's pipes is just too huge for someone snooping around to target you that easily. With the current advances in secure transaction technology, using your credit card is now safer than it ever was.

You'd feel better if you understood security, though

You're going to hear a whole lot about two types of security on the Web: Secure Sockets Layer (SSL) and Private Communication Technology (PCT).

These technologies make it possible to transmit data on the Internet that no one can intercept. You can send your credit card number to a secured Web server, commonly used for shopping, without a bit of worry. It's definitely safer than giving someone your credit card number over the phone, since most phone conversations can be tapped these days.

The technology behind the scenes isn't too important. What is important is for you to know that when you connect your browser to a secure Web server, anything you send to that server is confidential. No one else on the Internet can nab it. So, how do you know that you're actually talking to a secure Web server? Easy—look in the status line of your browser. If you're using Internet Explorer, you'll see a padlock in the bottom right corner of the window, as shown in Figure 18.1. You can also look at the URL of the Web page. If it begins with https (note the "s" on the end of http), you're communicating with a secure Web server.

Fig. 18.1
The padlock in the right-hand corner indicates you are talking to a secure Web server.

If you use Netscape, you'll see a key in the bottom left corner of the window with both halves connected together, as shown in Figure 18.2.

Fig. 18.2
If this was an unsecure Web page, the key would be split in half.

| ━━━□ | 88% of 13K (at 1.5K/sec, 1 sec remaining) | | ▭▭▭ | ✉? |

You can use a clearing house, instead

Clearing houses, or virtual payment systems, are a safe alternative to using your credit card on the Internet. You don't even have to connect to a secure Web server because you never send any information that you'd regret if some jerk intercepted it.

The payment system I describe in this system is called First Virtual. You have to set up an account with First Virtual before you can start shopping. To do so, point your browser to **http://www.fv.com**. You give them your credit card number, usually Visa or MasterCard. You do it over the phone, though, not over the Internet.

First Virtual works with your current e-mail system. When you buy something from a retailer on the Internet, you use a PIN (personal identification number). Much like the pin number you use with your ATM or calling cards. A few moments later, the virtual payment system sends you an e-mail asking you to confirm the sale. You reply with one of three responses:

yes   Confirm the sale

no   Cancel the sale

fraud   Immediately cancel your PIN because someone else is
            using your PIN

Don't get how this can be secure, yet? Let's look at the process:

1 You purchase something from a retailer, using your PIN number.

2 The retailer immediately contacts First Virtual with the details of the transaction.

3 First Virtual sends you an e-mail message to which you reply to confirm the purchase. Remember that no one else has access to your mailbox, right? The company you're buying from doesn't even know it. First Virtual can safely assume, then, that your reply is genuinely yours.

4 First Virtual charges your credit card for the purchase. Your credit card number was never, ever transmitted over the Internet.

NOTE **The only problem with systems such as First Virtual is that you** don't find a huge number of online stores that take it. Most of the better stores only do credit card transactions through secured Web servers. Second, since multiple payment systems exist, you may have to subscribe to more than one in order to be able to shop at all the places you want to shop.

How do I find cool places to shop?

I'd love to make a joke about how the different genders approach shopping; but, I'm male, and I'm an admitted shop-aholic. Regardless, online shopping malls and stores are very easy to come by. There are literally thousands upon thousands of places to spend your money on the Internet. And they're so close—right there on your computer.

Search your favorite index

Every single one of the online shopping malls wants to make sure that you can find it when you're ready to part with your loot. Given that fact, these malls make it very easy. They list their URL with all the different Internet search tools and indexes. Want to buy some flowers? Use Yahoo! to search for **shop** and **flowers**. How about some new tunes for that CD player? Search for **shop** and **music**. If you get so many hits back that you can't find what you want, throw the keyword **online** in the mix to limit the results to those entries that contain phrases such as "online shopping."

In addition, you can go directly to Yahoo!'s index of online shopping outlets. Open **http://www.yahoo.com/Business_and_Economy/Companies/ Shopping_Centers/** in your Web browser and chew your way through this list of almost a thousand stores.

Q&A *How do online shopping prices compare to street prices?*

Average. I haven't found any incredible steals while shopping on the Internet. Prices do tend to be a little lower, but you have to be careful sometimes. I have noticed that you can get good deals on items which usually require a large overhead to sell in a store. Bottom line? Don't shop on the Internet to save money, because you won't. Shop on the Internet because it's convenient.

Look at those advertiser sponsored sites

You see them all over the place now—those cute animated advertisements at the top of just about every single free Web service you visit. Many of those advertisements are for pretty darn good online shopping malls. The advertisements tend to be focused on the audience that they think visits their site. That is, if you're visiting an automotive Web site, you might see an advertisement for an online auto-parts store. If you're visiting a magazine targeted to women, you're likely to see advertisements for clothing or makeup outlets.

Still not sure? Watch this

Okay, I understand that you may still not be sure about spending your money on the Web. Security may not be the only issue. It's something new; you've not done it before. So, look at the following steps and figures as I make a purchase on Software.net, a Web site at **http://www.software.net** that sells software on the Web. See for yourself just how easy it is to purchase something on the Web:

1 I opened Software.net in Netscape, as shown in Figure 18.3. Then, I browsed the catalog of products to find just the product I wanted to buy: Norton's Your Eyes Only.

Fig. 18.3
You'll usually find many different catalogs to browse, such as a full listing, products by platform, or products by type.

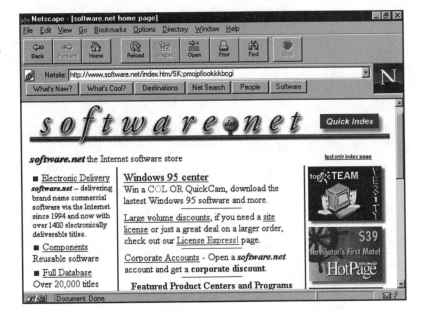

2 Then, I clicked the link to see more information about the product, as shown in Figure 18.4.

3 I clicked the link to order the package. In this case, I clicked Get It Now to order Your Eyes Only and download it immediately. You don't usually have this option when ordering other types of products, such as flowers or clothing. The result is the Web page shown in Figure 18.5.

Fig. 18.4
When purchasing software on the Internet, you can frequently download the software right then and there. Beats a trip to the computer store.

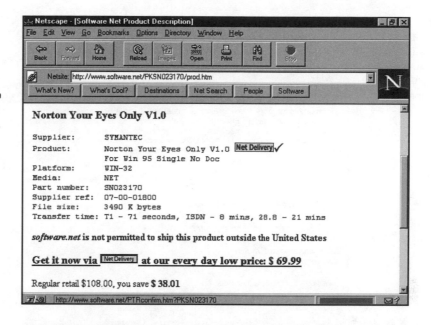

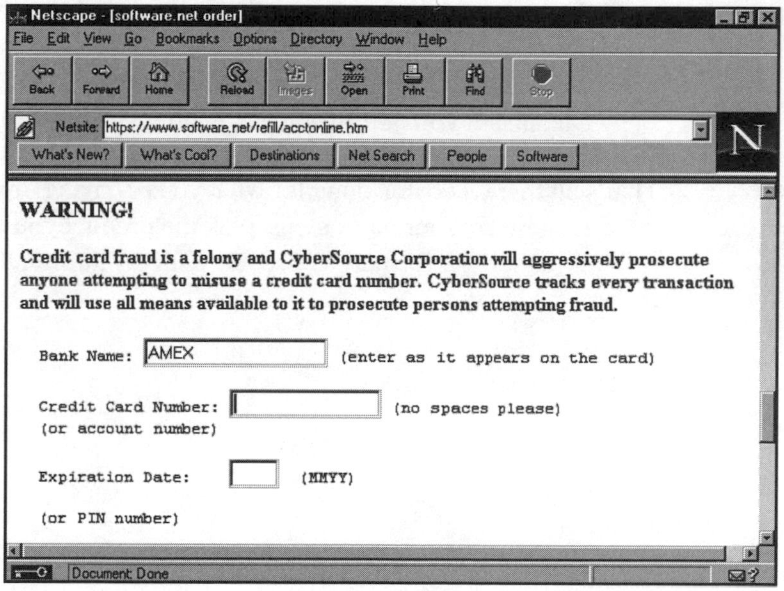

Fig. 18.5
This is where you actually have to give your credit card number. Notice that this is a secure Web site.

4 I filled in my credit card name, number, and expiration date. The next Web page confirms my order and displays a license agreement for me to review (see Figure 18.6). I clicked Accept to continue with my order.

Fig. 18.6
Even though I've already provided my credit card number, I can cancel my order by clicking Cancel.

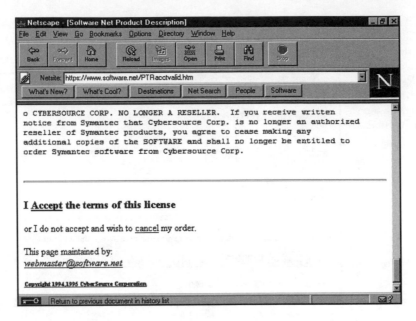

5 Since I'm ordering software that I can download, the next step is to download the program. When ordering downloadable software from Software.net, you have to wait for confirming information to be e-mailed to you before you can continue with the transaction.

That's all there is to it. No matter what you're buying or where you're buying it from, there are four basic steps: pick the product you want to order, provide payment information, provide delivery information, and confirm the order.

19

Plan Your Vacation or Business Trip

● **In this chapter:**

- **Where can I find packaged travel deals?**

- **Booking your own travel is just as easy, though**

- **Get to know the area to which you're traveling**

- **Learn how to best photograph your destination**

- **Get travel warnings from the State Department**

Travel agents, beware! The Internet makes it incredibly easy for ordinary folks to make their own plans. . . . . **>**

recently took a vacation in Scotland. Striking land. Lovely people. I took the entire family, too. Had a good time. We saw sights that the normal tourist in Scotland doesn't see. Out-of-the-way castles. Boulders scattered across hillsides by glaciers thousands of years ago. We saw a variety of other landscape features that I think many other tourists miss. The Internet made it all possible, too, because we found most of these gems online—before leaving the States.

Yes, I practice what I preach. I made all of our travel arrangements online. I scouted out the area on the Internet. I looked on UseNet to see what other folks recommended. I also printed a list of bed-and-breakfasts to take with us to Scotland. Overall, it was a very successful vacation. Your next vacation can be just as successful, too, if you spend a little time on the Internet before you take off.

Make your own travel plans

Making your own travel plans is easy. You'll need plane tickets, a place to rest your head, and perhaps a car. Other forms of transportation are available, too, such as trains and buses. Since you may not have ever booked your own tickets, you may be a bit timid about it. Don't worry, you'll put those travel agents out of business in no time.

If you're going on vacation, you can make it more productive and a lot less stressful if you check out the sites before you leave the house. Get on the Internet and see what the region you're visiting has to offer. Make a list of the sites that you definitely want to see. Maybe even prioritize that list so that you make sure to get the important stuff out of the way first.

 TIP **Travel consolidators are folks who offer deep discounts on airfare** and packaged vacations. There are a lot of them on the Internet. I've never found anything worth buying from these companies. Too many restrictions. As hard as I've looked, I've usually done better booking the arrangements myself.

Get your plane tickets

Although you can't necessarily book your tickets with all of the major airlines, you can, at the very least, look at their schedules and pick your flights. Take American Airlines, for example (see Figure 19.1). You can get flight schedules, fare quotes, service information, and information on packaged vacation deals.

Fig. 19.1
Point your Web browser to **http:// www.americanair.com**.

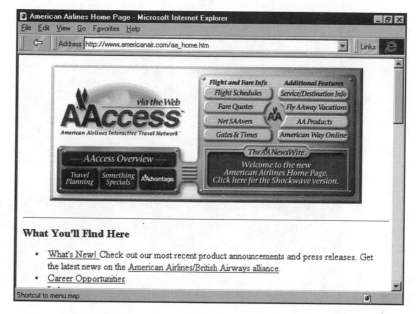

To get a fare quote on a flight from Dallas to Orlando, click Fare Quote. You'll see a page like Figure 19.2. Select the departing airport from the first list and the destination airport from the second list. Then, type the date that you want to leave, in the space provided. Note that the date starts with the day, then the month and year.

Click Submit and go get a cup of coffee—it can take a bit of time to return the results. American Airlines returns the results in a table that looks like Figure 19.3. You can click each heading of the table to see what's in that column. Each row represents a fare that you can purchase by calling American Airlines' reservation desk.

Fig. 19.2
If you're familiar with the airport codes, you can request a fare quote by using the codes at the bottom of the Web page.

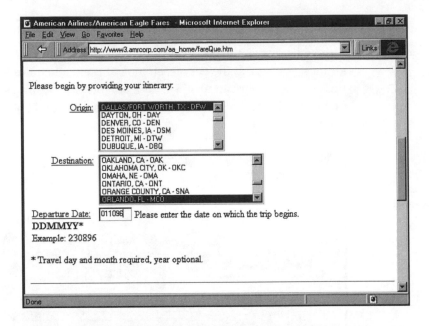

Fig. 19.3
American Airlines returns information about the type of service, fare basis, price one way, and other fare restrictions.

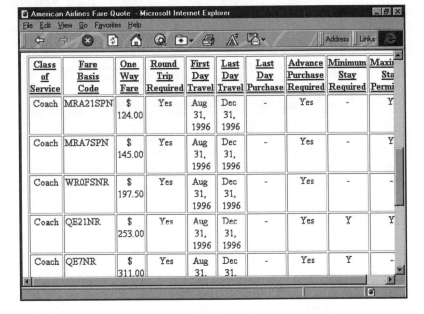

TIP   **Open http://www.amrcorp.com/cgi-bin/aans in your Web browser** to subscribe to American Airlines' Net SAAver Fares mailing list. This list notifies you weekly about special airfare, car, and hotel deals.

You'll find a variety of other airlines on the Internet, too. In fact, you don't want to rely on just one airline for all your travel needs. You'll find more discounts if you remain open to travel on a variety of airlines. For your convenience, here's a list of some of the other airlines on the Web:

America West	**http://www.americawest.com**
Continental	**http://www.flycontinental.com**
Delta	**http://www.delta-air.com**
Southwest	**http://www.iflyswa.com**
Trans World	**http://www.twa.com**
United	**http://www.ual.com**
US Air	**http://www.usair.com**

Getting Low-Priced Fares

American Airlines has some very good tips for getting the best possible fares. Here they are (plus some of my own observations):

- Purchase your tickets as far in advance as possible. You'll frequently get better fares 7, 14, and 21 days in advance.

- Remember that discounted fares are non-refundable. You can reuse the ticket on another trip, however.

- Low-cost fares usually require a Saturday-night stay at the destination.

- Spend a Saturday night at your destination. Airfares are frequently less expensive with a Saturday-night stayover.

- Don't travel on Friday or Sunday. These are often the most expensive days to travel.

- Fly at odd hours. Early morning and late evening flights are usually priced better than flights during the day.

- The season that you're traveling affects the price of the fare. For example, tickets from New York to Florida are more expensive during the winter months.

You're going to need a place to stay

If you're going on vacation, you may want to try the bed-and-breakfast scene, particularly in scenic areas and in Europe. B&Bs are homes that people have opened up to strangers with money. They're often very quaint and they make the trip much more memorable because you get to know the people really well. You can look for B&Bs in an index such as Yahoo! by pointing your Web browser to **http://www.yahoo.com/Business_and_Economy/Companies/Travel/Lodging/Bed_and_Breakfasts**. You can also try a variety of B&B directories, which you find by clicking Directories at the top of the Yahoo! page. The TravelASSIST Directory (see Figure 19.4) is an example.

Fig. 19.4
Point your browser to **http://www.travelassist.com**.

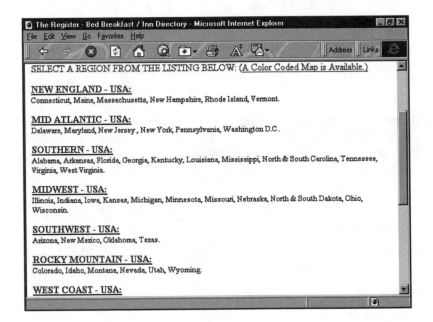

If hotels are more your cup of tea, or you're traveling on business, you can search for hotels in a particular region with services such as Accommodations Express (**http://www.accommodationsxpress.com**). Using this tool, you pick a city in order to view the major hotels in that city. Click a hotel's link to see a review, pictures, and reservation information.

TIP **The best way to find the best deals on a hotel is to watch the** current travel industry news with a news service such as NewsPage. You'll be the first to know if a hotel is launching a special promotion.

Better yet, use an all-in-one travel site like Expedia

Booking your travel directly with the airline, hotel, and rental car companies isn't the best way to spend your time. You have to do a lot of work to track down the best prices. You can better spend your time by using one of the Web sites that is designed to track down the best prices, regardless of the airline or hotel. Then, book all of your travel needs in one place and in one sitting.

Microsoft Expedia is one of those sites. Take a look; open **http://expedia.msn.com** in your Web browser, and you'll see a home page similar to Figure 19.5. With Expedia, you can book your flight, rent a car, and book your hotel room. You can also get up-to-the-minute travel news and information. Planning a vacation to New Zealand? Take a virtual trip through the illustrated guidebook first so that you can learn more about your destination. You can check out the weather, exchange rate, and local news in New Zealand, too.

Fig. 19.5
Open **http://expedia.msn.com** in your Web browser.

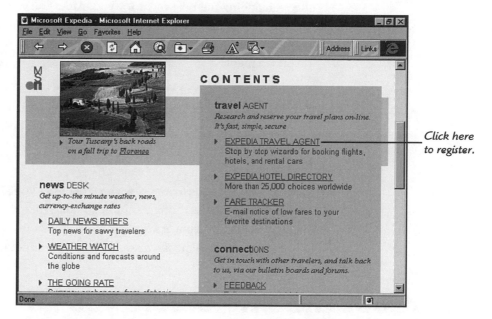

Click here to register.

Before you can start booking your travel, you have to Register. Expedia doesn't ask you for a credit card number up front; you can provide that later. All you provide is your name, mail address, and similar information. Click EXPEDIA TRAVEL AGENT, click Registration, and complete the registration information. After you've completed the registration, Expedia will toss you to the travel agent. The next time you click EXPEDIA TRAVEL AGENT, click Sign In; instead of being sent to Registration, you'll go to the Travel Agent.

From the Travel Agent, you can click Shop for Flights, Hotels, and Cars to make your travel plans. Click Subscribe to Fare Tracker to receive a regular update on fares to a particular destination, or click Update customer Information to update your vital information. The Travel Agent keeps track of all the itineraries on which you're working. For example, if you're booking, but haven't finished, a trip to London, you'll see that itinerary listed on this Web page. You click the link representing that itinerary to continue working on it.

You can also create a new itinerary by clicking Start a New Itinerary, which opens a Web page that lets you book flights, reserve cars, and book hotel rooms:

- Click Flight Wizard to open a wizard that walks you step by step through finding the best flight for you. After you've answered the appropriate questions, the Travel Agent displays a list of possible flights that match your requirements. You can add a flight to your itinerary or reserve a flight.

- Click Car Wizard to open a wizard that asks you a few questions about your car rental preferences, such as dates, airport, and car class. As a result, the Travel Agent displays a list of possibilities. Click one of the links beside that car to view more information about it, add it to your itinerary, or reserve it.

- Click Hotel Wizard to open a wizard that asks you about your hotel preferences, such as room rate, nonsmoking rooms, and location. Then, the Travel Agent displays a list of hotels. Click one of the hotels to view more information. You can also add it to your itinerary or reserve it.

Scout out the sites before you go

The best thing I ever did before trucking off to Scotland was to research the areas that we wanted to visit. I learned about the historical spots, the best places to eat, and the places to take the most striking photographs.

Two Internet resources will help you achieve that goal. First, touristy vacation spots almost always have good Web sites. Second, UseNet is a truly valuable resource when it comes to vacation planning.

Look at tourist sites on the Web

You can find them using any of the search tools. The best place to start is with an index for that area. An index is nothing more than a list of related Web sites. For example, you can search for an index of Web sites in Scotland with the keywords **Scotland** and **index**. Then, you can browse the index for sites that seem interesting to you. Figure 19.6 shows the index that I used to plan my holiday in Scotland.

Fig. 19.6
You can query this index, or you can browse the list at the bottom of the Web page.

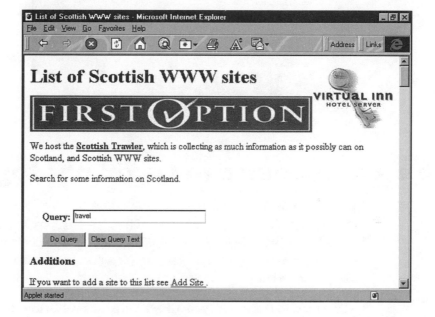

Get travel advice and ideas on UseNet

UseNet is definitely the resource to use when planning your vacation. You can go to a newsgroup dedicated to the region you're visiting and ask people that actually live there what they think are the best places to visit, and the best sites to see. Sure beats the travel agent's advice. The best way to find a newsgroup that discusses a particular region is to use Deja News, as described in Chapter 11, "Find Things on the Internet," to locate the group based upon the name of the region.

In many cases, however, you can go right to the appropriate newsgroup. Many of the regions around the world are represented in the **soc.culture** newsgroup hierarchy. For example, Scotland is in **soc.culture.scotland**. Figure 19.7 is the newsgroup listing, filtered so that it shows only the **soc.culture** hierarchy.

Fig. 19.7
Most other newsreaders, such as NewsXpress, provide a way for you to filter the newsgroup list.

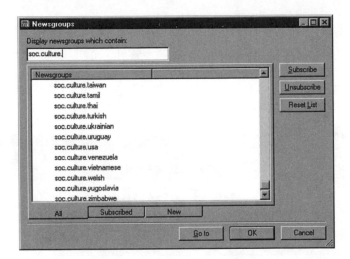

Take a crash course in travel photography

Imagine this. You spend thousands of dollars to take your family on vacation in Europe. You shoot twenty rolls of film. Landscapes. Portraits of your family in front of historical ruins. You snapped your camera at anything that didn't move. You get home, get your pictures processed, and they didn't turn out worth a darn.

Don't let this happen to you. Check with the pros before you go on vacation. The **rec.photo** newsgroup hierarchy contains groups to which you can post your questions, such as. **rec.photo.technique** and **rec.photo.equipment**. Here's the type of information you'll find in these groups:

- You can find out the best vantage points from which to photograph a particular landmark. Someone always knows where those postcard views are snapped.

- People will tell you about landscapes or objects you should not miss when photographing a particular region. For example, learn where you can find hidden waterfalls, ancient ruins, or villages.

- You can find out what type of film you need for a particular climate. Will a slow film work? Should I use a film with a warm cast?

- Discover what type of equipment you should take to a particular region. Do you need a tripod? What's the best choice of lenses?

- Do you need to take any special precautions before letting your film be x-rayed in a particular country?

Check with the government before you go abroad

You pay taxes, so you pay these folks' salary—right? So, why shouldn't you get some direct benefit from the information that the CIA and State Department gather? You can find out information, such as population, economy, or disputes, for any country in the world. The following resources will help you learn more about your destination.

The CIA

The CIA's World Factbook at **http://www.odci.gov/cia/publications/95fact/index.html** contains information about geography, people, government, economy, transportation, communications, and defense. The Factbook includes mostly technical and statistical information about each particular region, such as the number of miles around its border. You will find some useful information, however, such as how to address the nation's people (are they Scots or Scotsmen).

The State Department

If you'll be traveling overseas, check with the State Department's Travel Warnings and Consular Information Sheets at **http://travel.state.gov/travel_warnings.html**. For every country in the world, you can learn about entry requirements (visas, shots, and so on), medical facilities in that country, crime information, terrorist activities, drug penalties, and the location of the U.S. Embassy.

20

Have a Special Interest? Do It on the Internet

● **In this chapter:**

- ● **Learn how to exchange ideas with other people**

- ● **Find information about your hobby on the Web**

- ● **Learn more about your favorite celebrity**

- ● **Sample your favorite music online**

There are thousands of people all over the world that have the same interests as you. Learn how to connect with them . . . ⊙

A hobby that you can't share with friends and family isn't worth much. Don't believe me? Did you ever collect stamps? I'm sure it entertained you a lot, but wasn't it disappointing when you couldn't find anyone who was willing to talk about it with you?

I never did collect stamps, but I do have hobbies that my family just doesn't get into. Photography, for example. Nothing upsets my wife more than sitting there, holding a lens cap, while I carefully compose a photograph for the next hour. I'm not exactly sure why she can't get into this as much as I. Sheeze.

So, where do I go to find people to share my interest in photography? Well, since this is an Internet book, you'd have to think that's the answer, and it is. I've found people from all over the world who like to talk about lighting, exposure, and printing basics—just like me.

You can find people who have the same interests as you, too. Antiques. Bug collecting. Doesn't matter. I guarantee that you can find someone or something on the Internet to entertain you.

Exchange ideas with other people just like you

Whether you want to talk about the finer points of knitting, or want to share photographs of your antiques, you can do it with all sorts of people on the Internet. There are many different ways to do it, too. You can have an online conference in which you and the other hobbyists talk in real-time. You can share your interests at a slower pace on UseNet and with mailing lists.

Put together an online conference

You learned about some of the chat and conference programs for the Internet in Chapter 10, "Chat and Conferencing." You can use these tools to have your knitting or basketweaving conference.

Before you can have a conference, however, you have to invite people to it. The easiest way to do that is to mail friends who you think would be interested and ask them to join you online. If you'll be having your conference on IRC, you need to tell them the name of the IRC channel, such as **#Photography**.

The other way to find people to join your conference is to look them up in a white pages. Huh? Conference programs such as PowWow and NetMeeting have white pages that list their users. Frequently, these white pages list a person's hobbies, too, so you can search for people with a particular interest. Figure 20.1 shows you PowWow's white pages. You'll find NetMeeting's white pages at **uls.microsoft.com** (Microsoft calls white pages "user location servers").

Fig. 20.1
Point your Web browser to **http:// www.tribal.com/ wpsearch.htm**, or click the White Pages button on your toolbar to arrive here.

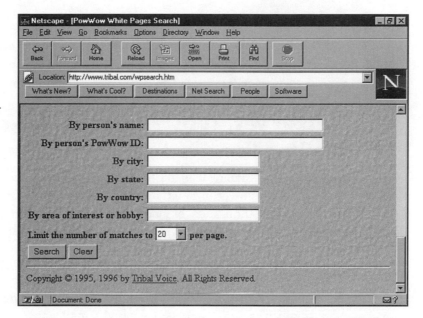

 TIP   **Online conferencing with programs such as PowWow or** NetMeeting are generally pretty safe for kids who want to share their hobbies with others.

You can find your hobby on UseNet

You've read a lot about UseNet newsgroups in this book. You should be an old pro by now. You can usually find a good newsgroup that relates to your hobby by searching for its name: **rec.photography**, for example. You can also use Deja News to discover in which newsgroups people discuss your favorite hobby. See Chapter 11, "Find Things on the Internet," if you need a refresher.

Curious? Here's a sample of what you'll find:

rec.collecting.sport.baseball

rec.models.rc

rec.toys.misc

rec.models.railroad

rec.gardens

 TIP **Can't find your hobby anywhere on UseNet? Look at the** newsgroup **news.announce.newgroups** to learn how to create a new group for your hobby.

Better yet, subscribe to a like-minded mailing list

You read about mailing lists in Chapter 7, "E-Mail and Mailing Lists." A mailing list is a powerful tool that people use to broadcast messages to hundreds, even thousands, of mailboxes. Each person on the mailing list has already expressed a desire to receive your messages, simply by subscribing to the list.

There are more mailing lists dedicated to hobbies than there are newsgroups. Many more. Unfortunately, you won't find a master mailing list in the sky. You usually have to run across one, or wait until someone tells you about a mailing list they think will interest you. In addition, you can point your Web browser at Publicly Accessible Mailing Lists to browse a comprehensive list of mailing lists by category.

Look for Web pages that express similar interests

The Web isn't really the best place to exchange ideas with other hobby enthusiasts. That's because the content, as exciting as it may be, is pretty static. It doesn't change much from day to day. Conferring with other enthusiasts isn't all that practical on the Web, either, although many folks have tried to set up chat areas on a Web page.

That doesn't mean that the Web isn't a valuable resource for you. Many folks like to publish what they know about their hobby on the Web. They do it, in part, because they like to share, but it's also fun just recounting everything you've learned about your hobby. The best way to find Web pages like these is to use one of the search tools, such as Yahoo! or AltaVista. Use keywords that fit your hobby. Table 20.1 shows you some suggestions for a variety of hobbies. You should get the idea from this table that the best choice of keywords comes from the description of the hobby.

Table 20.1   Keywords to find hobby pages

Hobby	Keywords
Stamps	stamp collecting
Model Trains	model train
RC Planes	model rc plane
Cross Stitch	cross stitch needlework
Home Brewing	beer brewing supplies

Stalk your favorite celebrity—online

You can definitely make a hobby out of stalking your favorite celebrity, band, author, etc. Now, I don't suggest that you hang out in front of their house, or follow them to work. I'm talking about following their activities on the Internet. Looking at their Web pages. Reading what other people say about them on UseNet—that type of stalking.

Here's how to find a celebrity's mail address

I'm going to get in trouble with a lot of celebrities here (author makes mischievous sounds). Want to get a celebrity's address? Well, you might first see if their name is on the list at **http://oscar.teclink.net/~chip1120/ email.html**. The next page provides a sample of who is on this list.

Brad Pitt	**CIAOBOX@msn.com**
Douglas Adams	**76206.2507@compuserve.com**
Ross Perot	**71511.460@compuserve.com**
Rush Limbaugh	**70277.2502@compuserve.com**
Scott Adams (Dilbert)	**scottadams@aol.com**
Tim Allen	**tim@morepower.com**
Wesley Snipes	**herukush@aol.com**

TIP **Do you collect autographs? E-mail a celebrity to see if they'll** contribute their autograph to your collection. Be nice about it, though.

Check out the fan newsgroups on UseNet

UseNet has an entire hierarchy dedicated to discussing your favorite celebrity. I can't think of a popular figure that doesn't have their very own newsgroup on UseNet—if not involuntarily. I'm talking specifically about the **alt.fan** hierarchy. Here's a sample of some of the groups you'll find:

alt.fan.alicia-slvrstone

alt.fan.bill-gates

alt.fan.dave_barry

alt.fan.douglas-adams

alt.fan.madonna

alt.fan.rush-limbaugh

alt.fan.tom-clancy

You'll also find a good number of newsgroups for your favorite musical artists. This newsgroup hierarchy is **alt.music**.

Don't forget those fan-dom Web pages

Another terrific source of fan information is the Web pages that people put up on behalf of a film or TV star. Terri Hatcher is a perfect example. She's an Internet phenomenon. People put up more Web pages on her behalf than any other personality I know of. I don't mean the type of Web site that contains naughtiness, either. I mean the type of site that tells you which films she's been in and where she was raised—the type of site that shows you pictures of Terri Hatcher from a variety of magazines and publicity shots. You can find Web pages for your favorite stars by searching for their name. You can also open **http://www.yahoo.com/Entertainment/Movies_and_Films/ Actors_and_Actresses** in your Web browser, browse the list of stars (hundreds of them), and click the star's name to see the fan Web pages available for them.

Sample your favorite music on the Web

I've grown very dependent upon the Web. No, I'm not an Internet junkie—I spend too much time on it for that. I use the Internet to check out something before I buy it. I especially like to check out a music CD before I run down to the music store to buy it.

Most, if not all, published artists have a Web page on the Internet. They don't always put the Web pages up themselves. Sometimes the recording studio does it. Other times, a really dedicated fan (fellow stalker) creates an "unofficial" Web page for that artist. Regardless, you can usually get background information about the artist, discography, lyrics, and of most importance to my buying decision, samples from the CD. Figure 20.2 (see next page) shows you an example of an artist's Web page, located at **http://www.bath.ac.uk/ ~ccsdra/enya/index.html**. This is an unofficial site put together by an individual for one of my favorite artists: Enya. You can find your favorite musical artists by using their names on one of the search engines, such as Yahoo!.

Fig. 20.2
Most fan Web pages also contain links to all the other fan Web pages for that person or group.

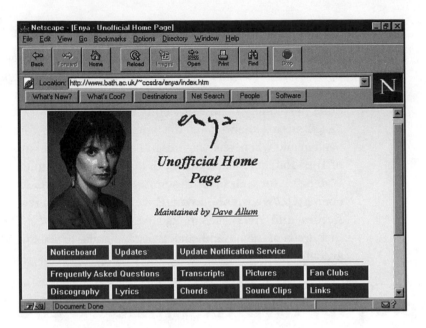

Flex Your Political Muscle

● In this chapter:

● You'll learn how to make your voice count

● I'm a Democrat/Republican. Where do I go?

● How do I stay on top of current events?

● Share your views with other folks on the Internet

The Internet has always been a hot spot for all sorts of political views. Express yours. . . . . >

This chapter isn't much about my political beliefs (don't have any—[wink]), or yours. This chapter is about becoming more politically active with the help of the Internet. Hopefully, the ideas you see here will spark you into action.

Before you move on, however, you need to understand my definition of being politically active. It doesn't mean that you have to participate in a sit-in or other kind of protest. You don't have to hurl stones at the next Democratic convention. You don't need to spend a bunch of money. You don't even have to belong to either political party. My definition of being politically active is that you stay aware of the issues, aware of the candidates' positions, spread the word, and, most importantly, vote. That, my fellow American, is how you make a difference.

Go to your corners

Democrat? Republican? Uh, Reform Party? Off to the corner with you. Your own corner, that is. All three parties have very good Web sites. You can find the Democratic National Committee at **http://www.democrats.org** (see Figure 21.1).

Fig. 21.1
The Democrats don't hold anything back at their Web site. They'll keep you up-to-date on all of the opponent's blunders.

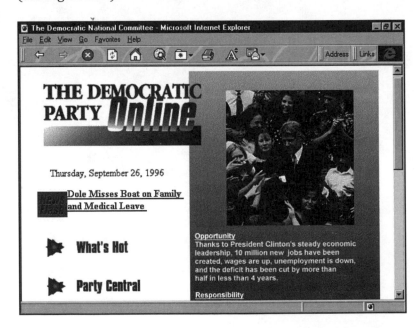

I can't play favorites, now, can I? Figure 21.2 shows you the Republican National Committee (**http://www.rnc.org**). It's quite an impressive Web site.

Fig. 21.2
You can read the Republican platform at this Web site.

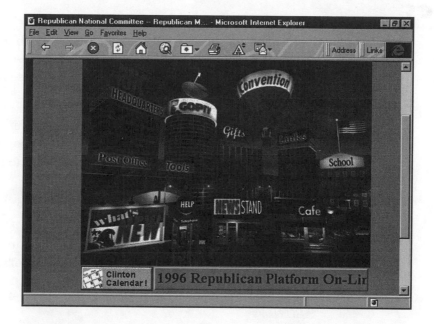

As a native of Dallas, I have to mention the Reform Party. Open **http://www.reformparty.org** in your Web browser and you'll see a Web page similar to Figure 21.3.

Fig. 21.3
Click Lend Your Support to register or volunteer to the Reform Party.

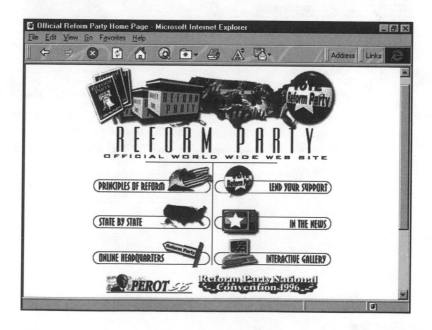

Stay informed with the Web's best political 'zines

The Web has a lot of politically oriented magazines (Web 'zines, E 'zines, whatever you want to call them). Most take a clearly liberal or conservative position—bashing the opponents, while singing the praises of their candidates. A few are a bit more objective.

There are other ways to stay informed, too. The best I can think of is to check in with the various Internet news sources that provide political news. You'll learn about these and other sources in the sections that follow.

PoliticsNow

PoliticsNow (see Figure 21.4) is a Web site that covers all of the political news you could want. Point your Web browser to **http://www.politicsnow.com**. It even has links to the latest polls. PoliticsNow gets its news from a variety of sources, including:

> *ABC News*
>
> *The Washington Post*
>
> *National Journal*
>
> *Newsweek*
>
> *The Los Angeles Times*

Slate

Slate has taken a lot of fire—for what, I'm not sure. Maybe because Microsoft publishes it. Slate is a good online magazine that's breaking a lot of ground, though. Not only can you read the online version, you can have it e-mailed to you as well. Take a look at Figure 21.5 to see the types of coverage you'll find in Slate.

Fig. 21.4
Besides the polls,
PoliticsNow has other
resources you can use,
such as the Almanac of
American Politics.

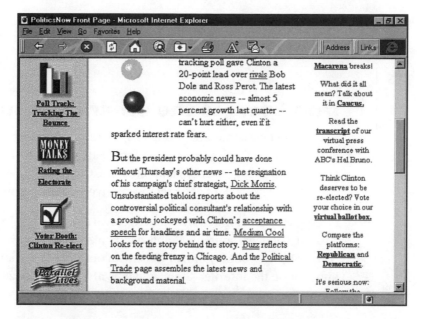

Fig. 21.5
Slate gives you deep
coverage of a variety
of issues.

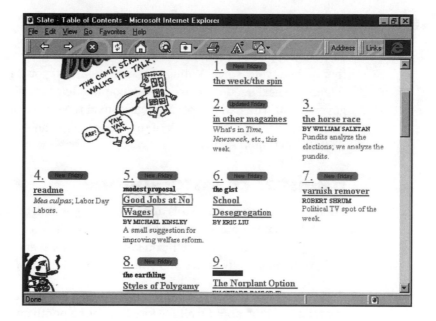

TIP   **Want to see a hilarious parody of Slate? Point your Web browser to http://www.stale.com. Get it?**

Don't forget the other news sources

Electronic magazines aren't the only source you can use to stay on top of the current issues. Don't forget to read the daily news. You can see your favorite candidate's daily successes and blunders. Check on the campaign trail. You can even keep track of your representative's voting record.

In Chapter 14, "Moment by Moment News and Weather," you learned about a variety of news sources. PointCast delivers it right to your desktop. NewsPage is probably one of the most comprehensive news sources that I know of on the Internet. Soon, you'll be able to have news specially packaged and delivered to your mailbox, too.

Make your voice heard: vote, vote, vote

The biggest part of being politically active is making sure that the powers-that-be hear your voice. Voting is one method, and you'll read my lecture on that in the next section. You can also communicate regularly with the folks in government. You can fire off an angry e-mail to your Senator if you don't like what's happening in your neck of the woods. You can even e-mail the President of the United States.

Register to vote—online

I don't know how to make this any clearer. If you don't vote, you're not heard. You don't vote, nothing changes. You don't vote, you don't send a message. You don't vote, well, you get the idea. First and foremost, if you want to be politically active and you want to be heard, vote.

Voting is a huge responsibility, though. You should not take it lightly. Some of my relatives brag about walking into the voting booth and choosing which-ever names they think had the better ring to them. This is totally irrespon-sible. Voting for a person because they are attractive, a great speaker, or charismatic, is also irresponsible. In order to vote responsibly, you need to understand the issues and understand the candidates.

TIP **You'll find information to help you cast an informed ballot** at **http://www.vote-smart.org**.

Before you can vote, however, you need to register. A lot of folks use this as an excuse: "I just don't have time to do it." Let me save you the trouble. Pop open your Web browser and point it to **http://www.rockthevote.org/and/ RockVote/ACTNOW/134/13_4.html**. Click Register to Vote Online, and follow the instructions you see on this Web page. You'll fill out a form, and they'll mail (snail mail) you a pre-filled voter registration card.

Send the President an e-mail while you're at it

Would you believe that you can actually send a mail message to the President of the United States? You can send the President a message and you'll get a computer-generated reply. The President and Vice President have people that sort through all of the mail messages they receive and prepare a report that summarizes what is on the people's minds. Your mail message, essentially, is rolled up with everyone else's into a collective mail message to the President. Here are the addresses:

President	**president@whitehouse.gov**
Vice President	**vice.president@whitehouse.gov**
First Lady	**first.lady@whitehouse.gov**

Get the facts before you vote

Your votes should be informed. You should know the positions of each candidate. You should know the party's platform, too. You can get all of this information on the Internet. For example, if you want to know how the candidates voted on a particular piece of legislation, check out the Web site at **http://pathfinder.com/cgi-bin/ congress-votes**. You can look up each bill, or you can enter your ZIP code to see how your Senators and Representatives voted.

You can learn more information about a particular candidate by looking up their Web page. Granted, it's usually slanted—after all, why would I write a biography that highlights my negative points? Use your candidate's name in one of the many search tools you learned about in Chapter 11, "Find Things on the Internet."

While you're at it, you may want to pop into the White House for a visit, at least on the Web. Take a look at Figure 21.6. It's a very intricate Web site that you can use to check out the President's family background, take a tour of the White House, and more. Well worth a look.

Fig. 21.6
Point your Web browser to **http://www.whitehouse.gov**.

Let your Senator or Representative have it

Keep your Senators and Representatives in check. They're working folks, and they work for you. Let them know what you think about their record, or about a current issue that's weighing heavily on your mind. Do you think they don't have all the facts surrounding an issue? Tell them.

Getting in touch with your Senator or Representative is a lot easier than you think. All you need are their e-mail addresses, which are probably published on the Web. You can use his or her name with one of the search tools, but it's easier just to go to Yahoo!'s index. To see a list of Senators' home pages, point your Web browser to **http://www.yahoo.com/Government/Legislative_Branch/Senate/Senators.** A list of Representatives' home pages is found at **http://www.yahoo.com/Government/Legislative_Branch/House_of_Representatives/Representatives**.

Share your political views with others

I'm no dummy. I've known enough politically active people to realize that half the fun of being politically active is having a really good scrap with someone of the opposite party. As we've seen lately, you can even get into a good scrap with someone in the same party.

So, if you're looking for a good debate, or you just want to share your opinions with other people, you can do it online. You'll find a number of UseNet newsgroups that get pretty hot sometimes. You can also find a bit of mud slinging going on in mailing lists, too.

 TIP Do you want to help your favorite candidate win? Spread the word. Let other people know where your candidate stands on the issues. Point people to interesting Web sites so that they can learn more about the candidate.

UseNet newsgroups

Political newsgroups are easy to find. If your newsreader lets you filter newsgroups by name, try filtering them using **pol**. That'll display a good list of political newsgroups whose names are usually self-explanatory, such as this very small sample:

Do politicians answer their e-mail?

Unequivocally, no. I'm willing to bet that some politicians don't even know that they have an Internet mail address. Most politicians have a helper who reads the e-mail and consolidates it into a report. Thus, you can still get your two cents' worth into the fray by mailing your Senator or Representative. Your thoughts will be compiled into a report, with hundreds or thousands of others, which will be presented to them.

To give you an example, I fired off messages to just about every Senator and Representative I could think of. To protect the guilty, I won't mention their names here. I asked that they share any information they wanted with you, the reader, about how the Internet affects politics, and how they use the Internet in their campaigns to stay in touch with their constituents. Don't be surprised when I tell you that I didn't get one single reply. I did get a handful of automatic replies (computer-generated), though, that said they took my issues and concerns very seriously and would look into the matter.

> **alt.politics.democrats**
>
> **alt.politics.usa.republican**
>
> **alt.politics.media**
>
> **alt.politics.perot**
>
> **soc.politics**

You can also use Deja News to see which newsgroups people use to discuss a certain issue. See Chapter 11, "Find Things on the Internet," if you don't remember how to do this. Searching for the keywords **Scandal** and **politics**, for example, told me that the best place to discuss scandal in politics is **alt.current-events.clinton.whitewater** (just reporting the facts here—see Figure 21.7) and **alt.fan.rush-limbaugh**.

Fig. 21.7
Also try searching for **Scandle** (misspelled) and **politics**.

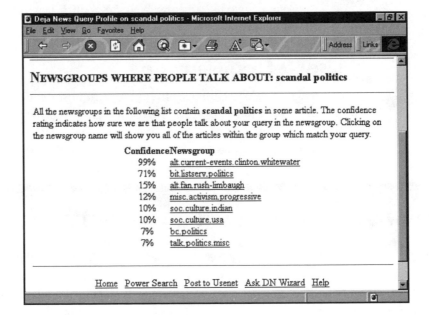

Mailing lists

In addition to the popular political newsgroups, you'll find a handful of politically oriented mailing lists. The best place to find these is in an index, such as Publicly Accessible Mailing lists at **http://www.neosoft.com/internet/paml**. You can go directly to a mailing list of about 75 names by pointing your Web browser to **http://www.neosoft.com/internet/paml/bysubj-politics.html**.

Appendixes

A

Great Internet Resources to Learn More

● **In this appendix:**

● Learn about other Internet books from Que

● Take a look at these Web sites for beginners

● What do I do if I have a specific question?

Don't stop with this book. The Internet is filled with resources for new users. . . . . ▶

This book is only the beginning of your Internet adventures. The first step. Everything that you'll eventually learn about the Internet can fill volumes of text. Technical details about how the Internet works. Nuances about using the Internet. Practical tricks for finding things fast. You'll impress yourself before you know it.

Some of what you learn will come from experience, but the rest will come from a variety of resources. Books. Web pages. Newsgroup postings. This chapter will help you get there quicker, though, by suggesting some additional books you can read and some additional Internet sites you can visit to learn more.

Take a look at these great books

Que has a huge number of books about the Internet. From the most general to the most specific topics. Interested in writing Web pages? Check out *Special Edition Using the Internet*. Interested in Java? Check out *Java by Example*. Here's a list of some of QUE's other Internet related books:

HTML by Example

Java by Example

JavaScript by Example

Special Edition Using Internet Explorer 3

Special Edition Using Netscape 3

Special Edition Using the Internet

Special Edition Using the World Wide Web

Using Netscape 3

Creating and Enhancing Netscape Web Pages

Visual Basic Script by Example

Here are a few Web sites for beginners and gurus

One of the best places to learn about the Internet is on the Web. The Web contains hundreds of resources for new Internet users, like yourself. Most of them are very well written and very attractive. Others aren't so well written, but contain valuable information nonetheless. Take a look at the following Web sites.

Learn the Net

URL Address: **http://www.learnthenet.com** (see Figure A.1)

Fig. A.1
Learn the Net is available in English, French, Italian, and Spanish.

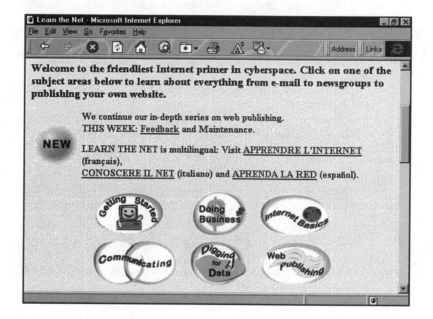

Learn the Net is one of the best Internet tutorials available on the Internet. It covers the most important things you need to know, including:

Getting Started   This section introduces you to the Web site. It tells you enough about your Web browser for you to comfortably use it to get around the Internet.

Doing Business   Doing Business discusses how to get your business onto the Web—how to make money.

Internet Basics   This section covers all the basics. How to get connected. How to use the Web. And, how to stay secure on the Internet.

Communicating   As you'd expect, this section shows you how to use the Internet to communicate with other people. It covers e-mail, chatting, and conferencing.

Digging for Data   Digging for Data shows you how to exploit the power of the Internet search engines. It also discusses downloading files and protecting yourself from viruses.

Web Publishing   Yes, this section tells you everything you need to know in order to hang your shingle out on the Internet. It also covers how to find a site to host your Web page and how to promote your Web page on the Internet.

Curious About the Internet

URL Address: **http://www.mcp.com/sams/samspub/e-books/30459-7/ httoc.htm**

This Web page is actually a SAMS (another Macmillan imprint) book—in electronic form. It's a terrific bit of information that answers the five journalistic questions about the Internet: who, what, why, where, and when. Examples of what you'll learn include the history of the Internet, what people do on the Internet, and where the Internet is headed.

Zen and the Art of the Internet

URL Address: **http://www.cs.indiana.edu/docproject/zen/ zen-1.0_toc.html**

This is one of those sites that isn't much to look at. It's also a bit old, published in 1992. Regardless, it's a wealth of information about the Internet. A lot of it is technical, too. One of the nice things about the Internet is that the underlying technology hasn't changed much over the last few years. Thus, this Web page is still a valuable resource.

Cyber Course™

URL Address: **http://www.newbie.net/CyberCourse** (see Figure A.2)

Fig. A.2
This Web site will
provide a good lesson
in navigating with
frames.

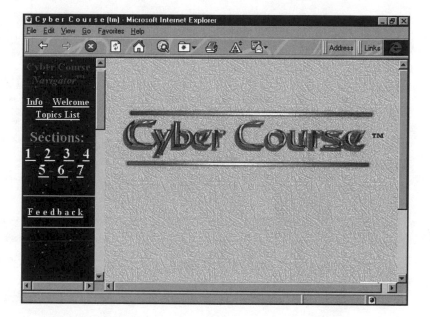

Cyber Course™ is another good resource for learning more about the Web. It goes into a lot of detail. You'll find that you have to dig a bit to find all the good stuff, but it's well worth it.

Imajika's Guide for New Users

URL Address: **http://www.cris.com/~ecfnw**

Imajika's Guide for New Users isn't a tutorial. Instead, it's an index that contains links to hundreds of guides for new users. Well worth a look.

The Internet Tourbus

URL Address: **http://www.worldvillage.com/tourbus.htm**

The Internet Tourbus is a cool way to get to know what's available on the Internet. It's a mailing list (see Chapter 7, "E-mail and Mailing Lists") that you subscribe to at its Web site. A few times a week, they send you a mail message containing a different site for you to visit.

Que's Internet Publishing Group

URL Address: **http://www.mcp.com/que/et** (see Figure A.3)

Fig. A.3
You can purchase Que books at this Web site, too (hint).

Que is a leader in publishing books on the Web. In particular, this Web site contains online versions of a lot of Que's most popular Internet related books. You can learn how to build your own Web page. Learn how to program with Java. Whatever. You can't curl up in the tub with an electronic book (shocking, eh?), but you can get a taste of what the book covers before you go out and buy it. You can also use these electronic books as quick reference guides that'll answer a tough question in a pinch.

Yahoo!

URL Address: **http://www.yahoo.com/Computers_and_Internet/Internet**

Yahoo! Is my favorite Internet index and search tool. The sites that it indexes are usually of good quality, and it filters out a lot of the noise that the other search tools have. Not only that, but you can search AltaVista from Yahoo! as well.

If you dig into Yahoo!'s categories, you'll find their collection of Internet related links. This is an extremely comprehensive collection of links to Web sites containing additional information about the Internet. If you want to see a list of links for new users, point your Web browser to **http://www.yahoo.com/Computers_and_Internet/Internet/ Information_and_Documentation/Beginner_s_Guides**.

Ask your questions on UseNet

If you have a burning question, and you haven't found an answer in this book or the other resources listed in this appendix, you'll do well to turn to the newsgroups. Whip out your newsreader, post your question to the appropriate newsgroup, and you'll probably get a reply in no time. By the way, be sure to read Chapter 8, "UseNet Newsgroups," before posting to a newsgroup so that you clearly understand the rules before you venture out into this territory. After that, address your questions to one of these newsgroups:

> **alt.internet.services**   This is the place to ask about Internet programs and resources.

> **news.newusers.questions**   This is the place to ask your questions about the Internet and using newsgroups.

Really stumped? Send me a mail message

It happens. Sometimes, you just get stuck. You can't find any information on the Internet to help you. No one on UseNet has answered your question. You're about to give up.

Wait! Don't give up. Send me a mail message and I'll be happy to help. Even if you don't have a question, let me know what you think of this book anyway. You can send mail to me at this address:

> **jerry@honeycutt.com**

B

Check Out the Author's Web Page

● In this chapter:

- You'll find links for all the URLs in this book

- You'll also find links for all the software

- Oh, yeah, don't forget any updates

The Internet moves at such a fast pace, you can't possibly keep up with it all. Let me help. . . . . ❯

By the time this book gets into your hands, some of its content is going to be out of date. That's not something we like to admit. We choke on those words. But, it's as unavoidable as taxes and Microsoft. However, you have to fight fire with fire sometimes, and that's what I intend to do with my Web page.

Figure B.1 shows my home page at **http://rampages.onramp.net/~jerry**. From here, you can acquire more information about me and my background. You can also skip this nonsense and go directly to the goodies by clicking the See My Latest Books from Que link. This link takes you to information about the books I've written for Que, including *Using the Internet, Second Edition*. You'll find updated information, software, and more, for each book I've written.

Fig. B.1
Click Tips for Windows 95 and the Internet to learn more about Windows 95 and the Internet.

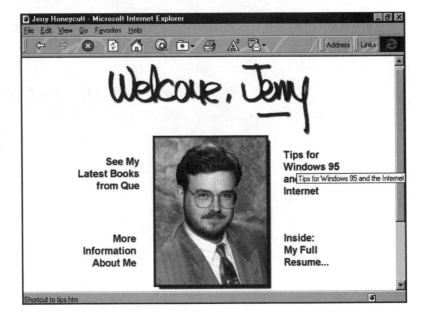

Now, scroll to *Using the Internet, Second Edition* and click the picture of the cover (you can also click the title). You'll see a Web page that contains three links: Links, Downloads, and Updates. Here's what you'll find when you click each:

- Click Links to load a Web page that contains links for all the URLs discussed in this book. Since URLs change and Web pages move, this is the place to check if you can't find a particular Web page. The list is organized by chapter, so you can easily find what you need.

- Click Downloads to load a Web page that contains links to all of the software you learned about in this book. It also contains links to other software that you didn't learn about in this book, but that is useful software nonetheless. The links almost always point to the files themselves so that you immediately download the file when you click the link. In some cases, a link takes you to the software vendor's Web site so that you can read the instructions for installing the product.

- Click Updates to load a Web page that contains any updated information. That is, any corrections we find, or any new information that you really should know about.

Locating an Internet Service Provider

In Chapter 3, "Here's How to Connect to the Internet," I suggested that the best way to find an Internet service provider in your community is to ask around. I definitely believe that you're going to end up with a better deal if you use other folks' experience with service providers to help you make a good decision.

On the other hand, you may not live in a community where you can do that. You might live in a small village. You just might not feel comfortable using the suggestions in Chapter 3 to find a service provider. Well, in that case, you can find a national or international Internet service provider to use.

This chapter lists some of the more noted service providers in Canada, the United States, the United Kingdom, and Australia. Some have local phone numbers in different communities, while others provide toll-free access. Just about all the service providers in this appendix offer a full range of services, including dialup and ISDN.

Canada and United States

American Information Network

1 800 779-6938

E-mail: **all-info@ai.net**

URL: **http://www.ai.net**

Covers all areas of Canada and the United States.

Anawave Software, Inc.

1 800 711-6030

E-mail: **sales@anawave.com**

URL: **http://www.anawave.com**

Covers all of Canada.

AT&T WorldNet

1 800 400-1447

E-mail: **wnettech@attmail.com**

URL: **http://www.att.com/worldnet/wis/**

Covers all of the United States.

ComStar Communications Corporation

1 800 426-6782

E-mail: **info@comstar.net**

URL: **http://www.comstar.net**

Covers all of Canada.

Delphi Internet Services Corp.

1 800 695-4005

E-mail: **service@delphi.com**

URL: **http://www.delphi.com**

Covers all of Canada and the United States.

EarthLink Network

1 800 395-8425

E-mail: **info@earthlink.net**

URL: **http://www.earthlink.net**

Covers all of Canada and the United States.

GNN

1 800 819-6112

E-mail: **support@gnn.com**

URL: **www.gnn.com**

Covers all of the United States.

The WELL, Inc.

1 415 332-9200

E-mail: **info@well.com**

URL: **http://www.well.com**

Covers the following area codes: 201, 202, 203, 205, 206, 207, 208, 209, 210, 212, 213, 214, 215, 216, 217, 219, 301, 302, 303, 304, 305, 309, 310, 312, 313, 314, 315, 316, 317, 318, 319, 334, 360, 401, 402, 404, 405, 407, 408, 409, 410, 412, 413, 414, 415, 417, 419, 423, 501, 502, 503, 504, 508, 510, 512, 513, 515, 516, 518, 520, 540, 601, 602, 603, 605, 606, 608, 609, 610, 612, 614, 615, 616, 617, 618, 619, 702, 703, 704, 706, 707, 708, 713, 714, 716, 717, 719, 770, 800, 801, 803, 804, 805, 806, 810, 812, 813, 814, 815, 816, 817, 818, 847, 888, 901, 903, 904, 908, 909, 910, 912, 913, 914, 915, 916, 918, 919.

UUNET Technologies, Inc.

1 800 488-6384

E-mail: **sales@uu.net**

URL: **http://www.uu.net**

Covers the following area codes: 201, 202, 203, 205, 206, 207, 208, 209, 212, 213, 214, 215, 216, 217, 219, 301, 302, 303, 304, 305, 309, 310, 312, 313, 314, 315, 316, 317, 318, 334, 360, 401, 402, 404, 405, 407, 408, 409, 410, 412, 413, 414, 415, 417, 419, 423, 501, 502, 503, 504, 508, 510, 512, 513, 515, 516, 518, 520, 540, 601, 602, 603, 605, 606, 608, 609, 610, 612, 614, 615, 616, 617, 619, 702, 703, 704, 706, 707, 708, 713, 714, 716, 717, 719, 770, 800, 801, 803, 804, 805, 806, 810, 812, 813, 814, 815, 816, 817, 818, 847, 901, 904, 908, 909, 910, 912, 913, 914, 915, 916, 918, 919.

ANS

1 800 456-8267

E-mail: **info@ans.net**

URL: **http://www.ans.net**

Covers all of the United States.

BBN Planet Corporation

1 800 472-4565

E-mail: **net-info@bbnplanet.com**

URL: **http://www.bbnplanet.com**

Covers all of the United States.

Camelot Internet Access Services

1 800 442-7120

E-mail: **cias@cias.net**

URL: **http://www.cias.net**

Covers all of the United States.

Cogent Software, Inc.

1 800 733-3380

E-mail: **info@cogsoft.com**

URL: **http://www.cogent.net**

Covers all of the United States and locally covers 213, 310, 714, 805, 818, 909.

Global Internet

1 800 682-5550

E-mail: **info@gi.net**

URL: **http://www.gi.net**

Covers the following area codes: 201, 202, 203, 205, 206, 207, 208, 209, 210, 212, 213, 214, 215, 216, 217, 218, 219, 281, 301, 302, 303, 304, 305, 307, 308, 309, 310, 312, 313, 314, 315, 316, 317, 318, 319, 334, 360, 401, 402, 404, 405, 406, 407, 408, 409, 410, 412, 413, 414, 415, 417, 419, 423, 501, 502, 503, 504, 505, 508, 510, 512, 513, 515, 516, 517, 518, 520, 540, 601, 602, 603, 605, 606, 607, 608, 609, 610, 612, 614, 615, 616, 617, 618, 619, 630, 701, 702, 703, 704, 706, 707, 708, 712, 713, 714, 715, 716, 717, 718, 719, 801, 802, 803, 804, 805, 806, 808, 810, 812, 813, 814, 815, 816, 817, 818, 901, 903, 904, 906, 908, 909, 910, 912, 913, 914, 915, 916, 917, 918, 919.

InfiNet Company

1 800 849-7214

E-mail: **sales@billing.infi.net**

URL: **http://www.infi.net**

Covers all of the United States.

Netcom

1 408 881-1810

E-mail: **support@ix.netcom.com**

URL: **http://www.ix.netcom.com**

Covers all of the United States.

NovaLink Interactive Networks

1 800 274-2814

E-mail: **support@novalink.com**

URL: **http://www.trey.com**

Covers all of the United States.

Pipeline

1 717 770-1700

E-mail: **support@pipeline.com**

URL: **http://www.pipeline.com**

Covers all the United States.

PowerNet

1 214 488-8295

E-mail: **www.@pwrnet.com**

URL: **http://www.pwrnet.com**

Covers the following area codes: 201, 202, 203, 204, 205, 206, 207, 208, 209, 210, 212, 213, 214, 215, 216, 217, 218, 219, 250, 281, 301, 302, 303, 304, 305, 306, 307, 308, 309, 310, 312, 313, 314, 315, 316, 317, 318, 319, 334, 360, 401, 402, 403, 404, 405, 406, 407, 408, 409, 410, 412, 413, 414, 415, 416, 417, 418, 419, 423, 441, 501, 502, 503, 504, 505, 506, 507, 508, 509, 510, 512, 513, 514, 515, 517, 518, 519, 520, 540, 541, 573, 601, 602, 603, 604, 605, 606, 607, 608, 609, 610, 612, 613, 614, 615, 616, 617, 618, 619, 630, 701, 702, 703, 704, 705, 706, 707, 708, 709, 712, 713, 714, 715, 716, 717, 718, 770, 800, 801, 802, 803, 804, 805, 806, 807, 808, 809, 810, 812, 813, 814, 815, 816, 817, 819, 847, 860, 864, 901, 902, 903, 904, 905, 906, 907, 908, 909, 910, 912, 913, 914, 915, 916, 918, 919, 941, 954, 970, 972

PSINet, Inc.

1 800 827-7482

E-mail: **info@psi.com**

URL: **http://www.psi.net**

Covers the following area codes: 201, 202, 203, 206, 207, 208, 209, 210, 212, 213, 214, 215, 216, 217, 219, 302, 303, 305, 312, 313, 314, 315, 317, 401, 404, 405, 407, 408, 410, 412, 415, 419, 501, 503, 505, 508, 509, 510, 512, 513, 516, 517, 518, 602, 603, 607, 609, 614, 616, 617, 619, 702, 703, 713, 714, 716, 717, 719, 801, 804, 806, 810, 813, 816, 817, 818, 904, 914, 915, 916, 918, 919.

Sprynet

1 206 957-8998

E-mail: **support@sprynet.com**

URL: **www.sprynet.com**

Covers all of the United States.

United Kingdom

CityScape

01223 566950

E-mail: **tony@ns.cityscape.co.uk**

URL: **http://www.citynet.net**

Covers +44.

IBM Global Network

1 800 775-5808

E-mail: **globalnetwork@info.ibm.com**

URL: **http://www.ibm.net**

Covers all Canada and the United States, as well as the following country codes: +27, +31, +32, +33, +34, +39, +41, +43, +44, +45, +46, +47, +49, +61, +64, +81, +90, +353, +357, +358, +599, +972.

AOL Bertelsmann

0800 376-5432

E-mail: **jaylaroch@aol.com**

URL: **http://www.aol.co.uk**

BT Internet

0800 800-0001

E-mail: **sales@btinternet.com**

URL: **http://www.btinernet.com**

BusinessNet

01252 318707

E-mail: **sales@businessnet.co.uk**

URL: **http://www.businessnet.co.uk**

CompuServe

0800 000200

E-mail: **74431.1374@compuserve.com**

URL: **http://www.compuserve.co.uk**

Covers +44.

Demon Internet

01306 732323

E-mail: **marketing@demon.net**

URL: **http://www.demon.net**

Covers +44.

Discovery Internet

01203 364400

E-mail: **solutions@discover.co.uk**

URL: **http://www.discover.co.uk**

Easynet

0171 681 444

E-mail: **postbox@easynet.co.uk**

URL: **http://www.easnet.co.uk**

Covers 0131, 0151, 0161, and 0171 in +44.

Entanet

0500 368-2638

E-mail: **james@enta.net**

URL: **http://www.enta.net**

Frontier Internet Services

0171 242-3383

E-mail: **sales@ftech.net**

URL: **http://www.ftech.net**

Covers 0171 in +44.

Global Internet

0171 957-1005

E-mail: **info@globalnet.co.uk**

URL: **http://globalnet.co.uk**

Covers +44.

Internet UK

01827 711722

E-mail: **sales@zipmail.co.uk**

URL: **http://www.zipmail.co.uk**

The Legend Internet

01274 743500

E-mail: **sales@legend.co.uk**

URL: **http://www.legend.co.uk**

Netcom Internet

01344 395500

E-mail: **sales@corp.netcom.net.uk**

URL: **http://www.netcom.net.uk**

Netkonect

0171 345-7777

E-mail: **sales@netkonect.net**

URL: **http://www.netkonect.net**

Planet Online, Ltd.

0113 2345566

E-mail: **info@theplanet.net**

URL: **www.theplanet.net**

Covers 0113 in +44.

PopTel

0171 923-9465

E-mail: **info@poptel.net**

URL: **http://www.poptel.org.uk**

Premier Internet

0181 213-1710

E-mail: **maria@globalnet.co.uk**

URL: **http://www.premier.co.uk**

PSINet UK

01223 577577

E-mail: Not Available

URL: **http://www.uk.psi.com**

Rednet

01494 513333

E-mail: **moreinfo@rednet.co.uk**

URL: **http://www.rednet.co.uk**

Sonnet Internet

0181 664-6000

E-mail: **enquire@sonnet.co.uk**

URL: **http://www.sonnet.co.uk**

U-Net

01925 633144

E-mail: **sales@u-net.net**

URL: **http://www.u-net.net**

Covers +44.

UUNet Pipex

01223 250100

E-mail: **sales@uunet.pipex.com**

URL: **http://www.uunet.pipex.com**

The Web Factory

01782 858585

E-mail: **sales@webfactory.co.uk**

URL: **http://www.webfactory.co.uk**

Covers 01782 in +44.

Zynet, Ltd.

01392 209500

E-mail: **zynet@zynet.net**

URL: **http://www.zynet.co.uk**

Covers +44.

Australia

Access One

1800 818391

E-mail: **info@aone.net.au**

URL: **http://www.aone.net.au**

Covers 02, 03, 06, 07, 08, and 09 in +61.

APANA (ACT Region)

02 9241 5888

E-mail: **act@apana.org.au**

URL: **http://www.act.apana.org.au**

Covers 06 in +61.

AUSNet Services Pty, Ltd.

02 241-5888

E-mail: **sales@world.net**

URL: **http://www.world.net**

Covers 02, 03, 06, 07, 08, 089, and 09 in +61.

DIALix

02 9948 6995

E-mail: **info@dialix.com**

URL: **http://www.DIALix.com**

Covers 02, 03, 06, 07, 08, and 09 in +61.

CompuServe Pacific

1800 025 240

E-mail: **70006.101@compuserve.com**

URL: **http://www.compuserve.com.au**

Covers most territories and states.

IBM Global Network

1800 645 336

E-mail: **webmaster@ibm.net**

URL: **http://www.au.ibm.net**

Covers most territories and states.

MagNet

1800 809 164

E-mail: **comments@magnet.com.au**

URL: **http://www.magnet.com.au/**

OzEmail

1800 809 164

E-mail: **info@ozemail.com.au**

URL: **http://www.ozemail.com.au**

Covers 02, 03, 002, 07, 06, 08, 09, 049, 089, 043, 042, 077, 070, 074, and 075 in +61.

Action Index

Getting Started

When you need to...	You'll find help here...
Choose a type of service	p. 31
Compare services	p. 40
Find a local service provider	p. 38
Get information from provider	p. 43
Learn about hardware you need	p. 32
Learn about Internet addresses	p. 29
Set up your connection for SLIP	p. 49
Set up your Windows connection	p. 51
Start your Internet connection	p. 49
Stop your Internet connection	p. 49
Troubleshoot your connection	p. 59
Use Windows 3.1 programs in 95	p. 30

Chatting

When you need to...	You'll find help here...
Choose a topic for a chat	p. 155
Get a chat client	p. 68
Learn about nicknames & channels	p. 154

E-mail

When you need to...	You'll find help here...
Attach a file to a message	p. 114
Communicate clearly in e-mail	p. 107
Compress files before sending	p. 113
Detach a file someone sent	p. 114
Find a friend's e-mail address	p. 176
Find a user in a company	p. 180
Find a user on a given server	p. 181
Find an e-mail address quick	p. 177
FTP files with e-mail	p. 78
Get a file from a list	p. 123
Get a list's FAQ	p. 121
Get off a mailing list	p. 121
Install WinZip	p. 113
Learn about mailing lists	p. 115
Learn about MIME	p. 112
Learn the rules for posting	p. 119
Manage your mail effectively	p. 105
Post a message to a list	p. 120
Reply to a posting	p. 120
Repost a lost mail list message	p. 120
Secure your e-mail	p. 103
Send a command to a list	p. 122
Send e-mail to a postmaster	p. 101
Subscribe to a mailing list	p. 116
Use signatures in e-mail	p. 109

FTP

When you need to...	You'll find help here...
Connect to an FTP server	p. 143
Decompress a downloaded file	p. 113
Download a file found by Archie	p. 147
Download free programs	p. 190
Download multiple files	p. 144
Find files by extension	p. 146
Find files on FTP servers	p. 146
Use a Web browser for FTP	p. 143
Use e-mail to get FTP files	p. 143

UseNet Newsgroups

When you need to...	You'll find help here...
Browse a newsgroup	p. 135
Find newsgroups you're missing	p. 133
Find newsgroups	p. 132
Get "real" news	p. 136
Learn about top-level categories	p. 132
Learn about UseNet online	p. 133
Practice posting to newsgroups	p. 136
Search newsgroups for topics	p. 132
Test a posting or upload	p. 134

World Wide Web

When you need to...	You'll find help here...
Find new stuff on the Web	p. 164
Get a copy of Netscape Navigator	p. 75
Get sound without a sound card	p. 92
Go to a Web page	p. 85
Learn about WAIS or Gopher	p. 81
Learn what's on the Web	p. 83
Play MPEG and QuickTime movies	p. 92
Play RealAudio files on the Web	p. 94
Play VRML files on the Web	p. 93
Search with AltaVista	p. 170
Search with Yahoo!	p. 165
Understand URLs	p. 86
Use Acrobat to read PDF files	p. 96

Using the Internet

When you need to...	You'll find help here...
Communicate with other people	p. 304
Download and install shareware	p. 200
Find a job using the Internet	p. 215
Find the news on NewsPage	p. 229
Find things to do in your area	p. 253
Find a good restaurant	p. 246

When you need to...	You'll find help here...
Get information about a celebrity	p. 307
Get the news on your desktop	p. 224
Learn about ASP and STAR	p. 189
Learn about shareware	p. 186
Look up a word in a dictionary	p. 206
Plan a vacation or business trip	p. 291
Print a map of your area	p. 251
Protect a computer from viruses	p. 266
Protect your children	p. 276
Protect your computer online	p. 264
Read a political magazine	p. 314
Read the news on Yahoo!	p. 238
Register to vote online	p. 316
Search a shareware collection	p. 192
Search trade publications	p. 211
See TV listings on the Web	p. 244
Shop safely on the Internet	p. 284
Use *USA Today* and other rags	p. 235
Write your senator or representative	p. 318

Index

Check out Que® Books on the World Wide Web
http://www.mcp.com/que

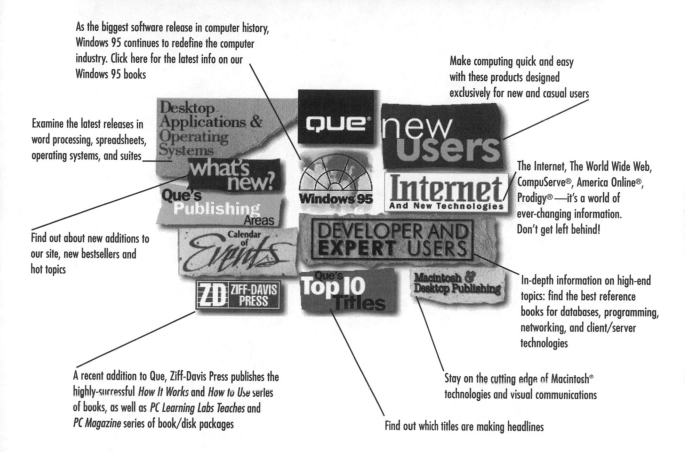

As the biggest software release in computer history, Windows 95 continues to redefine the computer industry. Click here for the latest info on our Windows 95 books

Make computing quick and easy with these products designed exclusively for new and casual users

Examine the latest releases in word processing, spreadsheets, operating systems, and suites

The Internet, The World Wide Web, CompuServe®, America Online®, Prodigy® —it's a world of ever-changing information. Don't get left behind!

Find out about new additions to our site, new bestsellers and hot topics

In-depth information on high-end topics: find the best reference books for databases, programming, networking, and client/server technologies

A recent addition to Que, Ziff-Davis Press publishes the highly-successful *How It Works* and *How to Use* series of books, as well as *PC Learning Labs Teaches* and *PC Magazine* series of book/disk packages

Stay on the cutting edge of Macintosh® technologies and visual communications

Find out which titles are making headlines

With 6 separate publishing groups, Que develops products for many specific market segments and areas of computer technology. Explore our Web Site and you'll find information on best-selling titles, newly published titles, upcoming products, authors, and much more.

- Stay informed on the latest industry trends and products available
- Visit our online bookstore for the latest information and editions
- Download software from Que's library of the best shareware and freeware

Complete and Return this Card
for a *FREE* Computer Book Catalog

Thank you for purchasing this book! You have purchased a superior computer book written expressly for your needs. To continue to provide the kind of up-to-date, pertinent coverage you've come to expect from us, we need to hear from you. Please take a minute to complete and return this self-addressed, postage-paid form. In return, we'll send you a free catalog of all our computer books on topics ranging from word processing to programming and the internet.

Mr. ☐   Mrs. ☐   Ms. ☐   Dr. ☐

Name (first) ☐☐☐☐☐☐☐☐☐☐☐   (M.I.) ☐   (last) ☐☐☐☐☐☐☐☐☐☐☐☐☐☐☐☐☐

Address ☐☐☐☐☐☐☐☐☐☐☐☐☐☐☐☐☐☐☐☐☐☐☐☐☐☐☐☐☐☐☐☐☐☐☐☐

☐☐☐☐☐☐☐☐☐☐☐☐☐☐☐☐☐☐☐☐☐☐☐☐☐☐☐☐☐☐☐☐☐☐☐☐

City ☐☐☐☐☐☐☐☐☐☐☐☐☐☐☐☐   State ☐☐   Zip ☐☐☐☐☐ ☐☐☐☐

Phone ☐☐☐ ☐☐☐ ☐☐☐☐   Fax ☐☐☐ ☐☐☐ ☐☐☐☐

Company Name ☐☐☐☐☐☐☐☐☐☐☐☐☐☐☐☐☐☐☐☐☐☐☐☐☐☐☐

E-mail address ☐☐☐☐☐☐☐☐☐☐☐☐☐☐☐☐☐☐☐☐☐☐☐☐☐☐☐

1. Please check at least (3) influencing factors for purchasing this book.

Front or back cover information on book .... ☐
Special approach to the content .... ☐
Completeness of content .... ☐
Author's reputation .... ☐
Publisher's reputation .... ☐
Book cover design or layout .... ☐
Index or table of contents of book .... ☐
Price of book .... ☐
Special effects, graphics, illustrations .... ☐
Other (Please specify): _____ ☐

2. How did you first learn about this book?

Saw in Macmillan Computer Publishing catalog .... ☐
Recommended by store personnel .... ☐
Saw the book on bookshelf at store .... ☐
Recommended by a friend .... ☐
Received advertisement in the mail .... ☐
Saw an advertisement in: _____ ☐
Read book review in: _____ ☐
Other (Please specify): _____ ☐

3. How many computer books have you purchased in the last six months?

This book only .... ☐   3 to 5 books .... ☐
2 books .... ☐   More than 5 .... ☐

4. Where did you purchase this book?

Bookstore .... ☐
Computer Store .... ☐
Consumer Electronics Store .... ☐
Department Store .... ☐
Office Club .... ☐
Warehouse Club .... ☐
Mail Order .... ☐
Direct from Publisher .... ☐
Internet site .... ☐
Other (Please specify): _____ ☐

5. How long have you been using a computer?

☐ Less than 6 months   ☐ 6 months to a year
☐ 1 to 3 years   ☐ More than 3 years

6. What is your level of experience with personal computers and with the subject of this book?

	With PCs	With subject of book
New	☐	☐
Casual	☐	☐
Accomplished	☐	☐
Expert	☐	☐

Source Code ISBN: 0-7897-0963-5

7. Which of the following best describes your job title?

Administrative Assistant .... ☐
Coordinator .... ☐
Manager/Supervisor .... ☐
Director .... ☐
Vice President .... ☐
President/CEO/COO .... ☐
Lawyer/Doctor/Medical Professional .... ☐
Teacher/Educator/Trainer .... ☐
Engineer/Technician .... ☐
Consultant .... ☐
Not employed/Student/Retired .... ☐
Other (Please specify): _____ ☐

8. Which of the following best describes the area of the company your job title falls under?

Accounting .... ☐
Engineering .... ☐
Manufacturing .... ☐
Operations .... ☐
Marketing .... ☐
Sales .... ☐
Other (Please specify): _____ ☐

9. What is your age?

Under 20 .... ☐
21-29 .... ☐
30-39 .... ☐
40-49 .... ☐
50-59 .... ☐
60-over .... ☐

10. Are you:

Male .... ☐
Female .... ☐

11. Which computer publications do you read regularly? (Please list)

_____
_____
_____
_____
_____
_____
_____
_____
_____
_____

Comments: _____
_____
_____

Fold here and scotch-tape to mail.

BUSINESS REPLY MAIL
FIRST-CLASS MAIL PERMIT NO. 9918 INDIANAPOLIS IN

POSTAGE WILL BE PAID BY THE ADDRESSEE

ATTN MARKETING
MACMILLAN COMPUTER PUBLISHING
MACMILLAN PUBLISHING USA
201 W 103RD ST
INDIANAPOLIS IN 46290-9042

NO POSTAGE
NECESSARY
IF MAILED
IN THE
UNITED STATES